GAINING
on the MARKET

Also by Charles J. Rolo

Radio Goes to War
Wingate's Raiders
The World of Aldous Huxley (editor)
The World of Evelyn Waugh (editor)
Psychiatry in American Life (editor)
The Anatomy of Wall Street (co-editor)

By Robert J. Klein

The Consumers Union Report on Life Insurance
The Money Book of Money

GAINING
on the MARKET

YOUR COMPLETE GUIDE TO INVESTMENT STRATEGY
Stocks, Bonds, Options, Mutual Funds, and Gold

REVISED EDITION

Charles J. Rolo
and
Robert J. Klein

An Atlantic Monthly Press Book
Little, Brown and Company   Boston ■ Toronto

Chapters 14, 15, 17, 19, 20, 22, 27, 28, and 29 were originally adapted from articles by Charles J. Rolo that appeared in *Money* Magazine © 1977, 1978, 1979, 1980, 1981, 1982 by Time Inc.

Library of Congress Cataloging-in-Publication Data

Rolo, Charles James, 1916–
    Gaining on the market: your complete guide to investment
  strategy: stocks, bonds, options, mutual funds, and gold / Charles J.
  Rolo and Robert J. Klein.—Rev. ed.
     p.   cm.
  "An Atlantic Monthly Press book."
  Includes bibliographical references and index.
  ISBN 0-316-75456-0
  1. Securities—United States—Handbooks, manuals, etc.
  2. Stock-exchange—United States—Handbooks, manuals, etc.
  3. Investments—United States—Handbooks, manuals, etc.
  I. Klein, Robert J. II. Title.
HG4921.R55   1988
332.6'78—dc19

                                    87-29758
                                        CIP

ATLANTIC-LITTLE, BROWN BOOKS
ARE PUBLISHED BY
LITTLE, BROWN AND COMPANY
IN ASSOCIATION WITH
THE ATLANTIC MONTHLY PRESS

10 9 8 7 6 5 4 3 2 1

FG

*Published simultaneously in Canada
by Little, Brown & Company (Canada) Limited*

Printed in THE UNITED STATES OF AMERICA

Foreword to the Revised Edition

The original edition of *Gaining on the Market* was a charmingly personal guide to investing, written by a man of letters who, well along in life, acquired a taste for investing, became a securities analyst, lost a fair sum in the market debacle of the early 1970s, and then set about in earnest to share with aspiring investors the lessons he learned from that debacle. Thus did Charles Rolo become a financial journalist and, as with so many other vocations that he had mastered, distinguished himself in his new career. My professional relationship with him was, first, as his editor at *Money* magazine and, within a very few years, as his fellow editor. But throughout our time together, he was always my mentor. When his widow, Bess, and his agent, Timothy Seldes, asked me, three years after his death, if I would be interested in preparing a new edition of *Gaining on the Market,* I accepted the assignment in the spirit of someone repaying a debt.

In those three years, the stock market topography had changed about as radically as that of Mount St. Helens after the eruption of 1980. Hyperinflation and high interest rates had driven masses of individuals and institutions into the shelter of Treasury and blue-chip corporate debt securities. There, returns of 12 percent or more were to be had at little or no risk. Since the average annual return on stocks over several decades was less than 10 percent, it took a genuine believer to counsel venturing into stocks. Charles counseled it, and he was right. Along with a few of his favorite security analysts, Charles zestfully foraged in the "hidden bull market" of small companies that seemed about to emerge as junior growth stocks. Above all, he believed that the small investor has a remarkable advantage over the professional money manager — an advantage rather like that of the horseshoe rabbit over the rhinoceros in walking on crusted snow.

The remarkable thing about this book is how valid its advice and strategies remain. Don't be deceived by what you may have learned in the six-year bull market that began — as Charles had expected — shortly before his death. Anybody could have made money in that market by picking stocks almost at random from the 500 companies that make up Standard & Poor's index. The S&P outperformed a large majority of mutual funds and other professional money managers. Emerging growth companies were left behind for many reasons, not the least being that institutional money managers from Japan, West Germany, and other foreign countries poured their money into the blue chips they knew and once again loved. But now that the easy profits have been taken, success will come to the investor who, in one way or another, follows an unpopular path laid out for him by Charles Rolo.

Revising Charles's book proved to be a humbling task. I took as my most important mission the preservation of his voice and his first-hand experiences in the market. No lover of the magisterial "we" or the standoffish third person, he wrote in the first person singular whenever appropriate. With two authors' names now on the cover, however, the first person becomes mostly invalid. I have attributed Charles's personal experiences to him, I have used the first-person plural to state jointly held views, and chapter 29's classic "Portrait of the Ideal Investor" is pure unbowdlerized Rolo. Rest assured that every time I changed a phrase or a thought or an example to replace outdated material, I listened for his voice as though he were standing over my shoulder (something he never did. He framed his thoughts and chose his words with painful deliberation; yet he accepted suggestions for changes gracefully and even gratefully). I hope that I have heard him right and heeded him well.

Most of the research that went into updating *Gaining on the Market* was done by Susan A. Siegler, a resourceful reporter who brought fresh insights to the task. My wife, Easy Klein, former editor of *N.Y.U. Business,* updated the chapter on gold. I could not have done the job without them, though even with their immense help, I take the rap for any mistakes.

Robert J. Klein
1987

Acknowledgments

My largest debt is to two former managing editors of *Money* — William S. Rukeyser [now director of international business development for Time Incorporated] and his successor, Marshall Loeb [now managing editor of *Fortune*] — who generously gave me time off to write this book and in other ways lent their support and encouragement. To Bill and Marshall I extend my warmest thanks. I must also thank Time Incorporated for permission to draw on articles of mine published in *Money*. None of the aforementioned, I must add, has edited or approved the manuscript; the responsibility for its opinions and shortcomings is entirely my own.

It is both a duty and a pleasure to thank the investment advisers and money managers whose ideas and writings are cited in the text. Those to whom I am especially indebted are Richard A. Crowell, David Dreman, Norman G. Fosback, George Lasry, and John Westergaard. I also wish to thank Edwin Caplin, an old friend and one of Wall Street's most conscientious stockbrokers, for answering a multitude of questions; Max G. Ansbacher, who helped me to unravel some of the complexities of options trading; and my colleagues at *Money,* Robert Klein and Michael Sivy, for patiently listening to my problems and coming up with valuable suggestions.

I am grateful to Arnold Ehrlich, my original editor at the Atlantic Monthly Press, for his enthusiastic backing of this project, and also to his successor, Peter Davison, who made perceptive suggestions and gave me the additional time needed to complete a book whose difficulties I had foolishly underestimated. My wife, Bess, endured with extraordinary grace the long-drawn-out rigors imposed on her by my immersion in this project. For the support she provided no words of appreciation would be adequate.

Charles J. Rolo
1982

Contents

III. Getting Advice and Information 53

IV. Analytic Approaches 97

V. Managing Your Money: Strategy and Tactics 139

VI. Conclusions 227

Appendixes 241

Foreword: What This Book Can Do for You

Many private investors feel that the cards are stacked against them in the stock market; they think they are doomed to be outgunned and outsmarted by the large financial institutions — banks, insurance companies, and the like. This discouraging belief, plausible though it may seem, is a myth that has been refuted by scholarly research. Studies cited in *The Changing Role of the Individual Investor,* a book by two distinguished professors of finance, Marshall E. Blume and Irwin Friend, show no long-range differences between the investment results that have been obtained by individuals and by institutions. Moreover, since those studies were made in the early 1970s, far-reaching changes in the investment world have worked to the advantage of individual investors — for reasons that our opening chapter will explain. *Nowadays, private investors actually have far greater chances than giant institutions of beating the averages used to measure the performance of the market.*

But to exploit his or her* advantages, the individual needs some market savvy. And many of the nation's 47 million stockholders lack sufficient knowledge to handle their investments effectively. This forces them to rely more or less blindly on the advice of others, usually brokers — a disconcerting and potentially dangerous dependence. We are not suggesting that a layman shouldn't seek the help of brokers and other professionals. But it takes some knowledge to choose such help wisely and to use it intelligently. So inescapably there is a do-it-yourself element in investing, and how well you cope with it could be of critical importance to your financial future. It follows that anyone who is seriously concerned with getting the best mileage out of his savings or inherited capital should master the fundamentals of investing. Any layman can do it. The main requirements are

---

* Fully half of all adult American stockholders are women. But our language has yet to devise a singular pronoun that stands for both sexes. So for simplicity's sake, and with apologies to female readers, this text will henceforward use the traditional "he" and "his" rather than the unmanageable "he or she" and "his or her."

common sense, a command of simple arithmetic — and, above all, a willingness to recognize that managing your money deserves some time and effort. Many people who spend hours shopping for sporting goods, furniture, or bargains in kitchen equipment make investment decisions in minutes. They call up their broker and say, "Just tell me what to buy. Don't confuse me with the facts."

This book is written for people who wish to know the facts and understand them. As Robert Metz, syndicated investment columnist and chief correspondent for cable TV's Financial News Network, has said, "If more individuals would learn to think for themselves, there would be fewer affluent brokers and more affluent customers." Our text won't overtax your mental muscles, but it will invite you to stretch them. It seeks to fill the gap between the two major categories of books on investing — those addressed to professionals or experienced investors and simplistic primers that give you a useful introductory course but don't really equip you to operate on your own. Unlike the advanced texts, ours doesn't take for granted any prior knowledge of investing or the jargon of Wall Street; investment terms, theories, and procedures are explained in simple English. This is therefore a book that can be read and assimilated by beginners. But it differs considerably from the typical primer. Here is precisely how it differs — and why.

1. **This book is action-oriented; it isn't a "what's what in the investment world" but rather a combined training course and combat manual.** I've shunned the conventional format — chapters that focus on the different types of investments: stocks, bonds, mutual funds, and so on. Understanding what they are is essential, but their anatomy really doesn't require lengthy explanation; *the bottom line is knowing how to use them.* Accordingly, the different types of investments are explained and discussed in the context of investment objectives — investing for growth or high income — and investment strategies.

2. **This book doesn't tell you what to do without telling you, wherever possible, precisely how to do it.** A common complaint about popular books on investment is that the advice they give is often too general. They say, for example: never fail to sell a stock that has risen so much in price that you think it is overvalued. But they don't explain with sufficient depth or precision how to judge whether a stock is overvalued or undervalued. The precept we

have tried to follow is: spare no effort to be specific. When we refer to information needed by investors, we tell you where to find it and, if it isn't free, what it will cost you.* When we discuss risk, we explain specifically how it can be measured and what are the methods for controlling it.

3. **This book goes far beyond the universe of popular guides to investing.** In varying degrees, such books dodge complexities that can't be dodged without slipping into glibness and dangerous oversimplification. Admittedly, simplification is desirable in any manual written for inexperienced investors. But there are times when, to serve the reader honestly, a writer must grapple with complexities and try to deal with them in language that is intelligible even to a novice. This can be done; popularization does not have to be pap. Accordingly, this book will not stop short at the elementary level, except in certain highly specialized areas that we don't consider vital for the average investor.

The approach taken here aims at showing the reader how to operate as much like a pro as possible without formal training and professional experience. The text summarizes and discusses what scholarly research claims to have discovered about the behavior of the stock market. It takes a look at modern portfolio theory — an investment doctrine that has become gospel to most high-level institutional money managers — and distills the doctrine's usefulness for the individual investor. It briefs the reader on the practical uses of contrary opinion theory, which concerns itself with the influence of human emotions on the stock market and highlights the role that psychology plays in successful investing. In sum, *our aim is to provide you with a step-by-step grounding in the fundamentals of investing and money management — how to judge the value of a stock; how to use tools that have proved helpful in trying to anticipate major movements of the market; how to choose and implement an overall investment strategy that suits your goals and your temperament.*

Clearly, this isn't a "how-to-make-a-bundle" book; it charts no easy shortcuts to fortune, because there are none. "How-to-make-a-bundle"

---

* Hundreds of addresses, telephone numbers, prices, and other specifics are given in the text. Inevitably, some will have changed by publication date and during the book's lifetime. We are sure our readers will agree it was preferable to give them the data required than to omit vital information because it is subject to change.

books are a menace to financial health; they exploit gullibility and encourage greed, an investor's two deadliest enemies. Their authors usually claim to have discovered an easy-to-follow system that ensures smashing success in the stock market. But anyone who had really devised such a system would keep it a fiercely guarded secret; for if any easily followed formula for coining profits were in the public domain, it would inevitably cease to work. Every share of stock bought represents a share of stock sold. So if too many investors were using the same formula for picking stocks, too few investors would be willing to sell those stocks at acceptable prices.

There are, of course, many ways to make a killing in the stock market. But none of them is easy or safe; they call for an unusual combination of skill, dedication, and foresight, plus the guts to take and live with inordinately high risks. Mark Twain said, "October is one of the peculiarly dangerous months to speculate in stocks. Others are November, December, January, February, March, April, May, June, July, August, and September." We see nothing wrong about speculation, provided you understand and can afford the risks you are taking. But never forget that if you lose 90 percent of your capital, you have to make a 900 percent profit on the 10 percent left in order to wind up back where you started — and 900 percent is awfully hard to make. The basic ways of shooting for speculative gains in stocks will be discussed. But we do not cover trading in commodities futures, because we consider it a game best left to professionals. The chances are overwhelmingly large that an amateur who plays the commodities markets will lose most if not all of his stake, and sooner rather than later.

The main focus of this book will be on strategies that seek the best available returns compatible with prudence. *By prudence we do not mean conservatism, a doctrine that dictates avoidance of risk.* Paradoxically, total avoidance of risk entails, in inflationary times, the certainty of loss — that is, loss of real purchasing power. From 1974 to 1984, a decade of runaway prices, the returns of "riskless" investments were substantially lower than the rate of inflation.

In contrast to conservatism, *prudence* is a way of handling yourself that involves taking justifiable risks for the sake of calcu-*

---

* For this and other valuable insights, we are indebted to George Lasry, author of *Valuing Common Stocks* (AMACOM, 1979), an original and illuminating treatise on investing.

lated returns based on reasonable expectations. Prudence involves understanding value, staying alert to opportunities for profit, and recognizing that the future is truly uncertain. That means not assuming that things will turn out for the best or the worst, but choosing a course that takes into account a set of rational possibilities. Putting all one's investment eggs into the basket touted by the prophets of doom is not exercising prudence. Ever since OPEC embargoed oil in 1973, they have screamed that catastrophe was around the corner; yet catastrophe is still no more than a cloud on the horizon. Nor is one exercising prudence by shunning the stock market at all times simply because stock ownership entails risks. Depending upon the circumstances, the exercise of prudence can lead to a cautious policy, an aggressive one, or something in between. A strategy based on prudence can, when conditions are favorable, bring splendid profits, and it should, at all times, protect you against intolerable losses.

This book, though not a textbook, will tell you all (or nearly all) you have wanted to know about how to invest — the what, the why, the when, and the where. It starts out, so to speak, in the first grade and takes you all the way through college, throwing in an occasional idea for those who might want to go on to graduate school. Our hope is that along the way an inexperienced investor, as he gains knowledge and understanding, will sense that learning to be his own investment manager is an exhilarating challenge. Managing money well is hard work — we won't kid you about that — but we also believe it can be fun. Nearly everybody enjoys a contest. And this one — as our opening chapter will show — isn't rigged. Its rewards are definitely within reach of all.

GAINING
on the MARKET

Introduction: The Individual Investor's New Edge

You, the individual investor, are better situated in the stock market than you think. In recent years, changes that this chapter will discuss have worked to your advantage; the strategic position of individuals has improved, whereas that of large financial institutions has worsened. If you have doubts about your ability to compete against the institutions, it is high time you got rid of them. They are probably based on myths and misconceptions that are still prevalent among investors who are leery of the market.

☐ Myth Number One

Institutions control the market and can manipulate it to their advantage.

☐ The Realities

If institutions could control the market, their results would be far better than those of private investors; yet scholarly studies have proved this isn't so. The notion that there is collusion between the institutions is a paranoid fantasy dreamed up by losers seeking a scapegoat for their misfortune. The truth is that institutional money managers are competing against each other in the market; what matters to them is how they perform in relation to their peers, not in relation to the John and Mary Does.

As for stock manipulation, it is a violation of federal securities laws and is punishable by fines and imprisonment. Over the years, the nation's major stock markets have greatly strengthened their self-policing procedures. They have set up elaborate electronic surveillance systems that instantly bring to light any suspicious or unusual activity in a stock — as, for example, when a stock that has been a sleeper takes a sudden run-up in price for no apparent reason. Exchange officials promptly notify the company and the brokers involved, and the exchange may suspend trading in the stock until the situation has been investigated. The stock markets are also policed by the Securities and Exchange Commission, whose function is to enforce the securities laws and protect the public interest. Stock manipulation still goes on, but it is increasingly difficult to get away with. The people who engage in it are either professional criminals or dishonest speculators acting in concert with shady brokers. They are certainly not institutional investors.

☐ Myth Number Two

Institutional investors profit from "inside" information. They are the first to learn about crucial company developments, and private investors are usually the last.

☐ The Realities

Over the past two decades, a string of court decisions has widened the application of the law that prohibits corporate insiders (defined as officers and employees) from trading on the basis of inside information — that is, information not publicly disclosed that could have an appreciable influence on the price of the company's stock. Following two landmark cases (*SEC v. Texas Gulf Sulphur* and *SEC v. Merrill Lynch*), *the same prohibition now also applies to any investor who obtains, or even innocently receives, inside information.* And judges have imposed stiff penalties on so-called tippees, who profited from inside information relayed to them by an analyst or a broker handling their account. In a 1978 ruling, Judge David Markun, an administrative judge of the SEC, set forth this guiding principle: "One who knows himself to be a beneficiary of non-public, selectively disclosed inside information must fully disclose it or refrain from trading." From the beginning of 1978 through 1985, the SEC pressed charges in 117 cases involving the use of inside information — three times as many as in all of the four previous decades. Passage in 1984 of the Insider Trading Sanctions Act made it still more hazardous to profit from inside information. This law empowers the courts to penalize insiders triple the profits from their deals.

Nevertheless, a wave of corporate mergers, acquisitions, tender offers, and other forms of buyouts — in the course of which the price of the targeted company's stock almost always rises sharply — tempted many insiders in the 1980s to buy shares of targeted companies before the public got wind of the deals. Noting that a stock often took off before a takeover move was announced, the SEC intensified its surveillance of insider trading. In 1985 a former deputy secretary of defense, W. Paul Thayer, was sentenced to four years in prison and made to disgorge more than a million dollars in stock market profits he had made by trading on information about a pending takeover that he had received as a director of Anheuser-Busch. In other cases, the agency has prosecuted corporate officers, financial printers, employees of law firms and investment banking firms representing companies involved in takeovers, and newspaper reporters who sold to brokers advanced word about stories that when published were almost certain to move the prices of certain stocks. The most spectacular case to date, in 1986, pitted the SEC against Ivan Boesky, the arbitrageur *extraordinaire,* and his network of informants about mergers and acquisitions.

Before the 1970s, institutions often profited from inside information. Now that kind of shenanigans is not only illegal, it is also foolhardy. To be sure, the prohibition is still widely flouted, but the culprits for the most part are individuals. Any institutional money manager who tries to take advantage of inside information would be risking his professional career, as the Boesky case makes plain.

Another development of recent years has lessened somewhat the difference between the quality of the research available to institutions and to individuals. The research-oriented brokerage houses that catered only to institutions were hard hit by the lower commissions they had to accept from institutions when fixed minimum commissions were abolished on May 1, 1975. Feeling shaky on their own, many of these research "boutiques" arranged to be taken over by nationwide brokerage houses that serve the public. Thus the earnings estimates and opinions of many top-flight institutional analysts have become available — in digests of their reports and through brokers — to individual investors.

□ Myth Number Three
Institutional investors are bound to handle themselves in the market with far greater skill than individuals because they represent the top investment talent in the country.

□ The Realities
In spite of their professional know-how, their prodigious input of information, and their arsenal of sophisticated investment tools and techniques, institutional investors as a group have an indifferent performance record. CDA Investment Technologies, a Silver Spring, Maryland, firm that specializes in tracking the performance of institutional money managers, reported that in the ten-year period to December 31, 1985, stock portfolios managed by banks achieved a

total annual rate of return — price appreciation plus reinvested dividends — of 13.8 percent; that was a shade under the 14.2 percent return on Standard & Poor's 500-stock index. In other words, the clients of these professional investors would have done better by simply buying and holding those 500 stocks.

Older surveys tell an even sorrier story. For example, in the 1970s decade 84 percent of the country's 3,000 largest pension-fund stock portfolios underperformed the S&P index. Perhaps the institutions are improving their performance, but improvement can go only so far. *Through no fault of their own, institutions collectively stand little or no chance of beating the market. The reason is simple: they can't beat the market because collectively they* are *the market, or a very large part of it.* Their share of the volume of public trading on the New York Stock Exchange has soared from 39 percent in the early 1960s to 65 percent and that of individuals has shrunk from 61 percent to 35 percent. Public volume excludes the trading that members of the exchange, mainly brokers and arbitrageurs, do for their own accounts. Counting all trading activity, only 10 to 15 percent of daily volume represents the participation of individual investors, according to H. Bradlee Perry and Brian F. Reynolds of David L. Babson & Co., Boston investment counselors.

An investor can underperform the market averages for two reasons: his timing is wrong — he buys when the market is high and sells when it is low — or he invests in stocks that do worse than those in the averages. The institutions as a group have often made both of these errors.

Evidence compiled by the SEC indicates that institutional investors did more buying than selling when the market was close to its highs in 1968, 1971, and 1972, and more selling than buying when the market was close to its bottom in 1974. In contrast, individuals sold heavily near the 1968 top and were buyers on balance at the market bottoms of 1970 and 1974. In the January 1981 issue of *Trusts & Estates,* Robert S. Waill, then a New York City investment counselor, wrote: "If one may generalize, at this moment the institutions represent the 'weak hands' and individuals the 'strong hands.' The impulsive old lady from Dubuque has steadied. . . . The institutions have become the nervous and irrational sellers."

Some of the horrendous mistakes in stock picking made by institutional money managers are cited in two excellent books by David N. Dreman, *Psychology and the Stock Market* (AMACOM, 1977) and *The*

New Contrarian Investment Strategy (Random House, 1982). At the third annual Institutional Investor Conference, held in New York in early 1970, the professional money managers picked National Student Marketing as the stock that would do best that year; five months later its price had dropped 95 percent, and the company later went bankrupt. In the early 1970s, *Institutional Investor,* a magazine addressed to stock market professionals, conducted annual polls that asked some 150 institutional money managers across the country to name their favorite stocks for the year to come. The ten favorites for 1972 rose on average roughly 1 percent, whereas the S&P index rose 15 percent; and the ten choices for 1973 dropped on average 40 percent, more than double the decline of the S&P stocks. Mercifully, the following year the *Institutional Investor* poll was discontinued.

What accounts for this startling record of bad judgment on the part of the institutional superpros? Charles Rolo's experience with institutions as a Wall Street analyst jibed with the explanation given by David Dreman: institutional money managers are led astray by groupthink, a herd psychology of their own. As members of the institutional herd, otherwise intelligent, rational professionals take leave of common sense and follow to extremes the investment fads and concepts currently in vogue among their peers. A flagrant example of this mindless conformity was the institutional craze of the early 1970s for the top-quality growth companies — nicknamed the "nifty fifty" — which included Avon, Walt Disney, Eastman Kodak, Johnson & Johnson, and IBM. Never before had so many money managers put so much money into so few stocks with such total disregard for the inevitable consequences of their folly. Their rationale was that the future earnings growth of these companies had "high visibility," meaning that their growth could be predicted for a number of years with assurance and considerable accuracy. A number of scholarly studies have shown that forecasts of earnings growth beyond the near future are highly fallible. This didn't faze the superpros. They dubbed their favorites "one-decision stocks"; the only decision was at what price to buy, because these stocks need never be sold. The tremendous buying channeled into the nifty fifty pushed their prices up to stratospheric levels. But when the market started to collapse in 1973, the "one decision" concept was instantly punctured. The institutions scrambled to sell, and the prices of their absurdly overvalued favorites went into a sickening and prolonged nosedive. In less than a year, IBM dropped 41 percent, Disney 63 percent, and "second team" favorites such as Clorox and Tropicana showed losses of 75 percent to 90 percent. Even in 1987, during perhaps the greatest bull market in history, most of the nifty fifty were still trading at prices far below their 1973 highs. By then, some of them looked like worthily priced investments.

Another aspect of institutional conformity — and a contributing factor in the institutions' poor investment performance — is the cult of limitless information. It rests on the notion that the greater the number of so-called inputs, the better the output — the investment decision — will be. But a variety of experiments designed to test man's cognitive capabilities have confirmed what common sense tells us — namely, that the information-processing capabilities of the human mind are strictly finite. At a certain level, additional information becomes useless or clouds the recipient's judgment. When Charles Rolo worked on Wall Street, he observed that the most highly specialized analysts — those who follow relatively few companies and whose knowledge of them is encyclopedic — were often poor judges of when to buy or sell their companies' stocks. Their preoccupation with detail, much of it trivial, blurred their perception of the crucial issues.

Since the 1960s, the brokerage industry has provided institutions with ever-increasing quantities of "in-depth research." Some of it is valuable, but much of it simply creates information overload and is therefore a hindrance to effective decision making.

☐ The Pygmies' New Edge on the Giants

It should be clear by now that individuals have no valid reason to doubt their ability to compete with the big institutions. In fact, they have a basic advantage — the advantage that nimble pygmies have over ponderous giants.

Sheer size has long been a serious handicap in the market to leading institutions such as the big city banks, and their resources keep on growing. The large institutions have such huge sums of money to invest that they are forced to concentrate their major stock holdings in a few hundred of the nation's largest companies. They can and do buy stock in smaller companies, but not on a scale that is significant in relation to the size of their portfolios. If they were to invest significant amounts in small companies, they would drive up the price of the stock by their buying and force it down when they sell. This constraint on their freedom of choice creates a problem for the money managers. The companies in which they make their big investments constitute the most exhaustively analyzed sector of the market. The stocks of these companies are so closely followed by so many of Wall Street's top analysts that just about everything there is to know about them is known, and new information is promptly reflected in the price of the stock. Consequently, the chances of detecting sharply undervalued issues in the institutional sector of the market are slim.

In contrast, an individual investor is free to choose from a universe of more than 7,000 companies, the majority of which are neglected by analysts in the major brokerage houses. And it is within this universe of underanalyzed companies that undervalued stocks are most likely to be lurking. A study made by finance professors Avner Arbel and Steven Carvell of Cornell University compares the annual performance of the 500 stocks in Standard & Poor's broad market index after grouping them according to the level of attention given a stock by security analysts. Over the ten years 1977 to 1986 the average annual total return for the group of stocks followed by six or fewer analysts was 25.6 percent, compared with 16.9 percent for the stocks tracked by more than 20 analysts. As Arbel concludes, in *How to Beat the Market with High-Performance Generic Stocks Your Broker Won't Tell You About* (William Morrow & Co., 1985), "The orphans eventually thrive and the wallflowers turn beautiful."

The underanalyzed universe isn't composed exclusively of companies that are small or little known. It includes large, long-established companies that are not intensively covered by Wall Street analysts because they happen to be out of favor with the institutions. At certain periods in the second half of the 1970s, a list of underanalyzed companies would have included Woolworth and the New York Times Company, both of which were among the nation's 500 largest corporations. A list of "Wall Street's Wallflowers" compiled in 1986 by the Institutional Broker's Estimate System (a compilation of earnings forecasts sponsored by the brokerage firm of Lynch, Jones & Ryan) had on it such stalwarts as Loews Corp., North American Phillips, and Castle & Cooke, a giant food packing company.

In addition to having greater freedom of choice than the large institutions, the individual has another important advantage — superior mobility in the marketplace. Managing a big institution's portfolio is like maneuvering a battleship in a canal. After the managers of billion-dollar portfolios have decided to buy or sell a stock, it may take them months to accumulate the half-million or more shares they want, or to unload their holdings, without sharply altering the stock's price by their buying or selling. The average individual doesn't trade enough shares to be bothered by this problem; he can jump in or out at a moment's notice, an especially valuable advantage at times of crisis or exceptional opportunity.

Private investors are free from yet another constraint that applies to institutions, the Employee Retirement Income Security Act (ERISA) of 1974. Under ERISA, managers of a pension fund can be sued by the fund's beneficiaries for behavior construed as imprudent; the definition of prudence boils down to doing what so-called prudent men are doing. Thus ERISA made groupthink and conformity more or less mandatory for money managers handling pension funds. In 1979, new regulations promulgated by the Labor Department seemingly gave pension fund managers considerable new latitude in their choice of individual investments so long as the overall policy was in accord with the concept of prudence. But even though ERISA is no longer the straitjacket it used to be, it still withholds from pension fund managers the total freedom that individuals enjoy.

Of all the changes on the investment scene, none has helped individuals more than the proliferation of specialized mutual funds, many of which have no sales charge and are known as no loads. The specialized funds have made it possible for small investors to own securities previously beyond their reach — for example, tax-exempt bonds, mortgage pass-through certificates (better known as "Ginnie Maes") and high-yielding money-market instruments that sell in denominations of $10,000 to $100,000, as well as securities that would be risky to invest in without the diversification that a fund provides — in particular, low-rated "junk" bonds and offbeat, speculative stocks.

Another tremendous benefit to individuals has been the introduction by mutual funds of the "switching" privilege. This allows investors to move from one type of fund to another within the same organization, usually without charge. The not-so-rich investor has thus gained a flexibility he never had before. When he becomes optimistic about the stock market, he can jump into an aggressive stock fund; when he turns pessimistic, he can take refuge in a money-market fund; and he can vary the proportions of his capital invested in stocks, fixed-income securities, and even gold mining shares as his perceptions of the economic outlook change. Switching no-load funds (see chapter 23) makes these moves possible at a moment's notice and without incurring brokerage commissions.

☐ How Are the Pygmies Performing?

Investment clubs are groups of the smallest investors who pool their resources and pursue a common investment policy. Many members are school teachers, housewives, and middle-echelon executives, and six out of seven have had no investment experience before joining a club. Taken together at the end of 1985, all the clubs that had been affiliated with the National Association of Investment Clubs for nine to 14 years had compiled a lifetime average annual compounded rate of return (including reinvested dividends) of 11.4 percent; that compared with 10.9 percent for the S&P 500 over matching periods. Clubs that had acquired 15 or more years of investing experience outdistanced the S&P by a dazzling margin of 11.3 percent to 8.6 percent. Top performer in 1985 was the Lorain County Club in Ohio; its members achieved a 35.6 percent one-year return versus 26.3 percent for the S&P.

So take heart. While the ability to make money in the market does not come quickly or easily, it isn't as difficult as the scared cats and the losers would have you believe. As one successful amateur investor has said, "You don't have to be a genius. You just have to avoid being a fool." The first step toward avoiding foolishness is to get to know the market better — to understand its language and what makes it tick.

Starting Points

1 | What, Precisely, Is "the Market"?

The U.S. stock market is composed of more than a dozen markets: the New York Stock Exchange, on which about 1,500 companies are listed; the American Stock Exchange (825 companies); the Boston, Philadelphia, Midwest, Pacific, and other smaller regional exchanges; the over-the-counter market, which isn't a place but a nationwide network of 2,800 dealers through whom stocks not listed on the registered exchanges are bought and sold; and the so-called third and fourth markets. The third market consists of firms that deal in listed securities, mainly with financial institutions, away from the floors of the regular exchanges, selling from and buying for their own inventory of stocks; the fourth market involves direct trading of large blocks of securities between institutional investors by means of a computerized service called Instinet.

The three major markets — the New York Stock Exchange (or Big Board), the American Stock Exchange (often referred to as the Amex) and the Over-the-Counter Market (OTC) — differ considerably in character. The New York Stock Exchange list includes most of the nation's largest and most mature companies; at the beginning of 1985, the market value of NYSE stocks — their price multiplied by the number of shares outstanding — was $2 trillion, *about 85 percent of the market value of all actively traded stocks.* The companies on the Amex tend to be smaller and younger, a mix of once and future growth stocks that featured, during the energy-starved 1970s, a stampede of oil and gas exploration companies. By 1986, however, energy issues represented only about 10 percent of the issues traded on the Amex. The OTC is the market for some 30,000 unlisted companies; it is here that new issues — companies making their first public offering of stock — are launched. Of the OTC's huge population, only 5,000 companies are actively traded. They fall into two categories, of which by far the larger one, numerically, consists of small to medium-sized companies, many of them relatively young. These include a large number of avant-garde technological companies with scientific-sounding names such as Avantek, Cermetek, Scitex, and Xidex. The other category is made up of large, often well-known companies that include

American Greetings, Apple Computer, and MCI Communications, a raft of banks and insurance companies, the South African gold mining companies and a handful of huge foreign concerns such as Cadbury Schweppes, Glaxo, and Fuji Photo Film. At the close of 1985, more than 4,000 actively traded OTC companies met the requirement for registration of their stock on the National Association of Securities Dealers Automated Quotation System, NASDAQ, which came into being in February 1971. More than 150 metropolitan newspapers now carry NASDAQ price quotations daily or weekly. This has given the OTC market much greater visibility than it used to have. Moreover, this market, which was considered somewhat disreputable in the 1960s, has gained respectability thanks to improved surveillance procedures by the National Association of Securities Dealers and increased disclosure requirements for its companies. It is the market in which an astute, aggressive investor has the best chance of detecting undervalued issues, because so many of its companies are too small or too obscure for most analysts to bother with.

2 Taking the Market's Pulse, or How to Read the Indexes

If you ask anyone, "How did the market do today?" his answer will almost certainly be that the Dow Jones Industrial Average was up or down so many points. The Dow is the oldest and best known of the market indexes, and it is the easiest to follow because it is so widely quoted in the media. But it is a mistake to assume, as some investors do, that the Dow's behavior accurately reflects the behavior of stocks in general.

The Dow Jones Industrial Average dates back to an 11-stock average first compiled by Charles H. Dow, editor of the *Wall Street Journal,* in 1884. It has since expanded to 30 stocks, and there have been many changes in its components; the most recent at this writing were the replacement in 1985 of American Brands and General Foods by McDonalds and Philip Morris (which acquired General Foods that year). The 30 Dow stocks are all of them "blue chips" — stocks of large, long-established companies that are leaders in their respective industries.

Originally, the Dow's level was computed by adding up the prices of its component stocks and dividing the total by the number of stocks in the average. But to maintain historical continuity, an adjustment had to be made for stock splits and changes in the composition of the average. Suppose, for example, that the 30 stocks' aggregate price at the close of trading on a given day was $1,500; the average would then have stood at 50 (1,500 divided by 30). But after the close, a $100 stock split 2 for 1, giving it a new price of $50, or a stock selling at $100 was replaced by one priced at $50; either change would have lowered the aggregate price of the 30 stocks to $1,450, even though no real decline had taken place. The simplest way of maintaining the average at 50 is to change the so-called divisor from 30 to 29. (1,450 divided by 29 equals 50.) This was the method chosen by Dow Jones & Co., which computes the Dow averages. Over the years, adjustments in the divisor of the DJIA have caused it to keep on shrinking; in May 1986, it was 1.008. With the divisor at 1.008, a 10-point change in the average represented an actual price change of $10.08.

The divisor is also used in computing the Dow's earnings per share, a figure that some investors have trouble understanding. If you read in a newspaper or brokerage house report that the Dow's latest 12 months' earnings were, say, $96.11, it means that the aggregate earnings per share of the 30 companies were $96.11 *after being adjusted by the divisor;* with the divisor at 1.008, the actual earnings were $96.88.

The total market value of the 30 Dow stocks in mid-1986 was $417 billion, or roughly 20 percent of the market value of all actively traded stocks. While the Dow encompasses a hefty segment of the U.S. economy, it significantly underrepresents the growth industries of the present and the future, and it overrepresents cyclical industries, those tied to the ups and downs of the economy. Analysts often refer to the Dow companies as Smokestack America because a significant proportion of them are in basic industries such as autos, chemicals, paper, and steel. Moreover, the Dow companies are among the aging or elderly giants of American industry.

The Dow's critics also point out that its behavior can be misleading because it is a "price-weighted" index. The movements of an "unweighted" index are measured by taking the *percentage* price changes of each of its components and calculating the average change, *a method that gives equal weight to the behavior of every* issue; when a $10 stock moves to $11 (10 percent), the impact on the average is the same as when a $60 stock moves to $66. But the Dow Jones Industrial Average is computed by adding up the actual dollar price changes of its components, the result being that high-priced stocks influence the average more than low-priced stocks because they have larger dollar fluctuations. The disproportionate impact of a few high-priced stocks was largely responsible for the Dow's surge to its then all-time high of 1,052 on January 11, 1973. And when the Dow was at a three-year low of 742 in February 1978, 60 percent of the drop from its high was due to fewer than one quarter of the stocks in the average.

We have dwelt on the anatomy and dynamics of the Dow because it is the average you hear about most, and it is the handiest index for the average investor to use; but keep in mind its shortcomings. Let's now take a look at ten other indexes that are often referred to in the financial press and investment advisory services. Each of them has a story to tell. And the divergences in their behavior can sometimes furnish useful insights into the mood of investors.

The Dow Jones Transportation Average (formerly the Railroad Average) consists of 20 companies — airlines, railroads, and truckers. It is closely followed by exponents of the Dow Theory, a market-forecasting system first formulated at the beginning of the twentieth century. The theory starts out with the observation that stocks usually fluctuate within a well-defined price range or "channel" for anywhere from several months to several years. Dow theorists hold that when *both* the Industrial and the Transportation averages break out of an established channel, they are signaling a new trend in the market — an uptrend if they penetrate the upper end of the range and a downtrend if they fall below the lower end. However, if a breakout by one of the averages is not "confirmed" by similar action by the other, the Dow Theory holds that the breakout is "false" and the average will drift back into its previous range. The rationale is that the Industrials represent the producing sector of the economy and the Transportation Average represents the distributing sector; so it is only when both averages break out of their trading range that they are signaling a change in economic expectations that will change the major trend of stock prices.

The trouble with the Dow Theory is that its exponents differ in their interpretations of what constitutes a real breakout, and when they do agree, the advance or decline in stock prices is already well under way. Nevertheless, the theory is worth knowing about, because its signals get attention in the press and its followers sometimes have a temporary influence on the market.

The Dow Jones Utility Average is composed of 15 public utilities; you'll find a chart showing its behavior over the previous six months on the third from last page of the *Wall Street Journal,* below similar charts of the Industrial and Transportation averages. The Utility Average is widely considered a barometer of the anticipated trend in interest rates: it tends to rise when rates are expected to decline and to fall when rates are expected to rise. The reason: utility companies must continually borrow huge sums of money to finance plant expansion, so higher interest rates hurt their profitability and they benefit when rates fall. The Utility Average flashed a prophetic signal when it peaked at 162 in early 1965 and then went into a long downtrend. We now know that 1965 marked the end of an era of low inflation and low interest rates and the beginning of a new era of recurring hyperinflation and surges in interest rates. The return of low inflation and low interest rates in the early 1980s seemed to mark the end of that era, heralded again by the Utility Average's climb to new high ground. This time, however, the non-nuclear sector of electricity companies was overbuilt and so heavily stocked with cash as to be temporarily impervious to any threat of renewed high interest.

Standard & Poor's 500-Stock Index is much more representative of the general economy and the market than the Dow Jones industrials; in addition to its 400 industrial companies, it includes 20 transportation, 40 utility, and 40 financial companies. Originated in 1923, the S&P index was subsequently linked to the Cowles Commission Index, carrying it back to 1893; thus it provides a continuous record of stock prices spanning nearly a century. Because it combines breadth and longevity, it is the index generally used by stock market professionals and academic researchers and the benchmark against which institutional money managers measure their performance.

Like the Dow, the S&P 500 is a weighted stock index, except that it is weighted by market capitalization. (A company whose stock is selling at $20 and that has 10 million shares outstanding has a market capitalization or market value of $200 million.) The index is computed by adding up the market capitalization of its components and dividing the total by the average market value of the index in the period 1941–1943, which stands for a level of 10. Thus the September

1987 level of 310 meant that the current market value was 31 times that of the base period. The weighting system causes the index to be strongly influenced by fewer than 40 stocks with huge capitalizations, such as Eastman Kodak, Exxon, General Motors, and IBM. The justification for weighting by capitalization is that an index so constructed reveals whether *the aggregate value of all the issues in it is rising or falling.* There is no such justification for price-weighting, as used in the Dow, because the market value of a company depends more on the number of its shares outstanding than on the price of its stock. In short, a capitalization-weighted index — though it does not accurately reflect the *average* percentage change in the prices of all stocks — reflects changes in *the total flow of investment funds* much more reliably than an index that is unweighted or price-weighted.

The New York Stock Exchange Composite Index, first published in 1966, includes all stocks on the Big Board and is a capitalization-weighted index, computed in the same way as the S&P 500; it was initially set at 50, which represents its market value at the end of 1965.

The American Stock Exchange Market Value Index replaced earlier Amex indexes on August 31, 1973; its base value is set at 50 (and it has been computed retroactively to January 2, 1969). Its flaw is that most of the Amex companies have small capitalizations, so a mere half-dozen large-capitalization stocks (out of 825) account for roughly 25 percent of the weight of index, and this can be misleading. For example, in the first nine months of 1979, the Amex Market Value Index rose nearly 50 percent, whereas the gain registered by an *unweighted* index of all Amex stocks was only 22 percent.

The unweighted index is compiled by Indicator Digest, an investment advisory service that also publishes an unweighted index of New York Stock Exchange stocks known as *The Indicator Digest Average.* The best known of the unweighted averages is the *Value Line Composite,* which tracks some 1,700 stocks analyzed by the *Value Line Investment Survey,* a leading advisory service that is profiled in chapter 14. About 85 percent of the stocks are listed on the Big Board, and the rest are traded on the Amex or over the counter.

The NASDAQ Composite Index, a market value index that includes about 3,750 over-the-counter stocks, was started on February 5, 1971, with a base value of 100. In September 1987, it stood at 436, up 900 percent from its 1974 low. This shows how well the smaller and less-known companies performed over that 13-year period; the Dow's rise from its '74 low was only 333 percent.

The most representative of all the indexes are those compiled by Wilshire Associates of Santa Monica, California, because they cover all actively traded stocks on U.S. markets on a given day. On April 24, 1987, for example, 5,900 stocks were represented in the indexes. The capitalization-weighted index (there's also an unweighted one) is published in *Barron's* and in *Forbes.* It is known as the Wilshire 5000 Equity Index, and its market value on that date was about 2.86 *trillion* dollars, up 394 percent since the end of 1974.

Let us try to sum up, now, what some of the leading indexes reveal about different sectors of the market. The Dow Jones Industrial Average, an all-blue-chip index, tells you how the mature giants of American industry are performing; most of its stocks are widely held by institutions and wealthy, conservative individuals. The behavior of Standard & Poor's 500, because it is strongly influenced by big capitalization stocks, is the best indicator of whether the major financial institutions are buying or selling. The Amex Market Value Index, the Indicator Digest Average, and the NASDAQ Composite represent the small-company sector of the market; these indexes reflect the behavior of aggressive investors — individuals or professionals managing relatively small pools of money. The Wilshire 500 Equity Index is by far the broadest of the indexes; it comes pretty close to representing the universe of stocks that are actively traded.

■ 3

A Company and Its Stock: A Case of Mistaken Identity

Inexperienced investors often make the mistake of thinking, "If I invest only in top-quality companies, I can't go too far wrong." It would take pages to list the top-quality companies that have been bad investments for long stretches of time. A stunning example is USX, formerly U.S. Steel. Once the bluest of the blue chips, it made its all-time high of 59⅜ back in 1976. During the bear market of 1982, it sank as low as 19, and during the first half of 1987, while the Dow was climbing to record levels as high as 2,400 in a bull market that had been raging for nearly five years, USX could rise no higher than 33¼.

To identify a company's reputation with the current investment merits of its stock is a dangerous fallacy. The quality ratings that Standard & Poor's assigns to a stock are, to be sure, based on the company's historical sales, earnings, and dividend record and present financial condition, but S&P warns that a high-rated stock "may be so overpriced as to justify its sale" and a low-rated stock may be on the bargain counter. Just because IBM is the colossus of a global growth industry, and its stock has the highest S&P rating (A+) doesn't mean that IBM is a sound investment at whatever happens to be the current market price. Eastman Kodak has long been and continues to be a superlative company, but the investors who bought Kodak stock anywhere near its 1973 high of 151¾ made a whoppingly bad value judgment; five years later, the stock hit a low of 28, a loss of 82 percent, and its best price from then until mid-1987 was only 84½ — just over one half of its peak price. On the other hand, the stock of Avco Corp., which like other conglomerates was rated a "junky" company in the early 1970s, soared from a price of 2 in 1974 to the takeover price of 50 paid by Textron in 1985, a gain of 2,400 percent.

A company may be great, good, mediocre, or lousy, but at any given moment, there is really no such thing as a good stock or a bad one; *a stock is either overpriced, underpriced, or fairly priced in relation to stocks in general.* Stocks can be judged only in terms of *value,* which of course is a matter of opinion. But value invariably hinges on price.

How to analyze stocks and judge their worth is the subject of a later chapter. But there's one yardstick used in valuing stocks that needs discussing now, because it is a basic term in the language of investing and will keep cropping up throughout this text. It is the price/earnings ratio.

4

All You Need to Know About Price/Earnings Ratios

Price/earnings ratios are the yardstick most commonly used — and misused — in valuing stocks. A stock's price/earnings ratio is its current market price divided by the company's annual earnings per share; if the price is $20 and the earnings per share are $2, the stock has a P/E ratio of 10 and is said to be selling at 10 times earnings.

You can find the P/E ratios of stocks traded on the New York and American stock exchanges, but not of those traded over the counter, in the daily stock-market tables in your newspaper. (When you see a stock with no P/E ratio, it means the company is operating at a loss.) Every Monday, the *Wall Street Journal* publishes, as an inset in its six-month chart of the Dow Jones Transportation Average, a table showing the price/earnings ratio of the Dow industrials and the other Dow averages at the previous week's closing prices and one year earlier.

Those P/E ratios and others reported in the press are based on the company's or the index's latest reported earnings for the previous 12 months, which are known as trailing earnings. But investors are vastly more concerned with the future than with the past — stocks rise and fall largely on the basis of *expectations.* So the P/E ratios most commonly used in stock valuation are based on estimates of earnings for the current year, and sometimes the year to come as well. The catch is that earnings estimates are fallible, however skillful the analyst making them may be. Here, then, is one of the limitations of P/E ratios: those based on trailing earnings are somewhat academic because they refer to the past, and those based on estimates of future earnings are frequently unreliable. That means they should never be the sole basis for valuing a stock but should be used in conjunction with other analytic tools discussed elsewhere in this book.

Before going any further, you need to know precisely why price/earnings ratios, which are commonly referred to as *valuations,* are a measure of value. Ownership of a share of stock gives you a claim to its earnings; typically, a portion of the earnings will be paid to you in the form of a cash dividend, and the balance, known as retained earnings, will be invested to finance the company's future development and contribute to the goal of earnings growth. The price you are willing to pay for a stock is, basically, a reflection of the value you place on ownership of its earnings, and that value will vary according to the rewards — increased dividends, a higher price for the stock, or both — that you think ownership will bring you. A stock whose earnings grow at an average annual rate of, say, 15 percent for the next five years will normally rise much more in price and have larger dividend increases than one whose earnings grow at a rate of 5 percent. If 15 percent and 5 percent are the growth rates you anticipate for two different stocks, you will be willing to pay significantly more for each dollar of the current earnings of the high-growth stock than for each dollar of earnings of the low-growth stock. The different values that investors, collectively, put on a dollar's worth of the current annual earnings of different companies are expressed in the price/earnings ratios of their stocks; hence, the term *valuations.* Another term for P/E ratios is *multiples,* because they represent a multiple of each dollar of earnings.

Historically, stock valuations or multiples have ranged from less than 2 times earnings to 100 times and more. But at any given time the range is not nearly that wide; in mid-1987 most stocks were selling in a range of 10 to 35 times earnings.

A stock's price-earnings ratio is influenced by every fact and belief that goes into the judgment of investors about the stock's investment merit. These include the company's past record of sales, earnings, and dividends; its prospects for the year ahead and for the longer term; its desirability as a merger partner or takeover target; the reputation of its management; its financial condition and accounting procedures; the principal industry or industries in which it operates; the extent to which its business is subject to government regulation; *and the current level of stock valuations in general.* A stock whose P/E ratio is 12 when the average P/E ratio for all stocks is also 12 is likely to sell at about 8 times earnings if the average multiple falls to 8 — unless, of course, the relative position and prospects of that particular company change significantly.

The general level of price/earnings ratios tends to be low (in relation to the recent past) at the peak of a boom and high at the bottom of a recession. This may sound wacky, but it is perfectly logical and easily explained. Investors, as noted earlier, are concerned with the future rather than with the past, and in actual practice they value stocks on the basis of estimates of future earnings. Thus, in the depths of a recession, P/E ratios based on the past 12 months' depressed earnings are high, because investors are expecting earnings to bounce back and move into an uptrend. Similarly, P/E ratios based on 12 months of boom earnings are low, because investors expect earnings to start heading down. At the end of 1982, for example, the Dow's earnings for that year were at a cyclical low point of $9.15 and its P/E ratio had risen to the incredible level of 114.4 in anticipation of a sharp earnings rise in the next 12 months. At the end of 1985, after three years of fairly steady profit growth, the Dow's earnings rose to $96.11 and its P/E ratio was down to 16.1.

Like the Dow Jones Industrial Average, the stocks of companies that are in highly cyclical industries — notably the airline, automobile, copper, rubber, textile, and steel industries — tend to sell at their lowest valuations when earnings are booming and at their highest valuations when earnings are acutely depressed. For example, from 1976 through 1985, the P/E ratio of General Motors stock averaged 6.7 in the years when earnings were high and 13.8 in the years when earnings were low.

The behavior of price/earnings ratios is altogether different in the case of so-called growth stocks — the stocks of companies whose earnings have increased even during recessions and are expected to remain in an uptrend for the next several years. Since the valuation of a growth stock is closely linked to a projected rate of growth, the valuation normally drops — often sharply — if that rate is not achieved. Conversely, valuation tends to rise if the growth rate is higher than investors anticipated. In a bull market for high-growth issues, their P/E ratios typically range from twice to four times the P/E ratio of the Dow Jones industrials.

☐ A BRIEF HISTORY OF PRICE/EARNINGS RATIOS

To use P/E ratios intelligently in valuing stocks, you need to be familiar with how they have behaved historically. Over the hundred-year period 1871 to 1970, the overall level of P/E ratios averaged 13.9 times earnings, but variations from this norm have been frequent and wide. (All P/E ratios cited in this chapter and elsewhere in the text are based on the previous 12 months' earnings, except when we refer specifically to estimated earnings.) Multiples were at their highest sustained level in history from 1961 through 1965 — the John F. Kennedy and early Lyndon Johnson era. During those years, the average P/E ratio of the Dow was about 19, but many stocks sold at 25 to 50 times earnings and multiples of 50 to 70 times earnings were not particularly rare. The euphoria underlying those unprecedented valuations stemmed from a then-prevailing myth that "fine tuning" of the economy by the administration would abolish recessions and keep business activity and corporate profits on a course of high growth.

Historic lows in P/E ratios were registered in mid-1949, when the Dow's valuation fell to 7 times earnings; in late 1974, when it fell to 5.8 times earnings; and in late 1979, when it fell to around 6 times earnings. In 1949 it was widely feared that the initial recovery from World War II would be followed by a global depression. When that fear proved totally unfounded, price/earnings ratios went into a long uptrend and stocks enjoyed their greatest bull market in history; with a few sharp but short-lived setbacks (in 1957, 1962, and 1966), that bull market lasted for roughly 20 years.

The 1974 collapse of P/E ratios was caused by runaway inflation, the Arab oil embargo, and drastic credit-tightening by the Federal Reserve Board, which together aroused fears that a major depression was in store. This time, too, the doomsday scenario did not unfold and stock prices shot up at the beginning of 1975. But recurring spells of accelerating inflation, accompanied by uptilts in interest rates, kept P/E ratios at the low end of their historical range from 1975 through 1981. Over that period, the valuation of the Dow Jones Industrials averaged less than 9 times earnings.

Once inflation and interest rates receded to their accustomed levels comfortably below double digits, the overall level of P/E ratios quickly reverted to the historic norm of about 14. With earnings of the Dow Jones industrials registering moderate growth, by the New Year's Eve ushering in 1987 the average was rising toward 2,000, with champagne corks at the ready. The Dow, like the calendar, was about to enter its third millennium.

II

What Makes Stock Prices Move

5 Every Share Bought Is a Share Sold

Unless some event of shattering importance occurs, the daily behavior of stock prices is the outcome of a tug-of-war between dozens of forces, some positive, some negative. These include economic, monetary, and political developments and rumors of developments; everything that is happening or believed to be happening in the corporate world; rulings by governmental regulatory agencies; court decisions that affect industries or individual companies; crop reports; scuttlebutt about what superstar money managers are buying or selling; the cash needs of investors (to pay bills or buy yachts), and so on. So trying to come up with specific reasons for the market's daily behavior is usually an exercise in futility. *Nonetheless, all changes in stock prices have an underlying rationale.*

Have you ever asked yourself what, basically, determines the price of a stock? The answer is: investors' expectations of the future returns — dividends and capital growth — that the stock will generate. So what makes stock prices move is changes in investors' expectations about future returns. What causes those changes can be summed up in three words: "Just about everything." *The behavior of the stock market reflects the collective knowledge, beliefs, hopes, fears, and fantasies of all investors. Facts, rumors, judgments, and emotions give rise to conflicting opinions about future risks and rewards. And those opinions assume concrete shape and size in the form of orders to buy and sell stocks; they are translated into demand and supply.*

There's a stockbrokers' saying about how to deal with a tiresome client who, whenever a stock of his falls even half a point, wants to know why — "Tell him there were more sellers than buyers." In the markets where stocks are traded, prices move in accordance with the law of supply and demand. When sellers wish to unload more shares of a stock than buyers are demanding at a given price, the price declines. When buyers are seeking more shares than sellers are willing to part with at a given price, the price rises. *Every share of stock bought represents a share of stock sold, which means that every transaction reflects a conflict of opinion.* When you buy a stock that you think is probably undervalued, it has been sold to you by somebody who thinks it is overvalued.*

The factors that influence investors' expectations of future returns — and thus determine supply and demand — fall into three categories: fundamental, technical, and psychological. The *fundamentals* include the earnings, dividends, and financial condition of companies, and trends in the general economy and the monetary system. *Technical* factors are those that most directly determine the potential demand for and supply of stock; the most important — others will be considered in Chapter 16 — is the size of the cash reserves in the hands of all investors. The *psychological* factors are, simply, fear and greed, and their influence on stock prices can hardly be exaggerated. We will take a closer look at each of those factors in the chapters that follow, *focusing on specific information that can help you to anticipate movements in stock prices.*

6 The Business Cycle, Profits, and Interest Rates

Investors' expectations of a stock's future returns hinge largely on the trend in the company's profits. So the trend in overall corporate profits is the most important of the fundamental factors that influence stock prices, and it is closely related to the ups and downs of the general economy. The economy's cycles, from peak to peak, have averaged 51 months. Since World War II, recessions or contractions have lasted on the average 11 months, and the subsequent recoveries and expansions 40 months; only two postwar expansions (1958 to 1960 and 1980 to 1981) lasted less than three years. Since investors try to anticipate the future, major declines in the stock market usually start while the economy is still booming, and major advances usually begin in the very depths of a recession. *In the eight business cycles between 1948*

---

* We have excluded from this discussion the important role of the exchange specialist, who is charged by the exchange's governing body with maintaining a "fair and orderly market" in the stocks assigned to him. The specialist can mitigate the impact of sudden drastic changes in supply and demand — but only temporarily. For a fuller description of his functions, see Appendix D, The Language of Investing.

and 1982, stock prices peaked and started to decline nine months on the average before the onset of the recession; the shortest lead time was five months, the longest 13 months; prices bottomed and started to rise about four months on the average before the beginning of the recovery.

☐ Those Influential Interest Rates

The relationship between interest rates and stock prices is in principle quite simple. Rising interest rates are normally unfavorable for the stock market for two reasons: (1) they increase the yields offered by fixed-income securities such as Treasury Bills, money market mutual funds and bonds, causing investors to switch money out of the stock market and into these securities, thereby depressing stock prices; (2) if interest rates rise steeply enough, they slow business activity by making borrowing expensive and perhaps difficult, and this causes corporate profits to decline. A sustained downtrend in interest rates has, of course, the opposite effects and is therefore extremely bullish for the stock market.

Major advances in stock prices usually begin either not long before or not long after an upward cycle in interest rates reaches its final peak and long-term rates start declining. But there is a long time lag between an upturn in interest rates and a major downturn in the market, and the lag varies considerably; the major market advances since World War II have lasted anywhere from seven to 44 months *after* interest rates bottomed and started rising. Moreover, in 1980 and early 1981, the principal market indexes (except for the Dow) climbed to all-time highs in the face of steep upsurges in interest rates. This unprecedented behavior suggested that, since inflation had become recognized as our number one economic problem, investors had developed a temporary tolerance for rising interest rates. They viewed them, or so it seemed, not simply as bad news for the economy, but also as reassuring evidence that the Federal Reserve Board was really committed to sticking with an anti-inflationary policy. However, during the bull market that began in 1982, investors again began getting the jitters at any hint that interest rates might climb. One thing is sure: when interest rates climb into the stratosphere and persist in staying there — as they did in the summer and fall of 1981 — investors become discouraged and stock prices drop. They have every reason to expect the persistence of extremely high interest rates to cause a slowdown in business activity and the onset of a serious recession.

7 Inflation and Stock Prices: Are Stocks a Hedge or Aren't They?

In the 1950s and early 1960s, when inflation averaged less than 2 percent annually, the conventional wisdom was that stocks were a hedge against inflation, because they represent ownership of real assets — property, plant, and equipment — whose values rise along with prices. This concept was seemingly demolished in the first half of the 1970s, when upward spirals in inflation were accompanied by two horrifying tailspins in stock prices. The disastrous losses suffered by most investors between 1969 and 1975 prompted some 5 million individuals to liquidate their stock holdings. By the mid-1970s, the consensus was that inflation is poison for the stock market.

The behavior of stock prices tended to support this view until 1978; prices rose when inflation declined and dropped when inflation tilted upward. Then something extraordinary happened: although inflation continued to heat up, the stock market embarked on a major advance that carried some of the popular averages to record-breaking levels in November 1980 and others (the Amex market value index and the NASDAQ composite) to new peaks in May 1981. Some analysts concluded that the view of stocks as an inflation hedge was back in favor. The question — are they or aren't they? — can best be answered by looking at the historical data on inflation and stock prices.

According to a study co-authored by Roger G. Ibbotson and Rex A. Sinquefield — *Stocks, Bonds, Bills, and Inflation: Historical Returns* (1926–1985)* — the total return on Standard & Poor's 500-stock index over the 59-year period was 9.8 percent compounded annually, and the annual inflation rate averaged 3.2 percent. So stocks provided a real return of 6.6 percent (before income taxes), and they were indeed a hedge against inflation. The real return on U.S. Treasury Bills was 0.3 percent — their annual return of 2.5 percent closely

---

* Published by the Ibbotson Associates, Chicago, 1986.

matched the rate of inflation. Long-term corporate bonds provided a nominal return of 4.8 percent and a real return of only 1.6 percent. However, the data on stocks for the extraordinary ten-year period of high inflation from March 1970 through February 1980 tell a very different story: the annual return on the S&P index was nearly 1 percent *less* than the 7.5 percent annual increase in the consumer price index. And over the four-year period 1973 through 1976, the rate of return on common stocks, adjusted for inflation, was *minus* 6.2 percent annually.

The Ibbotson-Sinquefield figures show that, over the very long haul, the total return on common stocks has substantially exceeded the rate of inflation. *But stocks have not been an inflation hedge in periods when inflation has persisted at exceptionally high levels.* These conclusions are supported by Steven Leuthold's book *The Myths of Inflation and Investing* (Chicago: Crain Books, 1980), which tracks stock prices and inflation rates all the way from 1872 through 1979. During those 108 years, there were 14 years of exceptionally high inflation (8 percent to 18 percent), and in nine of those years the total return on stocks was lower than the inflation rate. In two years of rampaging inflation immediately following Leuthold's study, the market produced a 32 percent total return and then a 5 percent loss. All in all, stocks achieved their best annual rates of gain in periods of price stability or mild deflation.

There are several reasons why, in principle, high levels of inflation have an adverse effect on stock prices. One is that *inflation has a negative impact on real corporate profitability,* a subject that became a burning issue in the accounting profession in the 1970s. Controversy continues as to how the so-called nominal profits that corporations report (and pay taxes on) should be adjusted to take into account the effects of inflation. But two adjustments made by the Department of Commerce are now generally considered standard procedure. The inventory valuation adjustment, or IVA, adjusts nominal profits by subtracting from them profits on inventory that are strictly due to rising prices; such profits are in effect illusory, because the company has to replace inventory at the current, higher prices. The capital consumption adjustment, or CCA, reduces nominal profits by increasing depreciation charges, which are based on the original costs of plant and equipment and are, therefore, too low in light of current replacement costs. Together, these adjustments take a big slice out of reported profits. In 1970, the difference in total corporate profits

before and after IVA and CCA was only 10 percent; the figures were
$37 billion and $33.4 billion. But in 1979, profits totaled $144.1 bil-
lion before IVA and CCA and $85.6 billion after; *the difference had
widened to 40 percent.*

A second reason high inflation tends to hurt stock valuations has
already been mentioned; as inflation escalates, interest rates rise, making fixed-income securities more competitive with stocks.

Third, a persistently high and rising level of inflation arouses fears
that the Federal Reserve Board will resort to drastic credit-tightening
measures that could cause a recession, a "credit crunch," or both. A
credit crunch — a critical shortage of available cash — is one of the
worst possible disasters for the market. When credit crunches have
occurred — as, for example, in 1970, 1974, and 1981 — the downtrends in stock prices that were already under way turned into catastrophic nosedives. On those occasions, investors feared that the Fed's
policies would result in overkill and throw the economy into a depression. Moreover, a credit crunch combined with rising prices forces
many investors, particularly those running businesses of their own, to
raise cash by withdrawing funds from the stock market — and money
is the market's lifeblood.

8 The Federal Reserve Board: A Fed-Watcher's Guide

At the corner of 20th Street and Constitution Avenue in Washington,
D.C., stands a massive neoclassical building with floors of travertine
marble and walls adorned with paintings of museum quality. Imposing
and aloof, this structure is an appropriate setting for its tenant, the
Federal Reserve Board, which is responsible for managing the nation's
supply of money and credit. Nowadays, no government agency is so
closely watched and so much discussed by Wall Street professionals as
the Federal Reserve Board, commonly referred to as the Fed. Interest
rates, inflation, and corporate profits are all of them strongly influenced by the policies of the Fed. Indeed some economists consider

the Fed's policies the most important single influence on the behavior of the stock and bond markets.

The Federal Reserve Board, created by Congress in 1913, is a government agency independent of the administration and the legislature. As the manager of monetary policy, the Fed has the awesome responsibility of trying to smooth the ups and downs of the economy, while fighting inflation and keeping an eye on the foreign exchange rate of the U.S. dollar. The Fed prides itself on its independence, and it has sometimes persisted in a course that was objectionable to the White House and Congress. But it is by no means insensitive to political pressures. A study by Robert Weintraub, a staff economist for congressional committees concerned with monetary policy, suggests that presidents since World War II have usually received from the Fed the policies they wanted. It is arguable that nothing is wrong with this, since the Fed, by cooperating with the incumbent administration, is in effect being responsive to the wishes of the electorate. But the Fed's critics have accused it of playing politics. They charge, in particular, that in presidential election years, the Fed is apt to pursue policies designed to stimulate the economy and thus to improve the incumbent's image in the eyes of the voters.

According to textbook theory, monetary policy should be stimulative when the economy is ailing and it should be restrictive when the economy is booming and threatens to become overextended. A stimulative policy is one that provides ample growth in the supply of money and credit, thereby pushing down interest rates. Easy credit boosts the demand for automobiles, housing, appliances, and other goods and services, and it encourages borrowing by industry for investment in plant and equipment, which creates jobs and thereby increases consumer income and spending. A restrictive policy tightens the supply of money and credit, which pushes up interest rates. Tight credit curbs consumer demand and discourages business investment, thereby causing unemployment and reducing consumer income and spending. For many years, the Fed's top priority as manager of monetary policy was to smooth the course of the U.S. economy and thus help to maintain a high level of employment. But when inflation becomes the nation's number one economic problem, the Fed finds itself confronted with a taxing dilemma, which we will try to explain as simply as possible.

A policy of easy money, which in principle promotes economic growth, can become highly inflationary when — as throughout the

1980s — the federal government incurs huge budget deficits. The government finances these deficits by selling Treasury securities, an action that is popularly though not quite accurately known as printing money. When Treasury offerings are larger than investors (mainly financial institutions) are willing to buy at the current rate of interest, the Treasury has to raise interest rates to attract buyers. Thus exceptionally heavy Treasury financing tends to push interest rates up to levels that could have stifling effects on the economy. The Federal Reserve, normally a big buyer of government securities, can help to prevent this by significantly stepping up its buying, thereby shrinking the amount that has to be absorbed by the public. But Fed purchases of Treasury securities release cash into the nation's monetary system; and when the purchases are extraordinarily large, their effects are inflationary. By thus helping the government to finance huge deficits without pushing interest rates too high, the Fed frustrates its own efforts to dampen inflation by curbing growth of the money supply — the total of all money sloshing around in the economy. One way out of this Catch-22 situation is to reduce the size of the federal deficit. But solutions to our macroeconomic problems are beyond the scope of this book. Our concern here is simply to explain the Fed's functions and influence in order to show how Fed-watching — which need only take a few minutes a week — can help the average investor to anticipate the behavior of the securities markets. So let's take a closer look at how the Fed manages monetary policy and at the specific signals that investors should watch for.

The Fed's chief policy-making body, its 12-member Open Market Committee, meets in Washington eight to ten times a year under conditions of secrecy that would do credit to the CIA. However, a so-called record of policy actions taken at a meeting (or in telephone conferences between times) is released to the press three days after the *subsequent* meeting — that is, usually with a time lag of about a month.

The most important and most flexible of the Fed's tools for managing monetary policy is *open-market operations:* buying and selling U.S. government securities in a market comprised of banks and other dealers in these securities. Open-market operations account for at least 90 percent of the Fed's daily activities. Banks are required by law to maintain a certain ratio, determined by the Fed, between their reserves and their deposits, which they use to make loans. For example, when the reserve requirement for demand deposits at large banks is 12 percent, $1,000 deposited in a checking account permits the bank to loan out $880. When the Fed's Open Market Desk in New York City buys, say, $400 milliion of Treasury Bills, its payments are deposited in member banks of the Federal Reserve System, increasing the banks' reserves and thus permitting them to increase their lending. On the other hand, the selling of government securities by the Fed siphons cash out of the money market, decreases the banks' reserves, and thus reduces their lending power. Through its open-market operations the Fed seeks to expand or contract the money supply to achieve a targeted rate of growth, determined annually by its policymakers.

There are several measures of the money supply. The one that gets the most attention, because it is considered the best measure of money in the hands of the public, is M-1 — currency plus most checking accounts, including interest-bearing checking accounts at banks and thrift institutions. Changes in the money supply are made public weekly after the close of the stock market on Fridays. They are reported in leading newspapers in financial centers and in *Barron's* on Saturdays and the *Wall Street Journal* on Mondays, along with an analysis of whether M-1 ran above analysts' expectations and the Fed's own annually announced target range. If the money supply is moving above target, there's a good chance that the Fed's open-market operations will seek to reduce money-supply growth, causing interest rates to tilt upward. Conversely, if M-1 is expanding at less than the targeted rate, the Fed may ease up on restraints; this would allow interest rates to fall.

In times when inflation is at exceptionally high levels, bulges in the weekly figures for the money supply are thoroughly bad news for the stock market, since they show that the Fed isn't succeeding in holding down inflationary pressures and will probably be tightening credit. By the same token, it is good news for investors when the weekly money-supply figures are in accord with, or below, the targeted growth rate. So by keeping an eye on these figures you can get worthwhile insights into how well the Fed is coping with inflation and also into the probable trend of short-term interest rates.

A second weapon in the Fed's arsenal is its power to change *bank reserve requirements* — the minimum level of cash reserves that banks must keep in relation to their deposits. Over the past half-century, the Fed has changed reserve requirements for large city banks fewer than 30 times. When it does change them, here is what investors can expect: *the market will rise over the 18-month period following a decrease in reserve requirements, and it will almost certainly decline over the 18 months following an increase.* Norman G. Fosback writes in *Stock Market Logic* (Fort Lauderdale: The Institute for Economic Research, 1986): "It may be stated categorically that a reduction in reserve requirements . . . for large city banks is the single most bullish event in the world of stock price behavior."

Another important indicator for investors is a change in the *discount rate,* the lending rate charged by a Federal Reserve District bank to its member banks. Since 1960, the discount rate has ranged from a low of 3 percent in 1960 to a high of 14 percent (plus a 4 percent surcharge for big borrowers) in May 1981. A decrease (or increase) in the discount rate is a signal that the Fed intends to ease (or tighten) credit, and *the historical record shows that the return on stocks has usually been higher than average in the 12 months following a decrease and slightly lower than average in the 12 months following an increase.* Changes in the discount rate occur relatively infrequently and are prominently reported in the financial pages, so it is easy to keep track of them.

Since the Fed limits the amount of borrowing that banks may do at its so-called discount window, banks tend to use it only as a last resort. They do most of their borrowing from other banks that have more than the required amount of reserves. The rate charged for such overnight loans is known as the *federal funds rate.* It is published in the *Wall Street Journal,* and *it is a key indicator of the demand for credit and therefore of the trend in short-term interest rates.*

A Fed-watcher's guide wouldn't be complete without a reference to *margin requirements.* The Securities Exchange Act of 1934 empowered the Fed to regulate the minimum amount that investors must put up when they buy securities on margin — that is, using funds borrowed from their broker. Since 1934, the margin requirement has been as low as 40 percent and as high as 100 percent (which means no borrowing is permitted). When the rate is, say, 50 percent — as it was when this book was written — an investor can buy $10,000 worth of stock by putting up $5,000. In theory, a margin rate hike should reduce the demand for stock by reducing the amount that investors can borrow, and a reduction should stimulate demand. But the record shows that a change in margin requirements is of little value as a stock market indicator. This is probably because margin requirements are usually raised only *after* the market has been booming for some time, and they are lowered only *after* the market has been in a prolonged slump.

However, margin requirements are one of three elements in *an indicator whose forecasting record, as of mid-1987, had been literally infallible for 70 years.* Its discoverer, Norman Fosback, calls this indicator "Two Tumbles and a Jump," and he formulates it as follows: *When any one of the Fed's three policy variables — the discount rate, bank reserve requirements, or margin requirements — is lowered twice in succession, stock prices will jump over the ensuing year. The two-tumbles signal was given 18 times between December 23, 1914, and June 1986. With a single exception, at the start of the Great Depression, the market was up six months, nine months, 12 months, 15 months, and 18 months later. The average six-month gain was 16 percent, the average nine-month gain was 21 percent, the average 12-month gain was 30 percent, and the 15- and 18-month gains were 34 percent.* Changes in the discount rate, reserve requirements, and margin requirements are reported in the *Wall Street Journal* and other leading newspapers. So a vigilant investor should be able to tell when the two-tumbles signal has been flashed. If he heeds the record, he will load up on stocks.

■9 The Cash in Institutional Coffers

Assessments of the market outlook in newspapers, brokerage house newsletters, and advisory services periodically refer to the size of the cash reserves held by institutional investors. High cash reserves represent latent buying power that could push stock prices up: low reserves mean that the institutions are already heavily invested in stocks and are therefore no longer a source of strong demand that could keep prices rising. The largest of the pools of institutional cash reserves is that of private (nongovernmental) pension funds. But pension fund figures are disclosed quarterly and may be out of date by the time they appear in the SEC's *Statistical Bulletin.* However, since financial institutions tend to behave roughly like one another, you can deduce whether pension and other institutional cash reserves are high or low from a figure published monthly — the mutual funds' cash-to-assets ratio. This is the percentage of the total assets of mutual funds — excluding money market funds — that is currently in cash or so-called cash equivalents (Treasury Bills, commercial paper, and other short-term securities). The cash/assets ratio is compiled for the last day of each month by the Investment Company Institute (1600 M Street, Washington, D.C. 20036), the principal trade association of the mutual fund industry; it is publicly released with a three-week time lag and usually appears in the *Wall Street Journal.*

Since the cash/assets ratio was first compiled in 1954, it has fluctuated between 4 percent and 14 percent; in the 1980s it has typically been 8 or 9 percent, of which about 2 percent is generally used to cover expenses and redemptions of fund shares. Consequently, brokerage-house market letters and advisory services will tell you that a ratio of, say, 10 percent is high and, therefore, bullish. This is misleading, because it doesn't take into account the current level of interest rates; fund managers tend to maintain above normal cash/assets ratios when they can get big returns on money market securities. Here's a formula, developed by Norman G. Fosback, to determine whether mutual funds' cash reserves are *really* high or low in light of the current rate of interest: add seven-tenths of the current Treasury Bill rate to the typical 2 percent liquidity reserve, and you get a cash/assets ratio that can reliably be considered normal. For example, when the T-Bill rate is 6 percent, the *normal* cash/assets ratio is 2 percent + 4.2 percent (seven-tenths of 6 percent), which equals 6.2 percent. The historical record shows that, *if the actual ratio reported by mutual funds is 2½ percentage points above the normal ratio, a substantial rise in stock prices is probable over the next three to six months.* On the other hand, a reported cash/assets ratio that is below the normal one is usually a bearish portent.

▪10 Fear and Greed

Fear or greed becomes the dominant influence on stock prices whenever investors cease to act as thinking individuals and surrender to herd psychology.* This occurs with unfailing regularity in the final stages of major bull or bear markets. In the euphoria generated by a long and powerful market advance, investors get carried away by the lure of instant profits, and greed takes command; even normally hard-headed professionals ignore rational yardsticks of valuation and join the frenzied buying that pushes prices up to preposterously high levels, from which eventually they come down with a crash. Similarly, at the tail end of bear markets, fear conjures up images of total catastrophe, and panic selling forces valuations down to fire-sale levels. Here are some examples of the enormous impact that greed and fear can have on stock prices.

In the 18 months leading up to the historic crash of 1929, Anaconda rose from 54 to 162, Montgomery Ward from 134 to 467, Radio Corporation from 95 to 505, and Westinghouse from 92 to 313. In the subsequent bear market, Anaconda fell from 162 to 4, Montgomery Ward from 467 to 4, Radio Corporation from 505 to 18, and Westinghouse from 313 to 16. At their peak prices in the bull market of the late 1960s, 30 growth stocks widely favored by institutions sold at a stratospheric average valuation of 84 times earnings — about five times that of the S&P 500. In the bear market of 1969–1970, the prices of these issues dropped on the average 81 percent from their bull market highs. Donald T. Regan, then chairman of Merrill Lynch and later President Reagan's chief of staff, said in his book, *A View from the Street* (New York: New American Library, 1972): "Institutional buyers, alleged to be . . . pretty cool customers making emotionless decisions, were just as susceptible to panic, if not more so, as anyone else." Institutions acted even more irrationally in the bear market of 1973–1974; 27 of the favorite institutional stocks dropped, on the average, 84 percent from their 1971–1972 highs. Avon Products plummeted from 140 to 18⅝, Walt Disney from 119⅛ to 16⅝, McDonald's from 77⅜ to 21¼, and Westinghouse from 54⅞ to 8. *Nothing was fundamentally wrong with these companies. Indeed, at their 1975 highs — that is, in less than a year — the 27 stocks were up, on the average, 221 percent from their 1974 lows.*

---

* The history of mass irrationality in investing is richly documented in Charles Mackay's *Extraordinary Popular Delusions and The Madness of Crowds* (1841), and in Gustave Le Bon's small classic *The Crowd* (1895), both of which are still in print.

Crowd psychology doesn't necessarily vanish from the marketplace at times when the market is neither booming nor collapsing. It can manifest itself in fads and fashions that generate speculative crazes from stock groups whose promise is either vastly exaggerated or entirely fanciful. Over the past two decades or so, fad-followed stock groups have included small business investment companies, companies in the bowling business, copycat fast-food franchisers short on assets and know-how, real estate investment trusts, high-technology camp followers, and other so-called concept stocks that put stars in investors' eyes and eventually took the shirts off their backs.

In the hope of making a quick killing people often buy fad stocks or other market favorites that their reason tells them are dangerously overvalued. They rationalize their greed with the greater fool theory, which says that you will be able to sell an overpriced stock to a greater fool at an even higher price. Occasionally, the theory works. But never forget that in the stock market fear displaces greed with astonishing rapidity, and all those fools who were frantic to buy suddenly become scared cats who are frantic to sell.

▪11 The Market Discounts the Future

Even though all investors don't act as thinking individuals all of the time, many investors act as thinking individuals much of the time. And as such they are constantly seeking, in their buying and selling, to anticipate future developments. That's what is meant by the dictum "The market discounts the future." In that saying is wrapped a key to understanding the behavior of stock prices.

A favorable (or unfavorable) development anticipated by knowledgeable investors causes a stock to rise (or fall) weeks, and sometimes months, *before* that development occurs; *by the time the development does occur, it has been taken into account in the stock's current price.* For example, when a $20 billion program to encourage the development of synthetic fuels was legislated by Congress in June 1980, the stock of companies that stood to benefit had already moved up appreciably in anticipation that the bill would be passed. Another example: after the market's close on October 27, 1980, General Motors announced a third-quarter loss of $567 million, until then the largest quarterly deficit ever reported by a U.S. corporation; the news had been so fully discounted that the following day General Motors stock actually moved up 3/8 to 49⅛. So don't rush to buy on good news or sell on bad news, as so many amateurs do; check first to see whether the news has been discounted. A recent runup in a stock's price is usually an indication that investors have anticipated good news, and a recent decline tells you that bad news has probably been discounted.

Developments that are unexpected or unpredictable cannot, by definition, have been discounted. If the event is of such importance that it could significantly affect the company's future, it often pays to act promptly. A case in point was the nuclear accident at the Three Mile Island plant of General Public Utilities in March 1979. In the two weeks following the accident, the company's stock declined from 17⅞ to 13, and it subsequently sank as low as 3⅜. When unexpected catastrophe strikes, the quicker you sell the better; but don't necessarily stay out of the stock forever. By 1986, General Public Utilities had restarted one of its reactors at the stricken site, and with the company under new management the stock price was selling above 20. Those who had been shrewd enough to buy at the bottom made a 600 percent profit in seven years. In much less time, Union Carbide shares recovered from the effects of a tragic leak of methyl isocyanate gas at a pesticide plant in Bhopal, India on December 3, 1984, that killed more than 2,000 people. In the next five days, the stock fell from 15¼ to 11¾, but by 1986 it was selling above 30, propelled up by GAF Corporation's unfriendly takeover attempt.

With the aid of computerized screenings of thousands of stocks, knowledgeable investors in the 1980s were able to anticipate hundreds of mergers and acquisitions by identifying companies whose assets were worth far more than the value of their outstanding shares. As knowledge of undervalued companies spread, their share prices discounted the desirability of the companies as perhaps imminent takeover targets.

Stock prices may also discount expectations related to the distant future. This is evident in the lofty and sometimes astronomic valuations placed on the stocks of young companies that are pioneering new technologies. Naive investors think they are getting into such companies on the ground floor; they fail to realize how stiff a price they are paying up-front for expectations of rewards that are still far distant and, in most cases, highly uncertain.

A historic example of reckless discounting of the future was the first public offering of Genentech, a pioneer in genetic engineering, whose prospects investors found intoxicating. Although the company had virtually no earnings when its stock went public at $35 a share in October 1980, investors who failed to get stock in the offering were so frantic to buy that Genentech opened for trading in the aftermarket at 80 and rose to a high of 89 on the day of issue. It closed at 71 — leaving everyone who bought in the aftermarket with a loss; three months later it had fallen to 36. The moral: even when a company's prospects are "Such stuff as dreams are made on," ask yourself coolly whether those dreams have not already been overdiscounted in the price of the stock. Whenever future promise grossly overinflates present price, the risks of future stocks are large.*

Once a novice has understood the market's discounting mechanism, he has taken a giant step toward losing his innocence. Among other things, this understanding will imbue him with a healthy skepticism about tips from friends or brokers who claim to know of an impending development that will make a stock jump. In such cases, you should immediately check on a stock's recent behavior; if it has had a run-up, the development has probably been widely anticipated. If the stock hasn't been climbing, there are, as Talmudists say, two possibilities: your informant may know something that hasn't been discounted — or his information may be phony. Your decision on how to act has to depend on how reliable you consider your source to be. But remember this: the chances that highly significant information about a company is not widely known are exceedingly slim — unless the company happens to be an offbeat one that few analysts follow.

---

* Six years later, although Genentech was barely profitable, the dream of a giant future company was reborn. The shares, having split 2 for 1 and having traded as low as 17 during the previous 12 months, had soared near 100. At that point, even someone who got in at the opening-day peak had more than doubled his money; hopes for Genentech were so buoyant that the price/earnings ratio had wafted to a dreamy 515.

12 The Academic Gospel: What's of Value in it for the Layman

It is now time to consider two related doctrines about the behavior of stock prices that are gospel in academic circles and have had a huge influence on institutional investors: the Random Walk Hypothesis (or Model) and its outgrowth, the Efficient Market Hypothesis. Random walkers hold that the past price behavior of a stock affords no clues to its behavior in the future; stocks move randomly, they do not move in trends. The Efficient Market Hypothesis goes much farther. It maintains that at any given moment a stock's price is the best available estimate of its value; consequently all of the efforts of analysts and investors to unearth undervalued stocks and anticipate market movements are completely useless. According to the Efficient Market Hypothesis, a 20-stock portfolio selected by a chimpanzee throwing darts at the stock tables in a newspaper has the same chance of outperforming or underperforming the market as a 20-stock portfolio selected by the top brains in Wall Street. This thesis — understandably abhorrent to most people in the brokerage business — runs counter to common sense and large amounts of documentary evidence. Nonetheless, the Random Walk and Efficient Market hypotheses contain important elements of truth. A thorough understanding of these doctrines will provide inexperienced investors with a professional perspective on the workings of the stock market. And it will furnish them with insights that have a crucial bearing on the way they handle their investments.

☐ THE RANDOM WALK THEORY OF PRICE MOVEMENTS

The theory gets its name from the unpredictable movements of microscopic particles suspended in fluids or gases. The concept that the random behavior of particles was paralleled by the price behavior of stocks and commodities was first formulated in 1900 by a French student of mathematics, Louis Bachelier. Bachelier's work was rediscovered by U.S. academic researchers around 1960 and tested by them in a succession of statistical studies. The evidence thus accumulated appeared to destroy the claims of technical analysis — a system for forecasting stock and commodity prices on the basis of past patterns in their behavior. The academicians' studies appeared to prove, again and again, that changes in stock prices occur independent of previous changes; consequently, past price movements offer no information that is of use in forecasting future movements. According to the Random Walk Model, a rise in a stock's price for five days in a row gives no indication of what it will do on the sixth day; the odds that it will rise rather than fall are 50/50 — just as the odds are 50/50 that a tossed coin that has come up heads five times will come up heads a sixth time. To put it more graphically, the behavior of stock prices resembles the walk of a drunk. No matter how closely you watch a drunk lurching this way and that, you can't predict in which direction or how far his next step will take him. The random walkers' conclusion: technical analysis is bunk.

This verdict has failed to shake the strongly entrenched position of technical analysis in the investment community. To the contrary, brokerage houses have expanded their budgets for technical research, and technically oriented advisory services have a larger following than ever before. In subsequent chapters, we will cite persuasive evidence that stocks do not move randomly all of the time; over the long term, trends in the market develop and persist. However, the random walk studies make it hard to reject the conclusion that *short-term price fluctuations* are random and unpredictable. We therefore believe that the efforts of technical analysts to anticipate short-term ripples in stock prices are worse than worthless; they are financially damaging in the long run to those who follow them. Typically, technical analysts who make short-term recommendations tell you to buy a stock at, say, $34 "for a possible move to 38," and to limit your losses by simultaneously placing an order to sell the stock if it drops to 32⅛. That kind of advice leads to incessant in-and-out trading, which makes brokers rich and leaves investors poor.

☐ THE EFFICIENT MARKET HYPOTHESIS: HOW TO PROFIT FROM INEFFICIENCY

Efforts by academic researchers to account for the supposedly random behavior of stock prices led to formulation of the Efficient Market

Hypothesis. The EMH carried the academic blitzkrieg into the realm of fundamental analysis, which seeks to determine the intrinsic value of stocks and project their future value on the basis of economic and financial fundamentals. The EMH holds that all available information that affects stock prices is known to and continuously analyzed by large numbers of investment professionals and concerned investors, and that all incoming information is evaluated almost instantly. Thus, at any given moment a stock is "efficiently" priced, which means that its price reflects all of the facts, opinions, and expectations that have a bearing on its value. As James Lorie and Richard Brealey, leading exponents of the EMH, succinctly put it, "Current prices reflect what is knowable." A stock's price may be too high or too low, but it is the best available estimate of what the stock is worth, because it represents the collective judgment of large numbers of informed investors, all of them competing in the search for values. Thus the EMH argues that there are no undiscovered values, precisely because analysts and informed investors work so hard at discovering them. And since stock prices at all times reflect what is knowable about values, no individual or team of professionals can consistently outperform the market. An investor may get lucky for a few months or even a couple of years, but over the long haul his rate of return will be about the same as that of a broadly based market index such as Standard & Poor's 500 — unless he is willing to assume above-average risks.

By taking above-average risks an investor can and indeed should obtain better than average returns, according to the Efficient Market Hypothesis. Its basic assumption is that investors act rationally at all times — that is, they constantly seek to minimize risk and maximize returns. Consequently, they would not invest in high-risk stocks or other high-risk securities unless such securities provided larger returns than those considered to be less risky. The argument applies only to a well-diversified portfolio of high-risk issues; it doesn't imply that *every* high-risk issue is likely to provide above-average returns. It recognizes, too, that a high-risk portfolio will have much larger price swings than the S&P index; indeed, there will be times when the portfolio shows a lower rate of return than the index or even alarmingly big losses. Nonetheless, in the long run a market that prices stocks efficiently will provide superior returns to investors who assume greater than average risks — and manage to survive. For those who don't take such risks, there is no hope of outperforming the market for any length of time.

Proponents of the EMH recognize that it hinges on a paradox.

Beating the market is an impossible dream only because so many smart investors are dumb enough to keep trying. If they recognized the futility of their efforts, they would cease to work so hard at digging for undiscovered values and evaluating incoming information, and the market's pricing mechanism would then cease to be efficient — prices would no longer reflect what is knowable. *Thus, for the Efficient Market Hypothesis to be true, investors and analysts must believe that it isn't true.* That paradox does not, in itself, refute the EMH. But there are compelling reasons for believing that the concept of efficient pricing — though it applies to part of the market much of the time — doesn't apply to all of the market all of the time.

1. For stocks to be efficiently priced, the collective judgment of investors must invariably be rational — an assumption whose absurdity was documented in an earlier chapter, "Fear and Greed." As the figures cited there show, it is farcical to maintain that stocks were efficiently priced at their 1972–1973 highs, their 1974 lows, and their 1975 recovery levels. Clearly, there are times when the collective judgment of investors goes haywire and the market as a whole becomes spectacularly inefficient.

2. The EMH assumes that all available information about stocks is known and all incoming information is instantly assimilated. Certainly, the presence of computers at the desks of almost all analysts and millions of private investors would seem to bolster that assumption. By way of telephone links to news and stock tickers, any investor can make himself the instant possessor of all information available to others. What is more, he can screen through thousands of stocks in a few minutes to identify discrepancies between a stock's selling price and the performance of its company.

Even so, the EMH adherents' assumption that all information is instantly assimilated can apply — common sense tells us — only to stocks that have been thoroughly analyzed and are closely followed by analysts and informed investors. Some proponents of the EMH concede that the stocks of small, offbeat companies — ignored by analysts and lacking a large body of shareholders — may be inefficiently priced; so it may be possible to discover among them issues that are undervalued. Having made that concession, they argue that such companies constitute a tiny and inconsequential subsector of the market. However, there's convincing evidence to the contrary; the requirements for efficient pricing apply, at most, to one-fifth of the 7,000 companies whose stocks are actively, or fairly actively, traded.

The intensive research done by brokerage firms is focused on fewer than 200 companies with large market capitalizations. Another 300 companies (including public utilities) have been thoroughly analyzed and are closely tracked by brokerage firms. Thus, there are roughly 500 stocks about which nearly all that can be known is probably known; these constitute the hard core of the efficient market (which, as we have pointed out, becomes spectacularly inefficient when investors get carried away by euphoria or panic). Knowledge of the 6,500 other regularly traded companies becomes sketchier. Lynch, Jones & Ryan, the brokerage house that combs analysts' reports for its widely used Institutional Brokers' Estimate System (IBES), reports that at a given time 800 of the 3,300 companies covered by its system are followed by fewer than three analysts and that 500 are totally neglected by analysts. In research based on data from IBES and other sources, Professors Avner Arbel of Cornell and Paul Strebel of SUNY Binghamton found that "at any given time in the last ten years [1974 to 1984], almost one-third of the companies included in the Standard and Poor's index received little regular coverage of any substance." Arbel, in his book *How to Beat the Market with Generic Stocks* (William Morrow & Co., 1985), concludes that "when you consider the whole investment opportunity set, including stocks listed on the American Stock Exchange and the Over-the-Counter market, the number of neglected stocks at any particular time reaches thousands of stocks."

These companies constitute an inefficient sector of the market. Admittedly, their total market value is only a fraction of that of the companies in the efficient sector. But, unlike the institutions, the individual investor doesn't have to invest in companies with large capitalizations. So, for individuals, the inefficient sector of the market is neither tiny nor inconsequential.

3. A third weakness in the Efficient Market Hypothesis has been forcefully exposed by David Dreman in his books *Psychology and the Stock Market* and *The New Contrarian Investment Strategy.* Dreman cites a succession of scholarly studies that prove that stocks with low price/earnings ratios have outperformed stocks with high price/earnings ratios over a large variety of time periods dating back to 1937. This shows that unpopular stocks — those on which investors put low valuations — tend to be underpriced. But if all stocks were efficiently priced, unpopular stocks would perform no better (or no worse) than popular stocks. *And there's decisive evidence that unpopular stocks, over the long term, have provided higher returns.*

4. The concept that all stocks are efficiently priced is also refuted

by abundant evidence that many investors — individuals, investment counselors, and managers of mutual funds of all sizes, from small to huge — have beaten the market for periods long enough to rule out luck and without taking inordinately high risks. A few examples: Over-The-Counter Securities Fund outperformed the S&P index by a margin of three to one over a 23-year period, stretching from late 1956 to 1980. (The fund is so widely diversified — it owns 350 stocks — that its overall level of risk is not especially high.) A fund run by Hugo Koehler of Train Smith, a top-echelon New York investment counseling firm, increased about tenfold in value between 1964 and 1980 — more than 13 times the increase in the S&P 500. Between 1975 and the spring of 1981, the less risky of two supervised lists of growth stocks recommended by Rauscher Pierce Refsnes, a Dallas brokerage house, achieved an average annual gain of 33.5 percent versus an average annual gain of 13.5 percent for the S&P index; the average annual gain of the riskier list was 61.2 percent. And from 1977 to 1987 the Fidelity Magellan mutual fund had an average annual gain of 35 percent. Few investors are likely to come close to matching those levels of performance, but achieving appreciably higher returns than the S&P 500 is certainly not an unrealistic objective.

This exposition and critique of the Efficient Market Hypothesis suggests conclusions and precepts that we will sum up here and now.

It is reasonable to assume that the stocks of the nation's largest and most exhaustively analyzed companies are probably efficiently priced much, if not most, of the time. *This has reassuring implications for the average investor. If you are contemplating purchase of a stock in the efficient sector of the market* — General Motors, Kodak, AT&T, Mobil, IBM, and the like — *you shouldn't consider yourself at a disadvantage because you know so much less about the stock than the experts do; everything that the experts know is reflected in the stock's current price, and the price that you pay will represent a fair estimate of the stock's value at that particular moment.*

Be skeptical if your broker advises you to switch from one efficient-market stock to a similar one in the same industry — for example, from Exxon to Mobil or vice versa. It is virtually certain that your broker's reasons (other than earning a commission) for recommending the switch are part of the available information already reflected in the prices of both stocks. It may make sense, however, to switch from one efficient market stock to another in a *different* industry to achieve better diversification.

If you set your sights on outperforming the market, your best chances of succeeding lie in following one or more of the following basic approaches (or variants thereof).

1. **The Intrinsic Value Approach:** you try to find sharply undervalued stocks in the inefficient sector of the market (which contains large companies as well as small ones).

2. **The Emerging Growth Stock Approach:** you try to find small high-growth companies that are strongly positioned in growth industries *before* their potential has been widely recognized and their price/earnings ratios are forbiddingly high.

3. **The Contrarian Approach:** you invest in large, well-known companies whose stocks are out of favor and are therefore selling at conspicuously low price/earnings ratios.

4. **The Market Timing Approach:** you confine your buying and your selling to periods when the market as a whole is inefficiently priced — that is, you buy when you think investors have surrendered to panic and you sell when you think that investors are getting carried away by euphoria. (How to implement these approaches will be fully discussed in later chapters.)

☐ MODERN PORTFOLIO THEORY: A PSEUDOSCIENCE

One more academic contribution to investment theory and practice merits scrutiny; it is an outgrowth of the Efficient Market Hypothesis called Modern Portfolio Theory (MPT). MPT defines risk as volatility — the extent of a stock's price swings (over a specified time) in relation to those of a supposedly representative market index, Standard & Poor's 500. A stock's volatility, which is calculated by computer, is expressed by the Greek letter beta. The S&P index, the benchmark, is assigned a beta of 1. Thus, a stock that has risen or fallen 15 percent whenever the index has risen or fallen 10 percent has a beta of 1.5; this means that its risk is 50 percent greater than the overall risk of the index. A stock that has risen or fallen 7 percent when the index rose or fell 10 percent has a beta of 0.70; it is considered to be 30 percent less risky than the S&P 500.

A stock's beta measures only that portion of its risk which is contingent on the behavior of the market. But stock prices also rise and fall because of company and industry developments. This type of risk, *not reflected in beta,* can be minimized by proper diversification, because price fluctuations caused by factors other than the market's behavior vary from industry to industry and company to company. For example, energy and computer issues will at times perform better and at times worse, in relation to the market, than stocks with the same betas in the food and cosmetics industries. Consequently, an efficiently diversified portfolio of, say, 15 stocks with an average beta of 1.5 is considerably less risky than a single stock with a 1.5 beta.

Constructing an efficient portfolio is what investing is all about, according to modern portfolio theory, which assumes that it is futile to look for undervalued stocks or try to anticipate advances and declines in the market. The portfolio manager's function (the theory holds) is to examine various combinations of stocks (or stocks and other securities) until his computer program — which analyzes betas and other measures of risk and return — determines the most efficient combination. That combination is the one that provides the largest expected return* for the degree of risk the manager is willing to assume.

An extreme form of applied MPT is known as passive management or indexing. The portfolio manager settles for the risk and expected return of Standard & Poor's 500-stock index, and he builds a portfolio that reflects as accurately as possible the composition of that index without including all 500 of its stocks; the portfolio gives each industry the same weight or representation as it has in the S&P.

The strategy (or rather, nonstrategy) of indexing has been enthusiastically seized upon by a good many large institutions as a remedy for their dismal performance. An indexed portfolio can't quite match the returns of the S&P index because of management costs and other expenses. Nevertheless, institutions managing billions of dollars have a justification for indexing; it doesn't make much sense for them to try

---

* "Expected return" is a theoretical formulation crucial to MPT and one most laymen will find difficult to grasp. Defined as simply as possible, the expected return (ER) of a security is the riskless yield offered by a Treasury Bill (T), *plus* the difference between the rate of return on the S&P index (RSP) and the Treasury Bill yield *multiplied* by the beta of a given security—the equation ER = T + (RSP − T)β. Thus, if T-bills are yielding 6 percent, the rate of return on the S&P index is 14 percent, and a portfolio's beta is 1.5, its expected return is: 6 percent + (14 percent − 6 percent × 1.5), which equals 18 percent.

to beat the market because, in effect, they *are* the market. Individuals can adapt the same strategy by investing in an index fund — a mutual fund whose portfolio is geared to the S&P 500. However, because we believe that individuals can beat the market, we see no point in that; they will be paying management fees simply to achieve guaranteed mediocrity. They would be far better off in one of the several growth-seeking mutual funds that have fairly consistently outperformed the market.

Modern Portfolio Theory represents an attempt by academics to replace qualitative judgments in investing with a supposedly scientific approach that consists in playing complicated statistical games with computers. But investing is not a science like physics or mathematics, and the scientific method has limitations when you apply it to a human activity that is subject to crowd psychology and the uncertainties of the future. After losing a bundle in the notorious South Sea Company, a red-hot stock speculation of 1720, Sir Isaac Newton said, "I can calculate the motions of heavenly bodies, but not the madness of people."

Notwithstanding its shortcomings, Modern Portfolio Theory highlights an important truth that many investors are either not aware of or unwisely disregard — namely, that proper diversification reduces the type of risk that is not contingent on the market's behavior but stems from industry and company developments. Most of the portfolios of individuals are not adequately diversified, according to surveys cited in *The Changing Role of the Individual Investor* (New York: John Wiley & Sons, 1978) by Marshall E. Blume and Irwin Friend, professors at the University of Pennsylvania's Wharton School. Predictably, small investors, excluding those who invest in mutual funds, diversify the least. For example, Blume and Friend found that the typical $13,000 portfolio contained only two stocks. They also found that over a 12-month period in the early 1970s, 63 percent of the investors who owned one or two stocks suffered losses, but only 32 percent of those who owned ten to 19 issues were losers.

How to achieve adequate diversification is discussed in a later chapter dealing with portfolio strategy. The good news is this: if you put an equal amount of money into five stocks in different industries exposed to different types of risk, you will eliminate about 80 percent of the diversifiable risk involved in owning one stock.

Getting Advice and Information

13 How to Pick and Use a Broker

Charles Rolo was a client of nine brokers and a broker himself for roughly equal periods covering 30 years, and he liked to say that his experience left him with strong but impartial views about the broker-client relationship. As a client, he often felt that brokers are a miserable breed. As a broker, he often felt that clients — with a few treasured exceptions — are an exasperating species.

Before going any farther, let Charles and me remind you of a prickly truth about the brokerage business: since brokers don't charge fees, their earnings come solely from commissions, so they earn money only when a client buys or sells. There's a cynical Wall Street joke about a sale of stock on which the client has lost a bundle: "The broker made money and the firm made money — and two out of three ain't bad."

The brokerage industry's compensation system saddles brokers with a conflict of interest from which the Wall Street establishment steadfastly averts its eyes. The conflict is flagrantly obvious. Basically, a broker is a salesman; he serves his employers and earns his living by generating commission business. But from a client's standpoint, a broker is supposed to be a professional investment adviser, and as such he shouldn't encourage clients to incur excessive commission expenses.

To play down the image of salesmanship, brokerage firms publicly refer to their brokers as "financial consultants," "account executives," or "registered representatives" (because they are registered with the stock exchanges, the National Association of Securities Dealers, or both). But intramurally, brokers are usually called salesmen or producers. To prosper or even to stay in business, a producer must produce; he must devote most of his working day to getting and executing orders. However, to serve his clients well he should devote a lot of time to activities that don't directly put a nickel into his pocket — for example, studying research material and keeping track of companies that he has recommended to clients. To achieve an ideal balance between his roles as salesman and investment adviser, a broker needs to be a well-organized workaholic, with a vast knowledge of the investment world, a flair for making wise decisions for investors with widely different objectives, and a strong sense of responsibility about the handling of other people's money. Such paragons are extremely rare, but probably no rarer than paragons are among insurance salesmen or real estate agents.

The attention you can reasonably hope to get from a broker — and the attention you can rightfully demand — is obviously related to the commission dollars you put into his pocket. So it is helpful to know precisely what you are paying a brokerage firm for its services and what portion of your commission dollars goes to your broker.

Since May 1, 1975, when the system of fixed minimum commissions was abolished by the SEC, brokerage firms have been free to set their own rates, and investors, if they have sufficient clout, can negotiate discounts from these rates. The standard rates for individual investors in 1987 were about 25 percent higher than the old, pre-May Day fixed commissions. Rates vary considerably, depending on the firm, the price of the stock, and the size of the order. Many firms have a minimum charge — it is usually anywhere from $25 to $40 — so you may find yourself paying a murderous 20 percent commission if you buy, say, 50 shares of a $4 stock. Rates are higher on small orders and decline as the amount traded grows larger. For example, when this book was written, the commission on a 100-share order of a $10 stock was typically $41, or about 4 percent; the commission on a 500-share order of a $50 stock was typically $406, or about 1.5 percent. The overall rate averages roughly 2½ percent,* with two-thirds usually going to the brokerage firm and one-third to the broker. Brokers with a sizable business get a slightly larger cut.

As a rule of thumb, most investors can assume that their broker's take is roughly 90 cents for every $100 worth of stock they buy or sell. So if an investor's annual trading averages $20,000 a year, his broker's annual earnings from his account are about $180. Most investors trade much less than that. A major brokerage house reported that, in a recent year, 80 percent of its retail clients — 957,000 individuals — generated on the average $130 each a year in commissions, which implies a trading volume of about $5,200. So typically a small investor is worth about $45 a year to his broker. And, nowadays, $45 buys barely half an hour of service from professionals in most fields, includ-

---

* Commission rates are higher on limited partnerships and mutual fund shares that are sold through brokers.

ing acupuncture and hair styling. So it is obvious that very small investors* can't expect a lot of tender loving care from a broker.

There are several ways of coping with this problem. For people of a strongly self-reliant bent, the most satisfactory course is to acquire sufficient investment know-how to make decisions without being overly dependent on a broker's time and guidance. An alternative course — one that has been chosen by many novices who are socially inclined — is to form an investment club. These clubs — of which there are an estimated 22,000 with about 15 members each and an average investment of $3,600 per member — are groups of compatible people who get together to buy securities on a small scale and to learn about investing. They make a modest start-up contribution to a common fund, select a broker, and commit themselves to investing a fixed amount monthly — typically about $25 each — in securities chosen by the club's members at their monthly meetings. Approximately one-quarter of the clubs belong to the National Association of Investment Clubs (P.O. Box 220, Royal Oak, Michigan 48068), a nonprofit organization whose annual dues are $30 per club plus $7 for each club member. For this, members get an 80-page manual on investing, two monthly magazines, a model portfolio containing a dozen stocks selected and followed by investment professionals, plus other services. Since investment clubs for the most part don't lean on a broker's advice, they can save on commission expenses by using a discount broker. As pointed out in our Introduction, well established investment clubs have outperformed the S&P 500. The club members we have met shared the sentiment voiced by Elizabeth Martz of Royal Oak when she was treasurer of the Investment Club of Michigan: "A club is a place where you can have fun, learn about the market, and make money."

The easiest course for small investors — and for many of them the soundest — is to buy shares in one or more no-load or low-load mutual funds: funds that have either no sales charge or limit it to 3 percent or less and that are not marketed through brokers. (Our only

---

* Regardless of how size is defined, the vast majority of this country's 47 million stockholders are small or very small investors. According to a 1985 survey made by the New York Stock Exchange, 64 percent of all investors then had stock portfolios worth under $10,000 and 15 percent had portfolios worth $10,000 to $25,000. Only 21 percent of stockholders owned portfolios worth $25,000 or more.

reason for favoring such funds is economy. The load stock funds marketed through brokers, their own sales forces, and financial planners typically charge sales commissions of 7 percent to 8½ percent. No-load and low-load funds deal directly with investors, who must contact them by writing for a prospectus. Their shares are sold, and can be redeemed at any time, at or very near their current net asset value per share — the market value per share of the fund's portfolio. Annual management fees and expenses, which are taken from income received on the fund's holdings, average less than 1 percent of an investor's share of the fund's total assets.* For that modest charge, an investor gets the benefits of diversification and professional management. Moreover, the fortunes of no-load and low-load fund managements are closely linked to the results they achieve for their shareholders. The earnings of these management firms depend on the size of the assets they manage. To some extent, companies that own a whole stable of funds build up their assets by advertising heavily in the financial press. But since no-loads and low-loads aren't promoted by brokers, they can best gain new shareholders through superior performance. In sum, even for investors who aren't in the "very small" category, mutual funds, which are more fully discussed in chapter 23, make a great deal of sense.

There are, however, some good reasons for using a broker in preference to mutual funds, provided your capital is not minute. When an investor buys mutual fund shares, he is buying a piece of a large and usually widely diversified portfolio, and there may be many stocks in it that he might reasonably not want to own, assuming that he has strong and informed opinions. With a broker, he can concentrate on the stocks that he likes best; he can move quickly into stocks he thinks will be winners and out of those that seem to have turned sour; and he can use options either to speculate or to hedge (see chapter 26). In addition, some people share our feeling that investing, for all its headaches and hard knocks, is an exhilarating challenge, and letting a fund manager call the shots for you takes away most of the fun.

---

* In recent years, however, many no-load funds have begun exploiting Section 12b-1 of the Investment Company Act, which permits them to finance advertising and promotional activities by taking money from their assets. This may add as little as 0.25 percent to annual management fees or as much as 1.25 percent. Moreover, several self-proclaimed no-load funds have added exit fees, also called back-end loads, which you must pay if you redeem shares in less than five years.

The more an investor knows about brokers, the better equipped he will be to use their services intelligently and guard against their shortcomings. So let's take a closer look at the species, which numbers about 85,000 men and women.

A composite profile drawn from a poll done for *Registered Representative,* a magazine for brokers, depicts the prototypical broker as a 38-year-old college graduate with seven years' experience in the securities industry. He or she — one in seven are women brokers — handles more than 300 accounts, but only a small portion of them are active. The average annual earnings of brokers who deal with individual investors were $97,100 in 1986, according to the Securities Industry Association. But a supersuccessful broker makes upward of $250,000. Small to medium-sized investors are likely to be best served by a broker who is earning a good living but not a fortune or a pittance. Big producers usually give most of their attention to their larger clients, and a marginal producer may be so hungry for commissions that he will try to churn (that is, overtrade) his clients' accounts.

Anyone of average intelligence and so-called good character can become a broker in a mere four months, provided he can convince the sales manager of a brokerage firm that he has the makings of a good securities salesman. To qualify as a registered representative, you have to take a four-month training course in a brokerage house and pass a six-hour multiple-choice test, most of which has to do with stock and bond trading procedures and industry regulations. James J. Needham, when he was chairman of the New York Stock Exchange in 1973, made the startling admission that a large percentage of brokers were "not adequately trained or sufficiently knowledgeable" to give investment advice.

Since Mr. Needham's day there has been some improvement in the training of brokers and a substantial improvement in the research available to them. But nowadays registered representatives in the big brokerage houses have a wider range of wares to sell — and therein lies a problem. The giant brokerage firms have transformed themselves into financial supermarkets, whose "products" (in addition to stocks, bonds, and mutual funds) include unit trusts, mortgage pass-through certificates, zero-coupon bonds, IRAs and Keogh plans, asset management accounts, options, commodities, gold coins, financial futures, real estate partnerships, deferred annuities, and life insurance. It stands to reason that a broker who handles a broad line of goods is spreading himself thin. "How on earth can you keep up with the stock market when you're selling Krugerrands and partnership units in a shopping center in Albuquerque?" asks a brokerage house executive who deplores what he calls "the deprofessionalization of Wall Street." No less worrisome is that broadening of the product line creates fresh conflicts of interest; brokers with underdeveloped scruples tend to promote the types of investment which are the most lucrative to them — for example, options and variable life insurance — but which may not be suitable for a particular client.

In spite of the present system's flaws, good brokers do exist, though they are heavily outnumbered by the mediocre and poor ones. To qualify as "good," a broker should be scrupulous, wise in the ways of the market, and truly anxious to do well for his clients. He should also give good service; that would include careful handling of orders, prompt action to correct clerical errors — which are appallingly frequent in the brokerage business — supplying clients with research material, keeping them informed about their stocks, advising them when to sell, and making sure that checks due to them are mailed without delay.

The obvious first step in looking for a good broker — whether you are doing it for the first time or making a switch — is to ask friends, relations, and business associates whether they have a broker they can confidently recommend. Tax accountants are a good source of referrals; they see how their clients are doing in the market and sometimes know the names of their brokers. And here is a tip worth heeding: a broker who is strongly endorsed by a doctor or dentist is probably a winner, because medical men are often avid players of the market.

You should not fail to interview the recommended broker or brokers. A worthy broker will start out by asking you for a full picture of your financial situation and investment objectives; the know-your-customer rule requires him to obtain this information. You, in turn, should find out as much as you can about his professional credentials, modus operandi, and approaches to investing. Questions you might ask include the following: How long has he been in the brokerage business? Does he have a large and varied list of clients, or does he concentrate on a limited number of substantial investors? Does he deal mainly in stocks, options, and bonds, or is he also heavily involved in commodities and other investments? Does he rely mainly on the recommendations of his firm's research department, or does he do much stock picking on his own — and if so, what are his sources? Does he consider himself conservative or aggressive, and what are the investment strategies he favors?

His answers should tell you whether he is the right sort of broker for an investor in your particular situation. For example, even if he accepts small accounts, a high-powered broker with a stable of wealthy clients might not be the best choice for a small investor. A broker who does his own research could be valuable to investors with the analytic know-how to check out his suggestions. But a novice would probably be better served by a broker who follows his firm's recommendations, which are made by trained analysts who devote all of their time to research and keep in close touch with the companies assigned to them. Whatever your situation, try to get a broker with experience, preferably one who has been through a few market debacles. A neophyte may give you more attention, but he will be learning his lessons with his clients' money, including yours.

Asking a broker about his track record is as silly as asking a maître d' whether he recommends the plat du jour. The broker will either tell you he's a winner, or he will take the modest tack: "We do OK." You can't expect him to give himself a failing grade. Most brokers, however, will supply references, and it is worth giving them a call.

If, for some reason, you aren't able to find a broker through referral, just walk into a brokerage house and ask to see the person who handles prospective clients; it may be the branch manager or the so-called broker of the day. You can get the names of firms in your area from the Yellow Pages, under "Stock & Bond Brokers." As a walk-in prospect, you will probably be assigned one of the firm's younger or less solidly entrenched brokers. If the interview leaves you with serious misgivings, ask to see a different broker or try a different firm.

Investors like to gripe about their brokers, but they seldom take the trouble to run a precise check on the performance of their portfolio, a chore that is worth doing once a year. Investment performance can be judged only in relation to the overall behavior of the market and the degree of risk you have chosen to take. Investors who are taking average risks should compare the performance of their portfolios with that of Standard & Poor's 500-stock index, preferably over a period of 12 months or longer. A broker whose recommendations match the performance of that index (taking into account commission expenses) is doing an acceptable job; a broker who keeps on beating the index should be considered outstanding. But if your broker, assuming that you hew to his advice, underperforms the S&P 500 consistently and by an appreciable margin, start looking for a replacement.

However badly a broker performs, he can't be held accountable for a client's losses, unless the client can show that he has been victimized by professional misconduct.* Such misconduct typically involves churning (overtrading an account) or ignoring "suitability" — that is, recommending investments that are too hazardous in light of a client's personal and financial circumstances. When such misconduct is flagrant, a client stands a good chance of obtaining at least partial restitution of his losses — provided he hasn't explicitly or implicitly approved the broker's course of action. His case will be shaky if his account shows a history of excessive trading and high-risk speculation and he failed to holler until he was badly burned. So act promptly if you think your broker is churning or otherwise mishandling your account.

If you have a complaint that you cannot settle with your broker, your first move should be to write to the chief executive of his firm. If that doesn't work, you can turn to either of two industry-sponsored dispute resolution centers. One is the Sales Practices Review Unit of the New York Stock Exchange (55 Water St., 23rd Floor, New York, NY 10005), which handles 3,000 complaints and inquiries a year and acts as an intermediary between investors and brokerage firms. If the Sales Practices Review Unit fails to get results, your last recourse is to ask it to refer your complaint to the Exchange's arbitration department, whose decision you must agree to accept as binding. The second dispute handling center is the Customer Complaint Department of the National Association of Securities Dealers (1735 K St. N.W., Washington, D.C. 20006), which refers complaints to 13 district offices. The NASD offers to arbitrate disputes between customers and brokers through its Arbitration Department (2 World Trade Center, 98th Floor, New York, N.Y. 10048). In 1985 the NYSE filed 1,095 arbitration cases, and the NASD filed 1,400.

When you sign an agreement with a brokerage house to open an

---

* When an investor has been accidentally penalized by a broker's goof such as failure to execute an order, any decent broker will make good on his mistake, provided it is brought to his attention promptly. If, for example, he has forgotten to enter a sell order and the stock's price has declined, he will make the sale in his firm's "error account" and credit you with the price at which the stock was trading when you placed your order.

account, you often agree to forgo the right to sue the broker and his firm. In 1987 the U.S. Supreme Court upheld this contract clause. Unless you strike it out before signing the agreement, arbitration will be your only way to settle disputes. But arbitration costs little, and you will probably get a verdict faster than by going to court.

□ A MINI-GUIDE TO BROKERAGE FIRMS

When they are looking for a broker, most investors are more concerned about the qualities of the individual who will handle their account than about the firm he works for, so long as its financial condition is sound. However, there are several different types of brokerage houses, and it is well worth considering which might suit you best. Here is a rundown of the main types that are hospitable to individual investors.

□ The Wirehouses

The best-known brokerage firms are the giant wirehouses, so-called because of their communication links with networks of branch offices throughout the country. The largest wirehouses are Merrill Lynch, Shearson Lehman Brothers, Dean Witter (owned by Sears Roebuck), Paine Webber, Prudential-Bache Securities, Thomson McKinnon Securities, and Smith Barney.

The big wirehouses are financial supermarkets that offer a full range of investment services. They have large research departments that follow hundreds of companies. The leader in 1985, as reported by W. R. Nelson & Co., was Merrill Lynch, which covered 1,149 companies. Some of the wirehouses are ranked in the top bracket for research by institutional money managers, according to annual surveys made by *Financial World.* In the 1985 survey, nine of the big national brokerage houses were among the 17 firms rated the best for research; they were Merrill Lynch, which ranked No. 1, Paine Webber (6), Kidder Peabody (7), Smith Barney (9), Dean Witter (12), Prudential-Bache (13), E. F. Hutton (14), Thomson McKinnon (16), and Shearson Lehman (17).

The wirehouses are hospitable to small investors because economics of scale permit them to turn a modest profit on accounts too small for many firms to handle on a break-even basis. Several of the national giants have special plans that enable small investors to buy and sell, subject to certain conditions, at discounts from the regular commission rates. And some — Merrill Lynch and Paine Webber, for example — have modestly priced programs tailored for small investors who need investment information and guidance.

☐ The Regionals

The major regional houses offer a narrower range of investment services than the nationals, and they follow far fewer companies. But their knowledge of local industry is a valuable asset. It enables them to spot emerging growth companies whose stocks are still cheap because they haven't yet been touted on Wall Street. In addition, since they concentrate on a limited number of companies, the regionals are able to keep especially close tabs on the stocks they recommend. The regional firms whose research we have followed closely and consider excellent include Rauscher Pierce Refsnes in Dallas, Prescott Ball & Turben in Cleveland, and Interstate Securities in Charlotte, N.C. Among the other regionals with a reputation for high-grade research are Robinson-Humphrey in Atlanta, Rotan Mosle in Houston, Wheat First Securities in Richmond, Va., Boettcher & Co. in Denver, Robert W. Baird Co. in Milwaukee, Crowell Weedon and Bateman Eichler Hill Richards in Los Angeles, and Piper Jaffray in Minneapolis.

☐ The "Carriage Trade" Houses

A third type of brokerage firm is the New York City "carriage trade" house, which caters mainly to investors with six-figure portfolios (though accounts smaller than that are generally accepted). The carriage trade houses maintain low profiles and high standards of service and professionalism. This league includes Morgan Stanley, Neuberger & Berman, L. F. Rothschild, and Wertheim.

☐ The Small Fry

A fourth category is made up of a multitude of smallish to very small firms, most of which welcome small investors. Their drawbacks are lack of expertise in many investment areas and minimal budgets for research — weaknesses that put them at a disadvantage in competing with stronger firms to obtain the better brokers. The attraction of small firms — a big one to some investors — is personalized service. In the brokerage business, small firms are analogous to the small-town general practitioner or family doctor in the field of medicine.

☐ The Discounters

The fifth category of brokerage firm is the discount house, which came into being when fixed minimum commissions were abolished in 1975. There are now more than 125 independent discount firms, plus about 3,000 discounters associated with banks. They have offices all over the country, and their share of the business done by individual investors is steadily growing. It exceeded 20 percent in 1986. The discounts these brokers offer on the rates charged by full-service brokers range from 35 percent to 90 percent, depending on the size of the order and the volume of trading done by the client.

It doesn't pay to use discounters for orders involving less than about $800, because discounters generally charge a minimum of $25 to $35, or for investment guidance, because they don't provide research or investment advice. Discounters simply execute orders, using salaried registered representatives who don't receive commissions, and provide routine services. For example, most offer Individual Retirement Accounts and Keogh Accounts for small business pension funds, and a few offer asset management accounts, which give you bank-style checking and credit card services along with a margin account for buying securities on credit. And all discounters provide custodial services — that is, they will keep your securities and collect dividends or interest, generally at no charge.

The discounters make a lot of sense for investors well equipped to do their own research and make their own decisions. The nation's largest discounter is Charles Schwab & Co., a boldly innovative firm with headquarters in San Francisco. In 1986, its expanding network of more than 90 offices served 32 states, all major American cities and Hong Kong. The conveniences that Schwab offers its clients include exceptionally long business hours — 8:30 A.M. to midnight, eastern time; price quotations 24 hours a day, 7 days a week, via a toll-free number; and automatic investment of idle cash in a money-market fund. Investors who deposit cash or securities or both in a Schwab No. 1 Account can withdraw cash or borrow against their securities by using a Visa card or writing checks, and any cash in the account earns interest at money-market rates. The minimum initial investment is only $5,000, whereas full-service brokers and banks offering similar accounts require $10,000 to $20,000.

Among the other major discount brokers, several of whom have branch offices in different parts of the country, are the following firms (with their home base in parentheses): Marquette De Bary, Quick & Reilly, and Whitehall Securities (New York City), Rose & Co. (Chicago), Brown & Co. and Fidelity Brokerage Services (Boston), Calvert Securities (Bethesda, Md.), Kennedy Cabot (Los Angeles), and C. D. Anderson (San Francisco). (The toll-free numbers of these firms can be obtained from directory assistance, 800-555-1212.)

The clients of all brokerage firms, including the discounters, are insured against loss resulting from a firm's bankruptcy by the Securities Investor Protection Corporation; SIPC is a nonprofit organization created by Congress in 1970, funded by the brokerage industry, and backed by borrowing power of $1 billion from the U.S. Treasury. The maximum amount covered by the SIPC is $500,000, but some firms have taken out added insurance on their own. Thus, nowadays, investors can entrust their securities to the custody of a brokerage house without fear of being wiped out if it founders. Nonetheless, you should check carefully into the firm's reputation and financial condition. When the Manhattan brokerage house of John Muir, an aggressive underwriter of small, highly speculative companies, went under in 1981, some of its clients suffered losses they could not recover through insurance because their accounts were frozen until they could be transferred to another firm. These clients were not able to sell stocks that they thought would decline — and which in fact did decline, at least temporarily. But assuming that the brokerage firm you deal with is thoroughly sound, there are considerable advantages in keeping your securities in a custodian account, especially if you are an active investor. You don't have to receive or send stock certificates through the mail whenever you buy or sell, and your monthly statement shows the market value of your portfolio and provides you with a documented record (for your tax return) of all the income you receive. Moreover, a custodian account with a brokerage firm that has its own money-market fund (or an arrangement with an outside one) enables you, if you so wish, to have your dividends, interest, and cash from the sale of securities automatically invested in the money fund — a service that is of value to many investors and for which there is no charge.

14 Information, Please

Information is the raw material out of which investment decisions are shaped, and the individual investor usually gets too little of it. (The problem of "information overload" that we referred to in a previous chapter mainly afflicts institutional investors.) Two kinds of data are indispensable — background information, which provides you with a frame of reference for your investment decisions, and up-to-date information about the general economy, the major industries, and individual companies. Much of the background information that you are likely to need is provided in this book. How much current information you require — and how much you should spend on it — depends, of course, on your financial situation, your investment objectives, and the extent to which you wish to be your own investment manager. An aggressive do-it-yourself investor who is hunting for neglected, undervalued stocks obviously needs more sources of information than a conservative investor whose goal is high income. Keep in mind that unfocused, intermittent perusal of a welter of investment publications is more likely to create confusion than to bring enlightenment. Your information-gathering should be concentrated on sources closely related to your individual requirements.

A great deal of investment information is available free or for a pittance — far more than most people realize. It includes brokerage-house research, company annual reports, and economic and financial publications issued by some of the leading banks. First let's discuss how to make the most of this material, then we will review selected sources of information and advice that you have to pay for — no longer, unfortunately, with tax-deductible dollars: the radical 1986 overhaul of the U.S. tax code did away with write-offs by most taxpayers, for subscriptions to financial publications and investment advisory services.

☐ RESEARCH FROM THE BROKERAGE FIRMS

Getting research material should be no problem for investors who do business regularly with a full-service broker. He will be pleased to send you reports on the types of investment in which you are particularly interested, and he can usually get his firm to put you on a mailing list for some of its "retail" research. (Retail, in Wall Street terminology, refers to business with individual investors as opposed to institutions. Some retail reports are digests of much longer reports prepared for institutions; others — often reports on companies not large enough to be of interest to major institutions — are conceived and written primarily for a firm's individual clients.) Whether you have a regular broker or not, you can get research material by walking into the nearest office of any major brokerage house. You will generally see a table or display rack on which recent reports and other pamphlets are stacked, and they are yours for the taking.

Another way to get brokerage-house research is by writing for the free reports advertised from time to time in big city newspapers or the *Wall Street Journal.* The purpose of these ads is to furnish leads to potential customers, so be prepared for a follow-up call from one of the firm's brokers, soliciting your business. However reputable the firm may be, it is generally unwise to do business with a broker who calls you up cold. If the caller touts a specific investment without inquiring fully into your financial situation, you can turn him off pronto: ask him to repeat his name, then tell him he is violating rule 405 of the New York Stock Exchange, the so-called know-your-customer rule.

Some people mistakenly dismiss brokerage-house research as simply a sales tool of the brokerage industry. It certainly is a sales tool — in Wall Street, research reports are sometimes referred to, intramurally, as "merchandise" — but it is not *merely* a sales tool. It is also a fruitful source of factual information and professional insights, and as such it can be valuable to investors who know how to use it intelligently. Remember, too, that the effectiveness of research as a business-getter is generally related in the long run to its quality. That's why major firms spend several million dollars apiece on their research departments and are willing to pay outstanding analysts anywhere from $250,000 to $750,000 a year.

Having read thousands of research reports during 25 years on Wall Street and at *Money* magazine, Charles Rolo observed that many analysts were incapable of expressing themselves in straight-forward, grammatical English. But the quality of stock market research is better than it was, say, 20 years ago, and for several reasons:

1. Sobriety in stock valuation — a rarity in the exuberant climate of the 1960s — has come back into style.

2. The training of analysts has been upgraded by the Institute of Chartered Financial Analysts, an offshoot of the Financial Analysts Federation; to earn the CFA designation an analyst has to pass three rigorous examinations, each requiring at least 120 hours of preparation, and has to have accumulated three years of experience in investment decision-making.

3. Because of greatly increased corporate disclosure, analysts now have official company figures to work with in appraising certain business operations, where they previously relied on educated but often inaccurate guesstimates.

Brokerage houses put out two kinds of reports that focus on individual stocks: technical and fundamental. Technical reports, which usually contain charts, pick stocks whose chart "formations" (patterns of price behavior) suggest that they are in an uptrend or about to enter one. When a technical analyst rates a stock as worth buying, he usually suggests a target price at which traders should cash in their profits, and he also gives an exact "stop loss" price; this is a price at which you instruct your broker to sell a falling stock to limit your loss. The fundamental reports concern themselves with a company's sales, earnings, profitability, financial condition, and other such basics. A fundamental analyst makes his recommendations primarily from a long-term standpoint; he is usually looking ahead anywhere from nine months to a couple of years or longer.

The most common complaint of investors about brokerage-house research — they are referring to fundamental research — is that it keeps telling you what to buy but seldom tells you when to sell. The gripe is valid, but there is one good reason outright sell recommendations aren't made more often in fundamental reports. An analyst who removes his buy rating from a stock — because it has risen in price or its immediate prospects look less promising — may still think that in the long run it will go higher and therefore shouldn't be sold by long-term investors; so he puts the stock on "hold." Other reasons analysts are somewhat reluctant to make blunt sell recommendations: they may be leery of ruffling their relationships with corporate managements, on whom they are vitally dependent for information; and they know that a "sell" opinion is more dangerous than a "hold" or even a "buy." If a recommended stock drops, an analyst can always argue that it will recover and that therefore the price drop has made it an even better buy. And time may eventually prove him right. But investors — and sometimes the analyst's employers — are apt to be unforgiving when a stock whose sale he urged at 20 has climbed briskly to 30.

Writers of brokerage-house reports employ a variety of code phrases to express negative opinions while sidestepping the naked four-letter word *sell*. Here are some examples, quoted in the unretouched jargon of Wall Street:

> "We would not expect the stock to be a better than average performer over the intermediate term."
> "We feel the stock lacks appeal at this time."
> "We would avoid the stock until the current uncertainties have been resolved."

When you read comments like these about a stock you own, you have only yourself to blame if you don't sell it and it performs badly.

How good — or bad — are brokerage-house recommendations? Several academic studies have concluded that their overall performance (not taking into account an investor's commission expenses) is roughly the same as that of the overall market. This finding was predictable, because the brokerage houses collectively recommend so many stocks that they are, in effect, recommending the market. However, some firms have better research than others or are especially strong in certain areas. In chapter 13, we named nine national and 11 regional firms that have fine reputations for research. A dozen firms at most — not counting those that cater only to institutions or very rich investors — might be added to that list; among them are Drexel Burnham Lambert, Donaldson Lufkin & Jenrette, and Oppenheimer & Co.

☐ How to Read a Research Report

A report may have been issued anywhere from a few days to several weeks before you get your hands on it. So start out by comparing the price at which the stock was recommended with its current market price; then look at its price range for the past 12 months, which should be in the front or back of the report. (If it isn't, you can find it in the stock tables in your daily newspaper.) If the price has risen appreciably since the report was issued, remember that every point gained has lessened your profit potential and has made your possible loss larger. And if the stock has had a large run-up in the previous 12 months, you can assume that its merits have been widely recognized and it is no longer cheap. Buying stocks that are already big winners can work well for a quick-footed trader when the market is off and running, but it is not a prudent policy for long-term investors.

Assuming that the stock's price is not out of sight, your next step is to judge the credibility of the report. That doesn't require special knowledge; it just calls for careful scrutiny and common sense. A report is not to be trusted if its flavor is more promotional than analytic. To test its credibility, ask yourself the following questions:

- Has the analyst taken a searching look at the company's problems?
- Do you feel that he has made a thoughtful assessment of how and when management expects to overcome them?
- Has he pointed out the unfavorable factors in the company's outlook and uncertainties that are potentially unfavorable?
- Has he built his earnings estimate by making specific estimates of how much each segment of the company's business will contribute?
- Has he clearly stated the assumptions — about the economy, the success of new products, raw material prices, and other matters — on which his estimates are founded?

In short, has he presented a tightly reasoned and well-documented case for his optimism about the company and his belief that its stock is undervalued? If all of your answers are "yes," it is highly probable that the analyst has done his homework and that his opinions have been conscientiously arrived at.

It doesn't necessarily follow that his recommendation will prove to be a good one; opinions conscientiously arrived at can be flawed by errors of judgment or invalidated by unforeseeable events. Nor does it follow that the stock meshes closely with your objectives; as an investment, it could be either too tame or too risky. To find out, you may have to do some further checking. You should be able to handle this on your own after reading the coming chapters on stock valuation and investment strategy. Nevertheless, with a credible and well-documented report in hand, it takes far less time and effort to determine whether a stock is worth buying than if you must analyze it from scratch.

There is one simple check you shouldn't fail to make if your strategy is to avoid overanalyzed companies: find out what percentage of the shares outstanding are held by institutions. The figures are given in Standard & Poor's monthly *Stock Guide,* and your broker can look them up for you in less than a minute. If institutional holdings amount to more than 20 percent of the shares outstanding, you can assume that the stock is widely followed by analysts. An overanalyzed issue such as IBM may be a sound long-term investment, but the chances of its being undervalued in relation to other stocks are exceedingly slim.

☐ THE (NOT SO) HIDDEN ASSETS OF ANNUAL REPORTS

You can usually obtain a company's annual report free of charge by writing to its corporate secretary or shareholder relations department. (The addresses of major corporations can be found in directories available in libraries.) Most annual reports are based on results for the calendar year and on the company's financial condition at the close of business on December 31. But fiscal years (reporting periods) ending at the close of other months are quite common. The time lag between the end of a company's fiscal year and the publication of its annual report is typically about 12 weeks.

As a starting point for this chapter, we asked professionals involved in the preparation and analysis of annual reports — corporate executives, security analysts, and consultants who advise companies on their relations with investors — how useful these reports can be to the layman. Here's the gist of what they said.

■ The conventional wisdom that annual reports are "puffs" for management and say little that's worth knowing is largely out of date. To be sure, the annual (as it is commonly referred to on Wall Street) is a biased document. Typically, it is designed to convey the company's story as favorably as the realities permit; indeed, now and then an annual soars above reality. But most chief executives, especially those of large companies, are wholly aware that excessive sugarcoating can cost them their credibility with investors and that distrust is damaging to a company's stock. Moreover, increased disclosure requirements mandated by the SEC have made annual reports far more revealing. Second to meetings with management, the annual is considered by security analysts to be their best source of information — better and more comprehensive than the company's 10K, a report containing the financial data that corporations are required by law to file with the SEC.

■ Most investors don't learn a fraction of what they could from annual reports. A layman with a feel for figures can wrest a lot of valuable information and useful insights from an annual if he makes some effort to acquire the know-how.

■ The annual report, by itself, is not a sufficient basis for making investment decisions; further research is necessary.

Investors typically spend five to ten minutes reading a report, according to Richard A. Lewis, chairman of Corporate Annual Reports, a New York City investor relations firm. Though most annuals are easy to scan, that isn't nearly long enough to find out what a report is really saying. Many lay investors skimp on their reading because they find annual reports hard to understand. Annuals have been made longer and more complicated by the SEC's widened disclosure requirements plus a slew of rulings by the Financial Accounting Standards Board (FASB), a professional body that sets accounting standards.

The SEC now requires companies to publish, among other things, a breakdown of sales and earnings by type of business, a five-year statistical summary of operations, a discussion and analysis by management of the company's operations in the year just ended and the year before that, and quarterly dividends paid and quarterly highs and lows for the stock price over the previous two years. In addition, a ruling by the FASB requires that unfunded pension obligations must appear in the balance sheet as a liability. Investors should not ignore pension obligations. If sufficient funds to meet future claims have not been set aside, the unfunded obligations could be a potential burden on future profits; conversely, plans that become overfunded because of rising stock and bond markets indicate that the company can restructure its pension fund and gain access to extra cash for business operations. Other FASB rulings have made the section called Notes to Financial Statements much longer and more complex. These footnotes now disclose such high-technology matters as the addition to capital of the cost of developing software products. As a heritage of double-digit inflation, about 1,300 of the nation's largest corporations have until recently been required to show the effects of rising costs on their assets and income. However, with inflation back under control, the FASB moved to phase out this requirement.

All of the new disclosures are potentially valuable to discerning investors, but some of them can be infernally confusing. The problem is that the nitty-gritty of annual reports is composed by accountants, lawyers, and financial executives, a troika with an inbred hostility to clarity. This chapter, used in conjunction with Appendix D, starting on page 307, should help you to cope. Help is also on its way from the companies themselves; a growing number of large corporations are working hard at making their annual reports more intelligible and more readable. Some have put them on audio cassettes. The 1985 annual of Telerate, a company whose business is to provide stock market quotes and other financial information, went to all 6,000 shareholders on a video cassette; tucked in the mailing sleeve was a small pamphlet putting SEC-required disclosures in writing. Annual reports don't make socko viewing material, but some people may prefer to do their investment homework by staring at the small screen instead of struggling with the fine print.

The annual report is a company's single most important communication to the public. To get the maximum mileage out of their reports, corporations include material that serves a variety of purposes — giving the company a more recognizable identity, building its image as a socially conscious concern, pitching its major products, throwing bouquets to its employees, or advocating political and economic ideas. Two examples: McCormick & Co., a specialty-food company, has proclaimed its identity to the reader's nose in a succession of annuals by impregnating them with the scents of its major products, spices. For 1985, shareholders got a whiff of Chinese Five Spice, an aromatic combination of anise, fennel, ginger, licorice root, cinnamon, and cloves. And in one of its annual reports, MacMillan Bloedel, a Canadian forest products concern, listed the names of 19,000 of its 24,000 employees.

There's a Wall Street saying that amateurs read annual reports from front to back and professionals read them from back to front, beginning with the footnotes. Like most smart-aleck generalizations, this one shouldn't be taken as gospel. A sensible approach for a layman is to let his most pressing concerns as a stockholder or prospective investor determine the sequence in which he studies the report.

For example, financial condition should probably be the primary concern in the case of a young company whose growth could be aborted by a shortage of funds, or of a large company wobbling under a huge burden of debt. But with a mature, gilt-edged company such as

IBM or Merck, the crucial concern would be its prospects of sustaining its rate of growth. The rest of this chapter takes a closer look at the most important sections of an annual report, focusing on what they can tell you about the four primary concerns of investors: a company's finances, performance, prospects, and management.

☐ Management's Message to the Stockholders

Often called the chairman's or president's letter, this opening section is where current problems and major developments are most likely to be discussed. It is usually easy to tell when management is being candid and when it is dishing out blah. Eastman Kodak was visibly pouring molasses on a sour story when it said, "The spirit and skill with which Kodak people went about their work was, without question, the highlight of 1977." The real highlight was that earnings per share were below their 1973 level for the fourth consecutive year, a distressing performance for a company long noted for its growth. A much younger growth company, Penril, earned the title of most artful dodger from Sid Cato's *Newsletter of Annual Reports* for a President's Message that stuttered: "1985 . . . was a year tempered by events under our control which have postured your Company for solid growth in the periods ahead . . . and a year during which external economic and market events, in their combined effect, produced an adverse impact on your Company's earnings." That was as close as the message of this electronics firm got to the central truth: earnings had dropped 98%.

A good example of the kind of candor that generates confidence is the comment made by the president of the L. S. Starrett Company, a leading industrial tool producer, in its 1979 report: "On a per-share basis, fiscal 1979 earnings amounted to $5.65. Now, so as not to kid anybody, I want to point out that . . . about $0.09 was due to the fact that there were fewer outstanding shares, and $0.39 was due to a reduction of Scotland's income tax."

The "message" is also the place where you will find management's comments on the company's prospects and, occasionally, a specific earnings forecast. For example, chairman Charles F. Luce predicted in Con Edison's 1977 annual report that earnings in 1978 would be below the 1977 level; as it turned out, they were $4.29 per share as against $4.53 in 1977. By studying the messages in a company's three most recent annual reports, beginning with the earliest, you can get a good fix on management's credibility and prescience.

☐ Income Statement

Also called the profit-and-loss (P & L) statement, this table sums up the company's performance — what it took in, what it paid out, and the crucial bottom line. Two sets of figures — for the year just ended and the year before — tabulate sales and other income, costs and other expenses, including interest charges and depreciation* (a bookkeeping charge that doesn't involve any outlay of cash), extraordinary gains or losses (such as those resulting from sales of property), income taxes, net income after taxes, and earnings per share.

You will sometimes find two different figures for earnings per share — "primary" and "fully diluted." Dilution occurs when convertible issues (bonds or preferred stock) are converted into common stock and when stock options or warrants are exercised; this increases the total number of shares outstanding, thereby reducing the earnings per share.† Fully diluted earnings are based on the number of shares that would be outstanding if all convertible issues were to be converted and all options and warrants were exercised. Since dilution could have an adverse effect on earnings per share in the future, it should be taken into account when you consider a stock's price/ earnings ratio. A $30 stock that has a P/E ratio of 5 based on primary earnings of $6 per share may not be as modestly valued as you think, if its fully diluted earnings are only $4 per share.

An analysis of the income statement is provided in a mandatory section usually headed Management's Analysis and Discussion. The SEC requires it to be strictly factual, and it is generally terse to a fault — but it does state reasons for the increases and decreases in items on the income statement. It also records significant developments such as major borrowings or repayments of debt.

---

* Depreciation is generally not itemized on the income statement. You can find the exact figure in a section of the annual report entitled "consolidated statements of changes in financial position."

† See glossary for definition of all these terms.

☐ Five-Year Summary of Operations

"The summary," as it is called, offers much of the same data as the income statement, but five years is a sounder basis than two for judging how a company is doing. First, look at the earnings record; in addition to showing past performance, it can provide important clues to the company's prospects. It could indicate that growth is accelerating or slowing or that a troubled company is making a comeback. It can also tell you something about the capabilities of management, provided you take into account conditions in the industry or industries in which the company is operating. For example, the dismal record of Chrysler from 1974 through 1978 was a strong warning that the company had serious management problems. By 1979, the automobile industry was sinking into a protracted slump. It was then that the directors brought in Lee A. Iacocca as chief executive. The five-year summary in the 1985 annual report celebrated Iacocca's success less flamboyantly but more eloquently than his best-selling autobiography of that year. In 1981 Chrysler had lost $5.54 per share. Two years later it was back in the profit column, earning $1.57. And in 1985 Chrysler netted $9.38. As for the stock, in the same five years it shot from 2¼ to 31⅛.

You should now check two basic measures of profitability. One is the *net profit margin* — the percentage of profit, after taxes, per dollar of sales. This figure is sometimes given in the summary; if not, you can compute it easily with the help of a pocket calculator; divide net income (excluding extraordinary gains or losses) by total revenues. The five-year pattern of the profit margin is a vital indicator of the health of a business. A slippage in the margin, which can occur even when earnings are rising, could mean that management is doing a poor job of controlling costs, or is unable to raise prices sufficiently to cover rising costs, or is encountering other difficulties. An improvement in profit margins is generally something to cheer about. However, if a company's margin is already high for its type of business, a boom in profitability may flash a cautionary signal that the profit margin has reached a peak because of abnormally favorable conditions. In such cases the price of the stock, too, is likely to be close to a peak, and it might be wise for holders to cash in their gains.

The second basic measure of profitability is *return on stockholders' equity,* often referred to as ROE. The equity or ownership interest of stockholders in a company is their original investment in it plus all earnings not paid out in dividends but reinvested in the business. Stockholders' equity appears on the balance sheet as a liability because it represents a claim on the corporation by the stockholders. You will find it shown as the sum of three itemized figures:

1. the "par" value of the outstanding stock, par being an arbitrary figure (often $1 per share) that bears no relation to the asset value of a share;
2. paid-in capital — the difference between par value and the capital actually received by the company from the sale of its stock;
3. retained (reinvested) earnings.

The return on stockholders' equity is often given in annual reports; if it's not, you can compute it by dividing net income by stockholders' equity. ROE is a measure of how well management has performed for the stockholders. Some outstandingly successful stock pickers have made it a rule only to invest in companies with a high return — 20 percent or more — on stockholders' equity. A high ROE generally indicates that the company is strongly positioned in areas of growth. Moreover, companies with a high ROE are better able to finance future growth out of their own profits than those with a low ROE; consequently, they are less dependent on borrowing.

☐ Breakdown of Sales and Earnings

These figures also cover a five-year period and they show what each major segment or division of the company has contributed. The breakdown tells you at a glance which are the strongest parts of a company's business and which, if any, are lagging or showing losses. A detailed discussion of each division's performance over the preceding year is found in the main text of annual reports.

☐ Balance Sheet

The balance sheet is a photograph of a company's financial position at an instant in time, the close of its fiscal year. The relationship between different parts of the balance sheet provides indications of the company's financial strength, which in turn can furnish clues to future performance. The stronger a company's financial condition, the greater is its ability to finance aggressive marketing strategies, develop new products, embark on expansion programs, or make acquisitions.

The two balance-sheet relationships that you shouldn't fail to check on are the current ratio and the size of debt in relation to the total capitalization (stockholders' equity plus debt). The first is the ratio of current assets (cash, marketable securities, receivables, and inventory) to current liabilities (all items payable within a year); the current ratio is a measure of a company's ability over the coming 12 months to meet its obligations and still have ample resources to run its business effectively. These resources — current assets minus current liabilities — are known as working capital. There is no single "correct" current ratio; 2 to 1 is widely considered a desirable minimum, but the figure varies from industry to industry.

The size of a company's debt in relation to its total capitalization has an important bearing on its ability to borrow more money. In the case of a typical industrial company, there could be cause for concern if debt amounts to appreciably more than 40 percent of the total capitalization.

Two other balance-sheet items that deserve attention are goodwill and book value. Goodwill is the cash value assigned to intangibles such as patents and franchises. It can also refer to the cost, over and above their tangible assets, of companies acquired before November 1, 1970. For acquisitions made after that date, the FASB has ruled that any excess of cost over tangible assets must be amortized over not more than 40 years. If the figure for goodwill is large, it is a blemish on the balance sheet.

Book value is total assets minus total liabilities (including the redemption value of preferred stock) divided by the number of shares outstanding. Theoretically, book value represents the value of a share of common stock if the company were to be liquidated. But in the real world assets are valued largely on the basis of what they earn. Historically, the stocks of flourishing companies have usually sold at prices substantially above their book value. When a stock's market price is significantly below its book value — as, for example, in the case of USX Corporation, formerly U.S. Steel, which in May 1986 had a book value of about $40 and was selling at 17 — it is usually an indication that a company's assets are obsolescent, that they are being poorly managed, or both. Assuming that the low price of a stock results from poor management and not from obsolescent assets, the company could become a takeover candidate; it may look bargain-priced to other managements who think they could run it more profitably.

□ Auditor's Opinion

These few paragraphs signed by an accounting firm usually state that the financial data in the annual report "fairly" represent the company's financial condition, "in conformity with generally accepted accounting principles, applied on a consistent basis." Sometimes, however, the OK is a "qualified" one. It may be "subject to" the outcome of a major uncertainty such as the verdict in a lawsuit, or the auditor may express reservations about some of the financial data. In any given year, auditors issue qualified opinions in the annual reports of about 12 percent of large U.S. corporations.

□ Notes to Financial Statements

It is worth struggling to try to decipher these pesky footnotes; the information they contain about a company's accounting practices and other matters enables you to judge the quality of reported earnings — a crucial issue that laymen all too often ignore. A stock that seems to be a bargain on the basis of its low price/earnings ratio may no longer look cheap when you take into account the poor quality of its reported earnings. As a rule, the quality of earnings is high if a company charges to current expenses all research and development costs that it is allowed to (by accounting rules) and depreciates assets as rapidly as possible; *such conservative accounting tends to understate earnings. Reported earnings are of poor quality — that is, overstated — if a company depreciates assets relatively slowly and treats research and development costs as capital investments, which are amortized over a period of years.* Reported earnings of $3 a share based on conservative accounting practices could be inflated to $4 a share or more by permissive accounting. In many cases reported earnings based on permissive accounting have been found to be nonexistent when recomputed on the basis of stringent accounting standards.

The quality of earnings is also affected by the method a company uses to price its inventory; this is disclosed in a footnote and is easily understood by a layman. The traditional method, FIFO (first in, first out) assumes that goods are sold in the order in which they entered the inventory. When inflation rates are low, inventory accounting has little affect on the quality of reported earnings. But in periods of rising prices, the earliest items in the inventory are the lowest in cost by a wide margin; consequently the FIFO method results in profits that are exaggerated by inflation, because the lowest-cost goods have to be replaced at the current higher prices. Moreover, these exaggerated profits are subject to income taxes. Thus, many companies have wisely switched to the LIFO (last in, first out) method, which assumes that each item sold was the last to enter the inventory. This reduces inventory profits stemming from inflation and saves the company money on taxes.

With the disclosures now made in annual reports an astute layman has a fair chance of spotting serious trouble. The most revealing figure, many analysts think, is return on total investment — that is, net income divided by stockholders' equity and long-term liabilities. If you find that over several years a company's total assets are producing shrinking returns, it's probably high time to sell the stock.

Studying annual reports is vital for do-it-yourself investors. But it is hardly less valuable to those who lean on a broker's advice. Investors who have learned enough about a company to focus on the crucial questions can make the most of the services that a broker and the analysts behind him can provide.

☐ THE INVESTMENT ADVISORY SERVICES: AN INSIDE GUIDE TO MARKET GUIDES

Through direct mail and eye-catching ads in the financial pages, investment advisory services claim they will guide you along the path to profit — in stocks and options, commodities and precious metals, in down markets as well as up markets. Some make extravagant claims that blatantly appeal to gullibility and greed. Others, more plausibly, invite you to benefit from their extensive research and expertise. Subscriptions range from $24 to nearly $900 a year; typically they cost $65 to $175 in 1987.

According to George Wein, president of Select Information Exchange, which publishes a catalogue of the services, there must be as many as 2,000 of them; the number doubled in the first four years of the bull market that began in 1982. Wein's best guess is that they have a total of about a million subscribers; the larger ones have more than 50,000, while many have fewer than 100.

The services cover nearly every conceivable approach to investing. More than a third of them are mainly or entirely technical. That is, they base their forecasts on past patterns of price behavior and trading volume and are primarily concerned with timing decisions. Many of the other services take the fundamental approach, including the three largest: the *Value Line Investment Survey,* Standard & Poor's *The Outlook,* and *United Business & Investment Report.* And a profusion of specialized services are devoted to options, stock charts, growth companies, foreign investments, mergers and acquisitions, mutual funds, and insider trading — purchases and sales of a company's stock by its own officers. (Such insider transactions are perfectly legal so long as they are not based on information not yet publicly disclosed that could significantly affect the price of the stock.) Finally, numerous services cover nonstock investments — the bond and money markets, commodities, precious metals, real estate, coins and currencies.

Some services can influence the price of a stock — at least temporarily. For example, a stock often has a runup when it is featured in *Value Line Investment Survey* as the "stock highlight" of the week. A few timing services with large and loyal followings can even swing the market as a whole. Joseph E. Granville, a celebrated soothsayer in his better days, flashed a sell-everything signal early in January 1981; the next day U.S. stocks lost $38 billion of their market value, and trading volume on the New York Stock Exchange rocketed to nearly 93 million shares, a record at the time. Publishers of advisory letters had to register with the Securities and Exchange Commission until the U.S. Supreme Court struck down that requirement in 1985. Today, freedom of the press prevails. There are no government qualifications or tests to restrain anyone from putting out an investment letter. In fact, publishers of them have included high school dropouts, an electrician, a textile designer, a hairdresser, and at least one convicted felon. Only two important limitations apply:

1. The publication may offer only impersonal advice, not guidance tailored to any specific person or group.
2. The publisher must not recommend stocks in a company he owns or stocks he is trading, and he cannot accept money for publishing recommendations. The SEC has obtained injunctions against services accused of scalping, which means buying a stock, featuring it as a hot tip, then taking a quick profit on the resulting runup. Unfortunately, the commission's staff isn't large enough to make sure no flimflam goes undetected. But the leading services have strict rules of their own governing securities transactions by their employees.

Charles Rolo was a reader of advisory services for nearly 30 years, first as a private investor, then as a security analyst and research director on Wall Street, and finally as a financial writer on *Money* magazine, where he scanned several dozen services each month; I read a dozen or so a week myself. From all this scrutiny come several points to keep in mind about the species in general.

- The services vary enormously in quality. Many are worthless and potentially harmful; some are excellent.
- The majority of the technical services are addicted to cloying self-congratulation. They often make fuzzy or cagily hedged forecasts and later boast that they have been right on target. Some of the habitually bearish services even have the gall to go on saying they're right when the market has for months or even years proved them wrong. Predictably, services that go easy on self-praise and admit errors are among the best in the business. The published performance records of advisory services don't take into account buying and selling commissions; consequently, they overstate gains and understate losses. The overstatement isn't significant in the case of services with a long-term investment strategy, because they don't do much trading. But ignoring commission expenses grossly inflates the results claimed by technical services that make short-term trades and recommend the use of "stops."* For example, a service that recommends buying a stock at $10 and later decides to sell it at $12 credits itself with a 20 percent gain. But typically, two-way brokerage commissions on 100 shares at those prices would add up to about $70. So an investor's real gain would be only $130, or 13 percent.

The major services that focus mainly on fundamentals are the most useful for the average investor. They provide statistics, earnings projections, industry and company analysis, investment strategies, stock recommendations, and model portfolios — a package of investment materials that you can't find assembled elsewhere in one place.

For a person with a few thousand dollars and a minimum of investment knowledge, an advisory service probably has no practical

---

* A stop is an order placed with a broker (or simply one you give to yourself) to sell a stock if it declines to a specified level.

value; that kind of investor is better off letting mutual funds manage his money. For investors with, say, $25,000 and up, a good service can be helpful. Substantial investors who are active in the market — people with a stake of at least $100,000 — might benefit from taking several services. The most you can expect from a service is that it provide a sound basis for your own decision-making; no service can make all the decisions for you.

How good are the advisory services as stock pickers? One newsletter, the *Hulbert Financial Digest,* 643 South Carolina Ave. S.E., Washington, D.C. 20003, has devoted itself exclusively to rating the performance of investment portfolios recommended by advisory services since June 1980. That span of time included a sharp downturn in the stock market followed by the bull market that began in August 1982 and was still riding high in mid-1987. On the sixth anniversary of his publication, editor Mark Hulbert measured the results of the 61 letters he was then following. There were 19 of them with full six-year records. During that period, the S&P 500 showed a total return of 191.3 percent — the results if all dividends had been reinvested. Hulbert had tracked all recommendations of the 19 letters for the same period. One, the *Prudent Speculator,* had dwarfed the S&P by gaining 682.1 percent. Five others also had beaten the market, though by much smaller margins: *Growth Stock Outlook,* up 255.9 percent; *Zweig Forecast,* up 252.5 percent; *Value Line OTC Special Situations,* up 210.2 percent, the *Dines Letter,* up 208.6 percent, and *Market Logic,* up 208.2 percent. These results certainly demonstrate that the better services have been able to select stocks that provided higher than average rates of return.

In choosing a service, you should first ask yourself what type best meets your requirements: one that concentrates on stock selection or market timing or one that offers a broad range of information or a specialized service. A look at the ads can help you weed out probable phonies. As a rule, services that promise you the moon belong on the garbage heap. Before committing yourself to a year's subscription to one of the services, it's a good idea to sample as many as you can. Most services offer trial subscriptions — often for not more than $10 or $15 — and some will send you a sample copy at no charge. The cheapest way of getting to know a variety of services is to write for the free catalogue published by Select Information Exchange, 2095 Broadway, New York, N.Y. 10023. The catalogue describes hundreds of services and offers you trial subscriptions to 20 services of your choice for $11.95. (Many services are not included in this offer.) If you then take a regular subscription to one of those you have sampled, your $11.95 is fully or partly deducted from the price.

Personal convictions about investment strategy are bound to influence one's judgment of a newsletter, whatever its performance rating. For example, our belief that for most investors in-and-out trading is a loser's game causes us to have a low opinion of technical services that cater largely to short-term traders. Another type of service that we have no use for is the messianic type, which preaches that God is on the investor's side or, at the opposite extreme, that apocalypse is at hand unless you follow a hard-and-fast recipe for survival. The favorite investment recommendations of the doomsayers — gold bullion, silver coins, and Swiss francs — did spectacularly well in the second half of the 1970s, but went sharply up and down over the first six years of the eighties. Moreover, these are investments that produce no interest or dividends and are therefore unsuitable for anyone who needs income from his capital. And much of the doomsayers' advice has been zany or mischievous — for example, stockpiling a year's supply of canned goods, buying arms and ammunition, selling your real estate to buy silver (and "bury it in some safe place"), and obtaining a forged passport so that you can flee the country when it turns into a police state. In addition, the devastating stock market crash predicted by the doomsayers had failed to materialize by mid-1987.

Our basic objections to the prophets of doom are that first, they systematically promote fear and paranoia; second, they delude their loyal followers into thinking that a basket of their favored investments offers safety and removes the need for further investment decisions. This is pernicious nonsense. Putting most of your capital into gold, silver, and Swiss francs is a high-risk strategy. The precious metals are extremely volatile. Not only could they drop precipitously — as both gold and silver did in 1980 and again in 1981 — they could also stay down long enough to make life nightmarish for people who have invested too heavily in them.

The services profiled in the rest of this chapter represent a cross-section of those that we consider to be the best for amateur investors. They were chosen because of their record for stock selection or market foresight, or because their coverage is broad and exceptionally informative, or because they perform a specialized function well. Limitations of space have prevented us from including many services that meet these criteria; it would take an entire book to cover the advisory industry thoroughly. In fact, an excellent one was published in 1986, *The Wall Street Gurus* by Peter Brimelow (Random House).

Price, too, has been a factor in our selection. With the exception of two services that we consider outstanding, we have excluded those that cost more than $450 a year. On the other hand, some services have been included because they are moderately priced and we rate them an excellent buy for investors who can't afford costlier ones. The subscription prices given are those in effect late in 1986.

☐ The Big Three

■ **The Value Line Investment Survey.** (Published weekly by Arnold Bernhard & Co., 711 Third Avenue, New York, NY 10017. One year, $425. Ten-week trial, $55.)

If we had to rely on one service only, we would unhesitantly choose Value Line. Its cost puts it beyond the reach of many small investors, but for anyone who can afford it — and who learns to use the incredible amount of information and guidance that it offers — the survey is invaluable.

With more than 108,000 subscribers, Value Line, founded in 1936 by Arnold Bernhard, is by far the largest of the advisory services. Each week its staff of 90 analysts and economists feeds into two big computers more than one million statistics on the general economy, 92 industries, and 1,700 stocks. Stocks are given two separate rankings of 1 (best) to 5; one ranking is for "timeliness" — that is, probable price performance relative to the market over the next 12 months — and the other is for safety. In a published report of its performance from April 16, 1965, to July 1, 1986, a period in which the Dow Jones industrials rose 109% and the New York Stock Exchange composite index was up 205%, Value Line showed that its Rank 1 stocks gained an almost incredible 13,012 percent. Rank 5 stocks showed a *loss* of 92 percent. The performance of the other three groups was also in line with their rankings; Rank 2 outperformed and Rank 4 underperformed the market. Rank 3 roughly matched it.

In response to a much earlier study showing comparable results, Professor Fischer Black, then at the University of Chicago — a leading exponent of the Efficient Market Hypothesis, which holds that no method of stock analysis can outperform the market — tested a portfolio strategy based on the Value Line rankings for timeliness. Black invested an equal amount in each of the stocks ranked 1, sold any of them that dropped to Rank 3, and reinvested the proceeds in the Rank 1 stocks. To his surprise, this strategy produced better returns than the overall market. His conclusion: "Most investment management organizations would improve their performance if they fired all but one of their security analysts and then provided the remaining analyst with the Value Line service."

The strategy that Value Line itself recommends is for an investor to pick from the stocks ranked 1 or 2 for timeliness those that best meet his safety and income requirements. For example, a conservative investor might confine his portfolio to the sometimes relatively few stocks in those groups that have a high ranking for safety and pay a respectable dividend. Stocks in the conservative category are listed in a special classifying screen, and data about them are easy to find in Value Line's weekly "Summary & Index," which lists, for example, stocks with the lowest price/earnings ratios, stocks selling below book value, stocks with the highest growth rates, stocks with the highest probable long-term (three-to-five-year) profit potential, and stocks that have performed best and worst over the previous 13 weeks. The main body of the *Value Line Survey* consists of more than 2,100 pages (in detachable sections) containing 1,700 continually updated company analyses that are both encyclopedic and compact. They assemble on a single page all of the data that an amateur analyst needs to size up the merits of a stock for himself. In sum, the *Value Line Survey* offers a comprehensive overview of the economy and the stock market, fully documented company reports, and a portfolio strategy that each individual can adapt to his particular needs. Its chief limitation is that its coverage includes relatively few small or little-known companies. That sector of the market is covered in a separate publication, the twice-monthly *Value Line O-T-C Special Situations Service,* which costs $350 a year extra. (A six-week trial subscription is $35.) Value Line Investment Services also manages four common stock mutual funds that base their stock selections on the Value Line rankings and are oriented toward different degrees of risk. The Leveraged Growth Fund and the Special Situations Fund aim at large capital gains; the Value Line Fund seeks growth and income; the Value Line Income Fund concentrates on earning dividends and interest. All are no-load funds available by mail from Value Line.

■ **The Outlook.** (Published weekly by Standard & Poor's Corp., 25 Broadway, New York, NY 10001. One year, $207. Eight-week trial, $29.95.)

Founded in the 1920s, this service — one that most brokerage houses subscribe to — is staidly conventional, with a cautiously bullish bias. Its strengths are that it is easy to read and digest, it doesn't encourage taking large risks, and it is backed by the large statistical and analytical staff of Standard & Poor's. Regular features include analyses of stocks "In the Limelight," lists of the best- and worst-acting stock groups, industry surveys, and a Master List of about 35 recommended issues graded in four categories on the basis of risk.

A study published in the *Journal of Portfolio Management* in 1977 concluded that over the previous six and a half years portfolios constructed from stocks recommended in the Master List had "generally outperformed the market on both an absolute and a risk-adjusted basis," even taking into account buying and selling commissions.

Typical subjects covered periodically in *The Outlook:* stocks for high income, stocks with high prospective earnings growth, low-priced stocks that look attractive. A weekly summation of the service's forecast and policy tends to be as bland as Pablum. A characteristic forecast (made February 25, 1981): "Conservative investors would probably be well advised to stay with a cautious policy pending clarification of economic and monetary trends."

■ **United Business & Investment Report.** (Published by United Business Service, 210 Newbury St., Boston, MA 02116. One year, $190. Six-week trial, $5.)

This 12-page service is similar in posture and coverage to *The Outlook* but devotes a page to Washington news. Regular features include reports on commodities, industry surveys, and buy-hold-or-sell opinions on stocks and bonds. The service's advice generally steers investors along a conventionally conservative course.

☐ Three Good Bargains

■ **Smart Money.** (Published monthly by the Hirsch Organization Inc., 6 Deer Trail, Old Tappan, NJ 07675. One year, $98, including special bulletins and the *Stock Trader's Almanac.* Three-month trial, $29.)

More like a small magazine for amateur investors than a typical advisory service, *Smart Money* is fun to read and at times has had a hot record as a picker of highly speculative stocks, including a category that it calls America's Most Undiscovered Companies. Between March 1979 and February 1981, a period of strength for small growth companies, the service recommended 82 stocks; taking losses into account, the average gain on the prices at which the recommendations were made was 96 percent. In the ensuing 12 months, stock prices declined and *Smart Money*'s track record slipped. But clearly the service has a flair for discovering dark horses that often finish up front. It also provides its readers with periodic reports on wave-of-the-future technologies such as genetic engineering and artificial intelligence. *Smart Money*'s editor and publisher, Yale Hirsch, doesn't concern himself with minor market fluctuations, but he tells you bluntly whether he is bullish or bearish on the major trend of the market. In 1986, for example, he was anticipating a revival of market interest in companies with small capitalizations. His forecasting record has been mixed since the service started in 1973, but that hasn't stopped him from guiding his readers into profitable stocks. Subscribers to *Smart Money* get a free copy of the *Stock Trader's Almanac* (retail price, $25), which contains a fascinating potpourri of historical lore and miscellaneous information about the stock market, including useful commentaries on seasonal and cyclical patterns of price behavior.

■ **Market Logic.** (Published twice a month by the Institute for Econometric Research Inc., 3471 N. Federal Highway, Fort Lauderdale, FL 33306. One year, $95. Two-issue trial, free.)

Working from econometric models (which apply mathematical formulas to forecasting) and on computer research, this inexpensive service provides in every issue projections of where Standard & Poor's 500-stock index will stand three, six, and 12 months hence, a review of what the market indicators are indicating, a list of the industry stock groups that are performing best and worst, and a forecast of the trend in the gold price. Other sections offer a digest of advisory service opinions, a guide to mutual fund selection, an extensive report on trading by corporate insiders, an options portfolio, and a master portfolio of recommended stocks — the basis used by *Hulbert Financial Digest* in ranking *Market Logic* as a market beater over a six-year span. This is among the lowest-priced services to provide its subscribers a hot-line telephone number to call for late-breaking commentary on the stock market. *Market Logic* updates this recorded message twice a week.

■ **America's Fastest Growing Companies.** (Published monthly by John S. Herold Inc., 35 Mason St., Greenwich, CT 06830. One year, $124. Three-month trial, $43.)

Formerly the *Johnson Survey, America's Fastest Growing Companies* has evolved into a publication of 36 pages with widely diversified coverage. Its centerpiece is a Guide to Investment Selection, which tabulates financial data on about 100 growth stocks and rates them on a scale of A to C. (For a cumulative list of 167 of these issues, including data about size, growth, and profitability, see Appendix A.) This guide is supplemented by about 15 pages of company progress reports. *America's Fastest Growing Companies'* policy is not to make investment recommendations or forecast the market's behavior. However, it keeps running accounts of two portfolios, each limited to stocks meeting certain growth qualifications, and compares their performance to those of the Dow Industrials and the S&P 500. The Midas Fund consists of a dozen or so companies with five-year average earnings growth of 30 percent or more. For example, leading entries in the spring of 1986 included Ultimate Corp., a maker of minicomputer systems, with a 92 percent growth rate; Price Co., a chain of members-only warehouse retail stores, with a 73 percent growth; the Limited, a women's clothing chain, 72 percent; and Dress Barn, off-price women's apparel, 62 percent. In the 52 weeks to April 1, 1986, an extremely bullish period, the fund as a whole gained 56.1 percent, compared with 45.8 percent for the Dow. The second list that *America's Fastest Growing Companies* tracks from month to month is called the AFGC Model Portfolio, 21 stocks chosen for high profit growth in relation to their price/earnings ratios. All in all, this service presents a large amount of well-organized information and opinion and invites you to decide for yourself.

☐ Growth Stock Services

■ **Equity Research Associates.** (Published twice a month by Equity Research Associates, a subsidiary of Ladenburg, Thalmann & Co., 540 Madison Ave., New York, NY 10022. One year, $360.)

ERA is one of the top services on junior growth companies — high-growth enterprises whose revenues, for the most part, are under $100 million. ERA's founder and president, John Westergaard, has been a leading analyst of junior growth companies for 30 years. A keen observer of the American scene, he is as concerned with ideas as with numbers: he primarily seeks underanalyzed companies whose growth is linked to changes in American life-styles, technologies, and business techniques. For example, he was among the first to recognize the exceptional growth potential of Flight Safety International, the leading independent supplier of pilot training services; Community Psychiatric Centers, which operates hospitals for acute psychiatric cases; and Datapoint, a pioneer in the development of data processing terminals linked to a central computer.

Westergaard monitors about 200 junior growth companies and focuses his reports on those he considers most promising. In recent years he has carried about 30 stocks on his recommended list (including some that have grown out of the junior category). In the decade from 1976 to 1986, the recommendations and managed accounts of ERA showed compounded annual growth in excess of 15 percent.

■ **Growth Stock Outlook.** (Published monthly by Growth Stock Outlook Inc., P.O. Box 15381, Chevy Chase, MD 20815. The subscription rate includes a quarterly supplement, *Junior Growth Stocks,* and a second monthly letter, *New Issues Digest.* One year, $175. Three-month trial, $65.)

This service tracks about 120 growth companies that it has recommended since it started in 1965; new recommendations are introduced with a concise analysis. A company whose earnings decline for three or four consecutive quarters is deleted — unless editor Charles Allmon believes its earnings are about to turn upward. The data tabulated in each issue include the stock's price range and earnings per share over the previous five years, its latest 12-month and quarterly earnings, and its book value, price-to-sales ratio (a leading indicator of stock behavior), return on stockholders equity, and four-year annual growth rates. In addition, stocks are ranked for attractiveness on a scale of A to C. As a possible model for its subscribers, *Growth Stock Outlook* manages a portfolio of selected growth stocks; when Allmon considers the investment outlook unfavorable, he sells stocks and parks the proceeds in money-market securities. Started in mid-1973 with an investment of $50,000, the model portfolio had a value of $473,304 (including reinvested gains and income) on June 15, 1986. That amounted to an 847 percent climb and a compound annual return of 18.9 percent. For the last six of those years, as calculated by the *Hulbert Financial Digest,* the return was 23.5 percent. In achieving those brilliant stock-picking results, Allmon takes a conservative approach. His policy is to ferret out growth stocks that have not yet achieved wide recognition and are still selling at low price/earnings ratios.

Junior Growth Stocks follows about 250 companies, while *New Issues Digest* keeps track of 80 to 100 initial public offerings for their first 18 months on the market. If they show promise, they move to the junior growth stocks group. Neither of these supplements includes stock recommendations.

☐ An Income-Oriented Service

- ▪ **Indicator Digest.** (Published twice a month by Indicator Research Group, 451 Grand Ave., Palisades Park, NJ 07650. One year, $175. Two-month trial, $25.)

The Income Investor, once a separate newsletter, now is an eight-page section of *Indicator Digest,* a comprehensive publication for individual investors. The *Digest* provides appraisals of the outlook for the stock market, interest rates, and precious metal. It suggests the proportions of money-market securities, common stocks, gold mining shares, and different types of bonds that investors should put in their portfolios. Special features cover convertible bonds, foreign government bonds, high-yielding common stocks that could become takeover targets, and options strategies for increasing your portfolio's income. The *Digest* also interprets a wide variety of market indicators, goes into investment tactics, makes stock recommendations, and compiles unweighted indexes of the New York and American stock exchanges that give an accurate picture of the average price changes on these markets. This is a well-rounded, imaginative, reasonably priced service.

☐ Mutual Fund Services

- ▪ **Switch Fund Advisory.** (Published monthly by Schabacker Investment Management, 8943 Shady Grove Court, Gaithersburg, MD 20877. One year, $140. Three-month trial, $57.)

Editor Jay Schabacker has a market forecasting system that uses a combination of more than a dozen fundamental and technical indicators. Each issue of his service gives fund switchers two kinds of market timing advice. One is based on the traditional concept of increasing or decreasing exposure to risk in accordance with market conditions; it tells investors the proportions in which to divide their assets between stock funds and money-market funds. The other tells those who take the all-or-nothing approach whether they should currently be fully invested in aggressive funds or completely out of the market. Schabacker also reports the performances and current yields of more than 400 no-load and load funds of all types, including tax-exempts, golds, and 63 funds specializing in single industrial sectors such as utilities, high technology, and banking. And he runs a model portfolio that is invested in four different categories of funds. His service is particularly helpful to investors who wish to follow a balanced-portfolio approach, using mutual funds rather than individual securities.

■ **Growth Fund Guide.** (Published monthly by Growth Fund Research Inc., Box 6600, Rapid City, SD 57709. One year, $85.)

Walter Rouleau, the editor, includes in each issue forecasts of how 40 stock funds will perform and how certain funds will do in bear as well as bull markets. Another regular feature lists the best- and worst-performing funds over the past one, three, six, nine, 12, and 24 months. A useful chart section shows the price performance, on a monthly basis, of the 40 funds over the latest three and a half years, and it gives their addresses, telephone numbers, objectives, and investment requirements.

■ **No-Load Fund Investor.** (Published monthly by No-Load Fund Investor, P.O. Box 283, Hastings-on-Hudson, NY 10706. One year, including an annual handbook, $95.)

The editor, Sheldon Jacobs, is so ardent an advocate of no-load funds that when one of the 470 or more funds whose performance he tracks in this newsletter adds a sales charge, he takes immediate note of the change; after giving his subscribers a few months to redeem their shares, he usually stops listing the fund. He seldom describes funds in much depth. The best performers are ranked in each issue for periods of one month to five years, and as many as 80 are recommended in each issue. The letter covers news and trends about mutual funds and the current state of the market. A market-timing service suggests percentages of assets to keep in stock funds and money-market funds. The annual *No-Load Fund Handbook* lists the addresses and telephone numbers of nearly 800 no-load funds, giving as many as 29 points of information about each. For example, it notes which funds have changed managers during the year.

☐ Technical Services

- ■ **The Professional Tape Reader.** (Published twice a month by Radcap Inc., P.O. Box 2407, Hollywood, FL 33022. Editor: Stan Weinstein. One year, $250. Five issues, $50.)

- ■ **Systems and Forecasts.** (Published twice a month by Signalert Corp., 150 Great Neck Rd., Great Neck, NY 10021. Editor: Gerald Appel. One year, $160. Three-issue trial, $25.)

- ■ **The Zweig Forecast.** (Published every three weeks by Martin E. Zweig, 900 Third Ave., New York, NY 10022. One year, $245. Three-month trial, $50.)

These three services — edited by well-known specialists in market timing — are among the best of their kind but are useful only for investors with faith in technical analysis and a grasp of how to use it. Appel, Zweig, and Weinstein address traders primarily, and their services are similar in format and content. They lead off with a commentary on the state of the market, a forecast (sometimes hedged) of its short, intermediate, and long-term trends, and a recommended portfolio strategy. Each service then gives its reading of numerous market indicators, makes brief stock recommendations based mainly on technical analysis, and follows up on previously recommended issues. The *Professional Tape Reader* and the *Zweig Forecast* (in that order) devote the most space to stocks. *Systems and Forecasts* has a proprietary feature: a rating system for mutual funds based on their performance in both downswings and upswings of the market. It covers about 80 funds, mainly those with little or no load, gives exact signal prices at which traders should move in or out of a fund, and maintains a model portfolio of funds.

☐ Miscellaneous Services

■ **Consensus of Insiders.** (Published weekly by the Consensus Group, P.O. Box 24349, Fort Lauderdale, FL 33305. One year, $199. Seven-week trial, $12.)

This unimpressive-looking service is designed for investors who wish to take their cue from corporate and stock market insiders. Once a month, it ranks 1,500 stocks from 9 (best) to 1 (worst), using a proprietary system based on the purchase and sale of shares and options by the companies' officers, as well as fundamental and technical data. Several academic studies have found that strategies patterned on trading by insiders produced higher returns than stocks in general (even though there is a time lag of 30 to 60 days before insider transactions are made public). Since 1962, editors Perry Wysong and his successor Barry Unterbrink have tracked the record of a model portfolio in which they buy stocks strongly favored by insiders and typically hold them for about six months. Through mid-1986, the portfolio appreciated by 1,873 percent (ignoring commissions and dividends) as compared with 190 percent for the Dow Jones industrials.

For market timing, Unterbrink uses two indicators: an index of buying and selling by market professionals (specialists and traders on the floor of the New York Stock Exchange) and a risk exposure ratio. When both indicators turn from neutral to positive, the service flashes a buy signal; when they turn to negative, it puts out a sell. The signals have an excellent but by no means infallible record for calling substantial swings in the Dow.

■ **New Issues.** (Published monthly by the Institute for Econometric Research, 3471 N. Federal Highway, Fort Lauderdale, FL 33306. One year, $95. Two-issue trial, free.)

Started in September 1978, this service has done a good job of covering the treacherous new issues market. The 150 recommendations it made from then to mid-1986 had an average gain of more than 90 percent from the initial offering price. Editor Norman G. Fosback describes forthcoming offerings, analyzes those he recommends, and draws attention to buying opportunities in the aftermarket — that is, after a new issue has been launched and is trading (usually over the counter). Fosback isn't averse to omitting recommendations when he considers forthcoming issues overpriced or is leery about the condition of the market. His service provides a calendar of offerings that gives the underwriter's name and address, the number of shares to be sold, their probable price, and the expected date of the offering.

■ **Investors Intelligence.** (Published every two weeks by Chartcraft Inc., 2 East Ave., Larchmont, NY 10538. One year, $108. Two-month trial, $24.)

This publication is the *Reader's Digest* of the advisory services. Each issue provides one-paragraph summaries of the market views of 30 services, culled from the 135 it monitors, and it gives a selection of their stock recommendations. Other features include advice to fund switchers on the allocation of their assets between stock funds and money-market funds, and a list of stocks that have been bought or sold by more than three corporate insiders.

Investors Intelligence is known for its "Bearish Sentiment Index," which shows the percentage of services that expect the market to decline. The number has been consistently largest (60 percent or more) at market bottoms and smallest (usually 15 percent or less) at market tops. Reason: most of the technical services are trend followers, so they tend to be wrong at major turning points in the market. The "Bearish Sentiment Index" has become widely recognized as a contrary opinion indicator; investors should be buying when sentiment among advisory services is exceptionally bearish and selling when it is strongly bullish.

Analytic Approaches

15 The Fundamental Approach: Judging What a Stock Is Worth

Investment analysis seeks to answer these two questions: *What* should I buy or sell? *When* should I buy or sell? The chapters that follow will show you how to use the three principal analytic approaches and a fourth that in recent years has attracted attention. The *fundamental approach* — the oldest and the dominant one in the investment world — concerns itself with value. The *technical approach* focuses on supply and demand and concerns itself mainly with timing. The *psychological approach* — generally referred to as contrary opinion theory or contrarian investing — concerns itself with groupthink and crowd psychology. Its goal is to discover opportunities for profit created by the irrational behavior of large numbers of investors. The connection between presidential politics and the stock market is the basis of a relatively new approach to market timing, which is known as *political cycle investing.*

Security analysis is an art that is struggling to become a science but isn't likely to succeed — because you cannot put a stock in a test tube. What security analysis can do is enable investors to separate realities and probabilities from vague hunches and unfounded hopes and fears. Through systematic assessment of the available facts, it arrives at specific estimates, which, though fallible, are vastly preferable to uninformed guesswork.

A stock's investment value, or intrinsic worth, as determined by fundamental analysis may be approximately the same as its market price, in which case the stock is said to be fairly or reasonably valued. If a stock is found to be undervalued or overvalued, fundamentalists assume that its market price will sooner or later come into line with the intrinsic value. That could happen in a few months or possibly a year, but it usually takes longer. Consequently, fundamental analysis is basically oriented toward long-term investing, though it also concerns itself with the intermediate term (three to 12 months).

The practical function of fundamental analysis is to determine

1. which issues, at their current prices, are undervalued or overvalued *in relation to others;*

2. whether stocks in general are undervalued or overvalued on the basis of their projected returns (dividends and price gains) and the returns offered by competitive investments — in particular, bonds and money-market securities such as Treasury Bills.

☐ A MINI-REFERENCE LIBRARY FOR AMATEUR STOCK ANALYSTS

Professional analysts draw on vast amounts of information, for which a major brokerage house typically spends upward of $500,000 a year, if you include computerized data services. But for less than $65 (at 1987 prices) you can assemble the reference materials described below. They provide the data you need to follow the analytic procedures described in this chapter and the investment strategies discussed later. There is one essential addition — the brief but extraordinarily comprehensive stock reports issued by Standard & Poor's. Your broker can usually supply you with an S&P report on a company you wish to analyze. Here is our suggested kit of reference materials for amateur analysts.

The Fortune 500 Directories contain investment data on the nation's 500 largest industrial companies, the nation's 500 largest service companies (diversified services, commercial banking, diversified financial, savings institutions, life insurers, retailers, transportation companies, and utilities), and the 500 largest international companies. Included are sales, net income, assets, return on stockholders' equity, total return to investors, earnings per share, and ten-year earnings growth rates. The directories appear serially each year in *Fortune* magazine in late April, early June, and early August, or they can be ordered separately by sending $8 per directory to Fortune Directories, 250 West 49th Street, New York, NY 10019.

The *Forbes Annual Report on American Industry* appears in the early January issue of *Forbes* magazine, which can be bought on newsstands; it cost $3.50 in 1987. A prodigious compendium of information for the do-it-yourself investor, this special issue starts out with reports on 30 or more industries and then measures the performance of more than 1,000 large companies over the previous 12 months and the previous five years. The data for individual companies include sales and earnings for the 12 months and their five-year growth rates; the past year's return and the 5-year average return on stockholders' equity; the number of shares outstanding and their total market value. The issue also ranks the companies on the basis of

1. profitability,
2. growth, and
3. market performance.

Barron's is a financial weekly that usually runs to more than 140 large pages; at this writing, it sells on newsstands for the bargain price of $1.50. Our $65 budget for reference materials allows $18 for the purchase of one issue of *Barron's* in the first week of each month. Here is a partial list of what you will get, in addition to excellent general articles: several reports on individual companies, a review of the past week on the stock and bond markets, a department on options, and about 60 pages of statistics. These include the prices and earnings of all stocks on the New York and the American stock exchanges and of the over-the-counter issues quoted on NASDAQ; the prices and current yields of all bonds traded on the New York and the American stock exchanges; the prices and yields of U.S. Treasury bonds and notes; the previous week's high, low, and closing prices of all options traded on the options exchanges; the week's closing level, and the percentage gain or loss for the year to date, of the Dow Jones Industrial Average, the S&P 500 index, the NYSE composite index, the Amex index, and many other useful stock and bond averages and indexes; the market prices and net asset values per share of closed-end stock and bond funds; the previous two weeks' reported figures for the money supply; all of the key short-term interest rates; and the latest week's figures for short sales by odd-lotters, the public, exchange members, and exchange specialists — their significance is explained in chapter 16. For a do-it-yourself investor, *Barron's* is invaluable.

The *Dow Jones Business & Investment Almanac* (Dow Jones-Irwin, $24.95; available in bookstores) contains surveys of 20 industries with financial data on major companies in them; data on the 100 fastest-growing smaller companies; the market performance of some 25 stock groups; the historical investment returns on stocks, bonds, and money-market securities; charts of the Dow Jones averages since the late 1940s and tables showing the behavior of other major stock averages; and sections devoted to mutual funds and to options. In addition, the almanac gives the *Hulbert Financial Digest* ranking of investment advisory services, listings of bank failures and corporate bankruptcies, federal government budget data, and other economic statistics.

The *Investors Information Kit* published by the New York Stock Exchange consists of several useful pamphlets including *Income Leaders on the Big Board,* which gives you the dividends paid by common and preferred stocks yielding 6 percent or more; *Understanding Stocks and Bonds; Understanding Financial Statements; Getting Help When You Invest;* and a glossary of investment terms (New York Stock Exchange, Publication Division, 11 Wall Street, New York, NY 10005. About $8 postpaid in 1987). Other background materials published by the New York Stock Exchange are distributed, free of charge, through brokerage houses.

The *Stock Guide,* issued monthly by Standard & Poor's, is a basic investment tool that brokers constantly refer to. Its $84 annual subscription cost is not included in the budget for our suggested reference library; however, if you have a friendly broker, he will be glad to send you an issue from time to time free of charge. This compact booklet covers 5,300 companies, and by running your eye across a single line you get most of the key investment data on a stock — its S&P quality rating; the size of institutional holdings; the price range over 16 years; the dividend yield and price/earnings ratio; the earnings per share over the previous five years, the previous 12 months, and recent quarters; and the company's financial position and market capitalization. A separate section provides investment data on more than 400 mutual funds. (Standard & Poor's Corporation, 25 Broadway, New York, NY 10004).

A source of free information that thrifty investors might welcome is a bank publication that discusses the state of the economy: the *Manufacturers Hanover Economic Report,* issued monthly except in July and August by Manufacturers Hanover Trust Co. (270 Park Ave., New York, NY 10017). It is edited by the bank's widely quoted chief economist, Irwin L. Kellner.

There are many other valuable sources of investment data, but the package of reference materials described above gives you, we think, the best mileage you can hope to get for under $65. If your budget for investment research is elastic, we suggest you take one or more of the investment advisory services described in Chapter 14 and a periodical that covers the investment scene. The magazines that, in our opinion, can be most helpful to individual investors are *Financial World* ($44.99 a year), *Forbes* ($42 a year), and *Money* ($29.95 a year), with the last of which the past writer was, and the present writer still is, associated.

Having assembled an adequate information bank, an amateur investor is equipped to tackle the nitty-gritty of security analysis. The procedures may at first sound forbidding. But all it takes to acquire a functional grasp of them — we are not suggesting that you aim at professional expertise — is common sense, patience, a command of simple arithmetic, and above all a strong desire to be self-reliant rather than blindly dependent on the judgment of others. Once you have mastered the basic procedures, they will enable you to make educated value judgments about a stock in much less time than you spend doing your income tax. This know-how is a tremendous asset for the layman. But even with it, inexperienced investors shouldn't try to operate entirely on their own. Do-it-yourself analysis will often raise questions that you should refer to your broker. If he doesn't know the answer himself, he may be able to get it from an analyst in his firm's research department or from the *Value Line Investment Survey.*

☐ Valuation Approaches

☐ Present Value

The reigning academic theory of stock valuation is that a stock's intrinsic value is the present discounted value of its expected future cash returns — that is, the future stream of dividends and the eventual sale price, discounted by the risk-free return on money plus an appropriate premium for risk.* The present-value concept has many applications in finance, and as a model for stock valuation it is totally logical. The catch is that the model makes assumptions that are divorced from practicality. Analysts' estimates of earnings for the next 12 months are notoriously fallible. It is therefore highly unrealistic to judge a stock's worth on the basis of projections of earnings and dividends stretching far into the future. To come up with the correct total cash return over, say, a ten-year period, an analyst would have to assess accurately a multitude of variables for each of those years: sales, profit margins, market reception of new products, strength of competition, state of the economy, and so on. He would also have to project correctly how much an investor would receive from the sale of the stock ten years hence. The present-value model ducks these real-life difficulties by expressing uncertain projections in

---

* The formula for discounting is as follows: if the discount rate is 7 percent, the present value of $1 one year hence is $1/1.07 = $0.93.

algebraic symbols. It then constructs an equation out of those symbols, and — hey presto — arrives at a mathematically "correct" figure for present value. But unless all of the projections are right, the present-value figure is phony. Like computers, present-value equations are subject to the GIGO principle: garbage in, garbage out.

☐ The Ben Graham Approach

Benjamin Graham (1894–1976) pretty much founded the discipline of security analysis in the mid-1930s when he and David L. Dodd published their monumental work *Security Analysis,* which has gone through four editions (New York: McGraw-Hill, 4th edition, 1962). In his later years Graham concluded that the more elaborate approaches to security analysis were of dubious value. In an interview with Patricia Dreyfus that appeared in *Money* magazine in July 1976, Graham distilled the insights of a lifetime devoted to analyzing stocks into two simple methods. One of them starts out by looking for stocks with low price/earnings ratios; Graham's requirement was about seven times earnings at a time when that valuation was 40 percent below the P/E ratio of the S&P index. Then comes the decisive test: *the company's current assets must exceed its current liabilities together with its long-term debt.* The second method ignores price/earnings ratios and focuses exclusively on current assets. The first step is to find companies whose current assets exceed their *total* liabilities — current liabilities plus long-term debt and the market value of their preferred stock, if any. The next step is to divide the difference between current assets and total liabilities by the number of shares outstanding; this gives you "net net working capital" per share. If the net net working capital per share is higher than the market price, the stock is undervalued. It is easy to see why. An investor is getting the company's property, plant, and equipment at zero cost, which means that he is buying the stock at less than its liquidation value.

Graham also provided simple, though controversial, guidelines for selling. He recommended setting a profit objective of between 50 percent and 100 percent and selling when that goal is reached; if it isn't reached within three years, the stock should be sold anyhow.

Graham's simplified valuation methods are fairly easy to use; all of the data required (except for the stock's current price) are in Standard & Poor's monthly *Stock Guide.* Both methods are bargain-oriented ones that focus on assets *and ignore growth prospects.* They are well suited for investors who concentrate on tangible value. But if you are venturesome, you are likely to find their requirements constricting. They will assuredly keep you out of the great growth companies of your era, because such companies have the kind of romance that commands high valuations. By Graham's yardsticks, the growth stocks of the 1950s and 1960s that are now mature giants — a Coca-Cola, an IBM, a McDonald's — were never undervalued. But thousands of investors made enormous profits in them.

□ The Value of Book Value

A company's book value is its total assets minus total liabilities (including the redemption value of preferred stock), divided by the number of shares outstanding. Since the difference between total assets and total liabilities is common stockholders' equity, book value is the same as stockholders' equity per share.

Book value has several uses in security analysis. For one thing, it can be an indicator of whether the general level of stock prices is abnormally high or low. There have been only a few periods between World War II and 1987 when the Dow Jones Industrial Average was priced below its book value — 1949, late 1973 and 1974, early 1978, early 1980, and the first seven months of 1982. Each of those periods was followed by a major rise in stock prices. On the other hand, from the late 1950s through 1968, the Dow sold on the average at 65 percent above book value. And that decade was followed by a long and severe bear market, at least for the vast majority of stocks. So it would seem that most stocks are undervalued when the Dow is selling at or below book value, and they are probably becoming overvalued when the Dow rises 40 percent above its book value. Your broker can get you the Dow's book value, and you need to update it only once a year. It was in the area of $1,000 in mid-1987, when the Dow towered above 2400 — 140 percent above it.

Book value is also the basic tool of some analysts who specialize in ferreting out sharply undervalued stocks. Unless the market is severely depressed, the stocks of companies that are prospering sell at appreciably more than book value; most of the stocks selling substantially below book value are deadbeats or weaklings — but not all of them. A hotly controversial New York analyst, Ray Dirks, wrote a book, *Heads You Win, Tails You Win* (New York: Stein and Day, 1979), which argues that focusing exclusively on stocks selling below book value is the safest and most profitable investment strategy. Dirks has a formula for avoiding the trash and homing in on the treasures: the stock must have an earnings yield* of 14 percent or more — which simply means a price/earnings ratio of about seven or less — and, preferably, it should have a "respectable" though not necessarily consistent or impressive earnings growth rate. Dirks's approach is somewhat similar to the first Ben Graham method described earlier, but not quite so exacting. Even so, a stock with a decent earnings record that is selling below book value and at seven times earnings or less is apt to be undervalued.

☐ Bargain-Priced Growth

An approach to stock valuation that is bargain-oriented but takes into account growth has been developed by Barry Ziskin, a New York money manager whose firm is called the Opportunity Prospector. Four times a year Ziskin screens 8,000 stocks to find out which ones meet his seven exacting and undeviating criteria. Two of them are related to consistency and magnitude of growth: pretax income from operations must show a growth rate of *at least 10 percent in each of the previous six years and total growth over the six-year period amounting to 20 percent compounded annually.* Three criteria are designed to establish that the company is in tip-top shape financially. The main requirements are:

1. the current ratio must be at least two to one, or working capital per share must exceed market price per share;
2. long-term debt must be covered by working capital or by the latest 12 months' cash flow (net income plus depreciation and amortization);
3. accounting procedures must be conservative. (These terms and ratios are explained in the discussion of annual reports in chapter 14.) The remaining criteria ensure that the stock has not achieved wide recognition — institutions must own less than 10 percent of the shares outstanding, and the P/E ratio must be less than ten times estimated earnings for the current year.

The merit of Ziskin's system is that it excludes subjective judgments. When a stock meets all of the criteria, it's a buy. It is then held until it flunks any one of the tests, at which point it is automatically

---

* A stock's earnings yield — its earnings per share divided by its price — is the reciprocal of its price/earnings ratio (price divided by earnings). So if a stock's earnings yield is 14 percent, its P/E ratio is 14 divided into 100, or 7.2.

sold. In the majority of cases, stocks are sold either because they have achieved wide recognition and their valuation has risen above ten times earnings, or because their growth shows signs of faltering. In the halcyon days for undervalued and under-researched stocks — the hidden bull market that extended from the early 1970s through 1981 — Ziskin's system excelled. According to his records from mid-1973 to December 1979, 112 issues that qualified as buys were subsequently disqualified and sold. Two were losers, three broke even, and 108 showed gains averaging 78 percent (before allowing for brokerage commissions); during that period the S&P index was up less than 2 percent. Ziskin's firm stopped keeping count, issue by issue, in the 1980s, but from 1980 through 1985, the accounts that he manages for clients earned an average of 19.45 percent a year, compared with 9.25 percent for the S&P. Clearly, this valuation system achieved remarkably good results. And even though amateur investors can't apply it to the letter — it calls for too much work — they will find its basic requirements an excellent guide to discovering undervalued growth companies. In sum, those requirements are:

1. a vigorous and consistent growth rate;
2. a strong financial condition;
3. low institutional sponsorship and a P/E ratio under 10.

□ Stock Valuation — Casting a Wider Net

While they have a proven record of success, the systems discussed thus far are limiting; relatively few stocks meet their requirements. A wider-angled approach to finding attractive stocks is to start by checking whether a stock appears to be overvalued or undervalued in relation to others. Then, if it seems to be undervalued, you try to analyze the company in the conventional way — that is, by looking into its earnings record, its profitability, its product line, the competition it faces, the prospects for its industry, and so on. The specifics of that approach will be described in the rest of this chapter.

The preliminary check — finding out whether or not a stock's relative valuation seems attractive — can be a tremendous time-saver. Why go to all the trouble of studying a company if its relative valuation shows that it is probably overpriced? There are two ways of establishing relative valuation. We will explain both of them, step by step, because they serve somewhat different needs.

The yardstick of valuation most widely used by analysts is the price/earnings ratio, which was fully explained in chapter 4. The P/E ratios given in newspaper stock-market columns are based on a company's latest 12 months' earnings. Professionals, however, base their P/E ratios on *estimates* of earnings for the current year, which you will find in brokerage house reports and investment advisory services. Though fallible, such estimates are usually a better guide to evaluating a stock than the previous year's results. For example, the stocks of fertilizer companies such as International Minerals & Chemical Corporation looked cheap in early 1976 on the strength of their booming earnings in 1975. But the outlook for the fertilizer industry suggested that earnings were about to decline — and they did, in 1976 and 1977. A P/E ratio based on past results is also highly misleading when a company has suffered a sharp drop in earnings because of temporary difficulties — for example, a strike; or when it has started to show a small profit after a period of losses. In such cases, the P/E will look forbiddingly high, but the stock may not be really overvalued on the basis of the company's more normal earning power — its average profits over the previous five years.

Amateur investors (aided and abetted by stockbrokers, who should know better) often make the mistake of concluding that a stock is cheap simply because its P/E is low — say, five times earnings. But P/Es vary from industry to industry. Furthermore the overall level of stock valuations and the valuations of industry groups have varied greatly over the past 35 years. So a stock's current price/earnings ratio is not, on its own, a reliable clue to whether the stock is undervalued, overvalued, or fairly valued. *What security analysts want to know is whether the P/E is higher or lower in relation to the overall level of P/Es than it has been in the past.* With the proper information at your fingertips, figuring out a stock's relative P/E takes only a few minutes.

First you calculate (from a Standard & Poor's company report, the *Value Line Survey,* or some other source) the stock's average P/E over the previous five years. Let's take, as an illustration, the stock of Carolina Freight, a trucking company traded on the New York Stock Exchange; its average five-year P/E in mid-February 1981 was about 6. Now you measure this figure against the average P/E of a leading market index over the same five years. Professionals use Standard & Poor's 500, but for most laymen it is easier to use the Dow, because its current P/E is published every Monday in the *Wall Street Journal.* The five-year average P/E of the Dow — a calculation you need make only once a year — was 8.5. So the historical ratio of Carolina Freight's valuation relative to the Dow's was 6 divided by 8.5, or 71 percent.

The final step is to measure the stock's current estimated P/E against the P/E of the market. (It is preferable to base the Dow's P/E on the prevailing estimate of its earnings for the current year, which your broker or his research department can give you.) In mid-February 1981, Carolina Freight, then selling at 14, had a P/E of 4.7, based on estimated 1981 earnings. The Dow's P/E based on per share earnings was about 8. So the ratio of Carolina Freight's current P/E relative to the Dow's was 4.7 divided by 8, or 59 percent. Now you have discovered whether your stock is selling at a lower or higher relative valuation than it has in the past. In the case of Carolina Freight, it was a shade lower — 59 percent against 72 percent. So there appeared to be a possibility that the stock was somewhat undervalued.*

A different and quicker way of determining relative valuation has been devised by George Lasry, the author of *Valuing Common Stock: The Power of Prudence* (AMACOM, 1979), and we have found it enormously valuable. The Lasry test is a lot simpler than it may appear at first sight to an inexperienced investor; with the necessary data at hand and a little practice, you can apply it to a stock in less than one minute. Before telling you how it works, we should explain its rationale.

The Lasry test uses two yardsticks — a company's return on stockholders' equity (ROE)† and the price/earnings ratio of its stock. Return on equity is a measure of profitability (of how well the company is performing) and the price/earnings ratio is the valuation investors put on a company's stock. So if you divide ROE by the P/E you get a number — Lasry calls it the "ranking number" — *that tells you whether a stock's valuation is high or low on the basis of its profitability.* The higher the ranking number, the lower the valuation, and vice versa. Let's assume, for example, that stock A has a return on equity of 21 percent and a P/E of 7; ROE divided by P/E gives us a

---

* The stock subsequently rose nearly 27 percent, to 17¾, and then slipped back. At the end of 1981, it had performed somewhat better than the Dow.

† The *Forbes* issue included in our suggested mini-reference library, "Report on American Industry," gives the recent and the five-year average ROE for more than a thousand companies. If you need to calculate a company's ROE, the easiest method is to divide earnings per share by book value.

ranking number of 3. Stock B has a return on equity of 14 percent and a P/E ratio of 7, so its ranking number is 2. Although both stocks are selling at the same valuation of seven times earnings, A is undervalued in relation to B because A's profitability is much higher — 21 percent as against 14 percent.

The Lasry test begins by establishing the average ranking for stocks in general; you do this by dividing the median ROE for American industry by the median P/E for stocks in general. As a surrogate for American industry in this case, Lasry prefers the Value Line Industrial Composite, a universe of 900 companies. Value Line publishes data on this composite twice yearly, in January and July. In its compilation, ROE is called "% earned on net worth." The five-year median ROE for Value Line's cross-section of American industry in 1985 was 12.3 percent. The median P/E ratio for the same 900 companies was 11.6 percent. So the median ranking number was about 1.

The next step is to calculate the ranking number of the stock you are investigating. If its return on stockholders' equity doesn't vary greatly from year to year, you can simply divide last year's ROE by the current estimated P/E ratio; in the case of companies with sharp swings in profitability, you should take the average return on equity over the past five years.

The final step is to compare the ranking number of your stock with the median ranking for the market in general. If, for example, the median ranking is 1, here is what the Lasry test tells you:

1. stocks with a ranking of anywhere from 0.9 to 1.4 are probably not appreciably overvalued or undervalued in relation to others;
2. a stock begins to look undervalued if its ranking number is close to 1.5 and it could be a bargain if the ranking is 2.5 or higher;
3. there's a strong possibility that stocks with a ranking of 0.8 or less are relatively overvalued.

The Lasry test has one important drawback: the stocks of high-growth companies selling at fairly high price/earnings ratios almost invariably come out either overvalued or at best fairly valued. If the median ranking is 1, a stock selling at 32 times earnings would have to have an ROE of 32 percent merely to match the median ranking — and relatively few companies have a return on equity of more than 30 percent. So the Lasry test will keep an investor out of high-growth issues with high P/E ratios. But there are periods when such issues are the stellar market performers — for example, from 1978 through mid-1981.

Lasry's rejoinder to this objection is that most high P/E stocks are always relatively overvalued. They may indeed be stellar performers at times when the market environment is favorable, provided that their earnings growth at least matches expectations. But, Lasry argues, high P/E stocks are apt to get clobbered when their earnings are disappointing or the market suffers a major setback. His test, he says, was devised to serve an investment policy based on discovering stocks that are *sharply undervalued* — not on the basis of uncertain estimates of future growth but on the basis of their *actual* return on equity. Judging from Lasry's record, his policy has been extremely successful. However, if you want to invest in stocks in the high-growth category, you should use the relative P/E method to check on their current valuations.

The Lasry test and the relative P/E test provide what lawyers call prima facie evidence that a stock may be undervalued or overvalued. But that isn't sufficient. For example, if a stock's relative P/E ratio is currently below its five-year average, you would want to know whether the change is justified by a deterioration in the company's position and prospects. The further evidence you need to reach a reasonable verdict on the merits of a stock must be pieced together by giving the company a general checkup. Here is how the average investor, who isn't in a position to visit the company and interview its management, might go about doing this.

A logical starting point is to determine whether the company is predominantly in growth sectors of industry or in cyclical ones, or whether it is about evenly involved in both. (See Appendix C.) You will find a breakdown of a company's sales and earnings by sector or industry in its S&P report or its annual report. If the company is cyclical, check on whether the underlying earnings trend is upward — that is, whether profits in recent up years were generally higher than profits in earlier up years and profits in recent down years were higher than profits in earlier down years. As a rule, a cyclical company that doesn't have an underlying pattern of growth should be avoided by long-term investors.

In the case of growth companies, the earnings record gives you instant answers — positive or negative — to several crucial questions. Has the annual percentage increase in earnings been accelerating or slowing down in recent years? How much has profit growth been affected by recessions — slightly or substantially? Has the growth rate been consistent, or does it show pronounced variations? (Investors pay high premiums for consistency.)

Now compare the pattern of sales with that of earnings. If sales gains have not been keeping pace with profit growth, it is most unlikely that profit growth can be sustained. But what if sales have been increasing conspicuously faster than earnings? That is a warning that the company needs to trim costs or eliminate unprofitable operations.

Turn next to the dividend record and calculate the average percentage of earnings that the company has paid out in dividends over the years. A large dividend payout is attractive to investors whose primary goal is high current income, but for growth-minded investors it is undesirable. Dividend income is subject to double taxation. As a stockholder you have in effect paid the corporate income tax rate on your share of the company's earnings, and then you are hit with personal income taxes on the dividend payout. So the smaller the dividend payout, the greater is your share of earnings that escape double taxation and are reinvested for you in the business, causing your equity as a stockholder to grow.

Your next target is the company's earnings prospects, perhaps the most vital factor in stock valuation. For companies in highly cyclical industries, these prospects tend to be closely related to the future course of the economy. Since the behavior of stock prices tends to anticipate major moves in the economy by roughly six months, the time to consider cyclical stocks is when you think a recession has hit bottom or even sooner; their prices usually start rising well before economic recovery is discernible. Conversely, you should be thinking about selling cyclical stocks some time before the economy seems to be reaching a peak — unless you expect the next business slowdown to be mild and short-lived.

In assessing the prospects for a high-growth company, you run into a problem if its earnings gain in the previous 12 months was well below its average annual gain — or, worse still, if profits declined. In such cases, the stock has often dropped so far in price that it would be a bargain provided the company regains its momentum in the fairly near future. But if it doesn't — and this kind of prognosis is often tough even for the pros — the stock could be a catastrophic investment. Since the stocks of high growth companies usually pay inconsequential dividends and are therefore unattractive from the standpoint of income, there's not much limit to how far their stocks can decline if earnings stop growing. A horrific example: when the profits of Levitz Furniture peaked in 1972, it was selling at 242 (adjusted for a subsequent one-for-four reverse split); by 1974, it had fallen to 6. Seven years later, it was selling at only 29, even though its profits started rising again in 1976. (In 1985, Levitz bought back all its stock and went private.)

Assuming that a high-growth company is running true to form, you still have to ask yourself some questions about its future. Is it maintaining or enhancing its profit potential with new products, expansion programs and perhaps acquisitions? Is there a serious threat of mounting competition? (Xerox, for example, found the going tougher after IBM, Kodak, and the Japanese joined its earlier competitors in the copier market.) Do its major markets continue to offer opportunities for robust growth? Is its growth menaced by changes in government policies or regulations? You can find the answers, or clues to them, by studying the company's annual report, by questioning your broker or knowledgeable business friends, and by combing through recent issues of business and financial periodicals in a well-stocked library.

A major factor in stock valuation is a company's profitability. The principal yardsticks: its operating margin (the pretax amount earned per dollar of sales, excluding both income from investments and outgoing interest charges); its net profit margin (income after taxes divided by total revenues); its return on stockholders' equity (net income divided by the total balance-sheet value of the shareholders' ownership in the company).

You can gauge the company's profitability by comparing its margins and return on shareholders' equity with averages for its industry (which you will find in the suggested reference materials or in the annual *U.S. Statistical Abstract,* available in libraries). A company's profitability, together with its sales and earnings record, gives you a reliable reading on the quality of management. Meeting a company's top executives, as professionals do, is sometimes not a help in judging their competence. Many Wall Street analysts bear scars of the mistakes they have made by overrating, or being misled by, a charismatic chief executive.

Your next exercise is to run through the company's balance sheet, which shows its assets, liabilities, long-term debt, and other financial data at the end of the previous fiscal year (or most recent quarter). Your first checkpoint: *the ratio of current assets to current liabilities.* The excess of current assets over current liabilities is the company's working capital — the funds available to run the business. The adequacy of working capital depends on the industry in which the company is operating. As a rough rule, it is desirable for current assets to be twice as large as current liabilities, or nearly so, but utilities, supermarkets, and other industries that generate prompt cash payments get by on less. When in doubt, ask your broker whether a company's ratio is comfortable. A company that has impressed you with its earnings growth could prove to be strapped for working capital because it has expanded too rapidly — and that could spell trouble.

Another key ratio is that of long-term debt to stockholders' equity. A high debt-to-equity ratio makes earnings extremely volatile because of the high fixed charges for bond interest. Take, for example, a company with a million shares outstanding that is earning $1 million and has fixed annual charges of $500,000 for bond interest (computed after taxes). Its earnings per share will be $1 million minus $500,000 divided by a million shares — that is, 50 cents. But if total earnings drop 20 percent, earnings per share will drop 40 percent. The math then becomes $800,000 minus $500,000 divided by a million shares, or 30 cents. Such companies are said to be highly leveraged, and their valuations tend to be relatively low because their earnings are extremely volatile. Moreover, a succession of losing years could drag such companies into bankruptcy. Chrysler, Navistar, Lockheed, and Pan American World Airways are examples of companies whose survival has been endangered in bad times because they are so highly leveraged.

Your next checkpoint on the balance sheet is *book value;* it was discussed a few pages back as well as in chapter 14. That chapter also briefly covered a subject that is important in security analysis — a company's accounting practices and how they affect the quality of its earnings. Reported earnings may be overstated or understated depending on whether accounting practices are permissive or conservative.

You will need one more crucial piece of information before you weigh the evidence — *an estimate of earnings* for the company's current fiscal year and, if the year is halfway through, a tentative projection of earnings for the next year. Your broker can get you earnings estimates for companies that are well covered by analysts, but you may sometimes have to make an earnings estimate yourself.

There is a mechanical way of forecasting earnings that gives you what might be called a well-educated guesstimate: *simply multiply the current book value by the five-year or three-year average return on stockholders' equity.* If book value stands at $10 and average ROE was 20 percent, estimated earnings per share will be $2. If the company's ROE has been improving steadily, you can refine your estimate by using last year's ROE or even a slightly higher one instead of the average. The mechanical method shouldn't be applied, however, to highly cyclical companies whose earnings fluctuate sharply.

There's another rough-and-ready method for forecasting earnings. Look at the total revenues for the past few years and the net (after-tax) profit margin. Then, drawing on everything you have learned about the company, estimate revenues and the profit margin for the current year. By multiplying these two figures you'll get net income, which, divided by the number of shares outstanding, gives you earnings per share. If estimated revenues are $100 million, the net margin is 6 percent, and there are three million shares outstanding, then the indication is that net income will be $6 million and earnings per share will be $2.

To wind up your analysis you should try to figure out *the ratio of risk to possible reward,* a crucial factor that amateur investors often fail to evaluate. There are several ways of doing this. Let's illustrate a crude but useful one with a hypothetical stock, Testcorp Inc., and let's say Testcorp had earnings per share (EPS) of $3.65 last year, is expected to earn $4 a share this year, and is selling at $24.

First, you make a projection of a price to which the stock might drop within the next 12 months if things turn out badly; then you make a reasonably optimistic price projection; then you compare the possible percentage loss and gain. A moderately pessimistic projection for Testcorp might be based on EPS of $3.50 × 5, or $17.50 — 27 percent below the current price. A rational projection based on favorable assumptions might be that the stock will sell at eight times EPS of $4 or $32 — about 33 percent *above* the current price. The ratio of possible reward to risk — 33 percent to 27 percent — is not inviting. If you're trying to beat the market, you should look for stocks whose potential gain appears to be twice their possible loss.

Some of the procedures described in this chapter undoubtedly sound formidable to a beginner, and at the start such a person certainly will find them taxing. But they really aren't difficult to learn. And even a novice, once he gets organized and has the data at hand, will quickly pick up speed and proficiency. Madelon Talley was a New

York housewife with no financial experience when she joined the Dreyfus Corp., a large mutual fund organization. While performing statistical chores, she taught herself to analyze stocks and so impressed management with her acumen that she was soon promoted to portfolio manager. Within a few years, Mrs. Talley was a recognized star. Another brilliant stock picker with no formal training in economics or finance is Charles Allmon, a money manager who became fascinated by the stock market while working as a photographer for *National Geographic.* The losses Allmon suffered as a result following brokers' advice prompted him to develop his own investment strategy in the 1950s. The best opportunities, he concluded, lay in the smaller companies that analysts had overlooked. This strategy proved so successful that friends started asking him to manage their investments, and before long he found himself with a stable of clients.

Another amateur who learned to analyze stocks with remarkable results and went on to become a professional is Robert S. Morrow of Dublin, Ohio. Morrow, an electrical engineer, had no interest in the stock market until his wife badgered him into joining an investment club that calls itself the MMMDCX Stock Club. From 1976 to 1982, he recommended 14 stocks at the club's bimonthly meetings and the club invested in all of them. During the periods the club held them, they rose an average of 64 percent a year after commissions; over the same six years the Dow finished down 10 percent. Only two of Morrow's picks were losers. How did Morrow achieve these phenomenal results? He used a market timing approach and confined his stock picking to high-technology issues, which, as an engineer, he was well-equipped to understand. In 1983 he became a registered investment adviser and began managing private accounts. He prepares audio and video tapes on investments, appears regularly on Financial News Network, and publishes a monthly newsletter (the *High Tech Growth Forecaster,* Muirfield Village, 8547 Pitlochry Court, Dublin, OH 43017; $195 a year).

Clearly Madelon Talley, Charles Allmon, and Robert Morrow are exceptionally gifted people; moreover, they didn't retain their amateur status. But all three are self-taught, self-motivated, and sterling examples for any investor willing to concentrate on fundamentals.

A final word about stock valuation. Don't waste your time analyzing overanalyzed stocks that represent the most efficient sector of the market. The chances are virtually nil that you can discover anything about a Kodak, an Exxon, or a Philip Morris that isn't known and reflected in the price of the stock. Confine your homework to lesser-known or underanalyzed companies, which are by no means always small ones. If you are good at handling numbers and have an inquiring mind, you should find stock analysis an intriguing form of detective work. And it can be a lot more rewarding than solving whodunits.

·16 The Technical Approach: Focusing on Supply and Demand

There's much in technical analysis that smacks of abracadabra, but its underlying premises are ones that common sense can readily accept: the behavior of investors tends to repeat itself, so past trends or patterns in buying and selling can provide valuable clues to future price movements. While the best policy for most amateur investors is to rely mainly on fundamentals in their choice of investments, an understanding of some of the tools of technical analysis can be of considerable help to them in deciding when to buy and when to sell. Before getting down to specifics, let's briefly review the case for and against technical analysis.

Technical analysts don't deny that fundamental factors — earnings, interest rates, trends in the economy, and so on — influence the actions of investors. But, the technicians claim, EVERYTHING that influences investors — including fear, greed, and crowd psychology — is precisely reflected in the behavior of stock prices and trading volume, recorded on charts or in the output of computers. The purists of technical analysis argue further that the fundamentals are irrelevant and indeed misleading, because they don't tell us anything about the dominant force in the market: the emotions of investors. It follows that the only winning approach is to go straight to the heart of what really makes stock prices move: the interplay of supply and demand. The messiahs of technical analysis insistently reiterate that the data they heed are "the language of the market," and "only the market tells the story."

The trouble with this credo is that the market speaks "with forked tongue"; its language is often so ambiguous that it tells different stories to different technicians. For example, when Joseph E. Granville flashed his notorious "sell everything" signal on January 6, 1981, the market was telling another cardinal of the technical hierarchy, veteran analyst Edson Gould, that its trend was still upward. Indeed, Granville himself was bombastically bullish only three days before he pushed the panic button; his market letter of January 3, headlined "Straight Up," urged investors to do "some aggressive new buying." Thus from a practical standpoint, a major drawback of technical analysis is that the data it studies are subject to divergent interpretations. And when technical gurus give conflicting advice, you have to be an expert in the abstruse "language of the market" to judge which of their readings seems to be the more persuasive. In contrast, when fundamentalists differ, the evidence they present — earnings records, product information, profit margins, and so on — is of a kind that an intelligent layman can weigh for himself.

The most far-reaching attack on technical analysis has come from the Random Walk Hypothesis (discussed in chapter 12). But the random walkers claim too much, or so their critics charge — in our opinion, rightly. The most that the random walk studies have proved is that the particular technical tools they tested — past patterns of price behavior — failed to produce worthwhile results. That does not prove that past prices *coupled with volume data — figures showing patterns of money flows into stocks and out of them* — are of no value in predicting price movements. Nor do the mathematical concepts applied by the random walkers prove beyond a reasonable doubt that stock prices move randomly *all of the time.* Common sense and the perceptions of countless investment professionals suggest that stock prices, at least part of the time, do move in trends. That view is supported by a study* conducted by two students at the Wharton School of the University of Pennsylvania, Edward L. Bishop III and John R. Rollins, and published in the fall 1977 issue of the *Journal of Portfolio Management.* Bishop and Rollins measured the results of

---

* "Lowry's Reports: A Denial of Market Efficiency," December 30, 1975. I could find no updated study to confirm this one. However, the Lowry Management Corporation handsomely outperformed the stock market from 1980 through 1985, with an average annual audited return on managed accounts of 19.6 percent.——R. J. K.

buying and selling the shares of five mutual funds in accordance with the signals given by a well-known technical service, *Lowry's Reports Inc.,* chosen because its timing system is clearly defined and all of its signals have been a matter of public record since 1938. The study covered nine different periods between 1950 and 1975 and led its authors to the following conclusions.

1. Purchases and sales made in accordance with the Lowry signals "resulted in over double the gains achieved through buy-and-hold strategies" (taking into account commission costs).

2. "Trends in the market do seem to exist . . . and can be discovered in advance using weak form [technical] data." Complete randomness is not a correct description of how prices behave.

3. Trends develop and persist only when significant changes in investors' expectations substantially increase the flow of funds into or out of the stock market. The rest of the time stocks move randomly, and even during an extended uptrend or downtrend, there are trendless interludes when price movements are random.

☐ Trends and Countertrends

A basic concept of technical analysis stems from Newton's First Law of Motion, which says that a body in motion, left to itself, will continue to move in the same direction. Applied to stock prices, this means that a trend in force will persist until a significant change in investors' expectations (about the market or an individual stock) causes it to reverse itself; the odds are better than even that a market (or stock) in a well-established uptrend will continue to advance, and that one in a clear-cut downtrend will continue to decline.

Technical analysts identify three kinds of trends: the long-term (also known as the primary or major) trend, which may last anywhere from nine months to several years or even longer; the intermediate-term or secondary trend, which typically lasts from two or three months to nine; and the short-term or minor trend, which is measured in days or weeks. A primary uptrend is usually interrupted by intermediate-term corrections (downtrends) and a primary downtrend by intermediate-term rallies (uptrends). Similarly, intermediate-term trends are punctuated by short-term movements running counter to the trend. Some technical analysts concentrate on the primary and the intermediate-term trends; they wisely issue buy and sell signals only when they anticipate a swing of at least 5 to 10 percent for the Dow. But many technicians address themselves to in-and-out traders; they try to catch minor fluctuations, which are probably unpredictable and certainly not predictable enough to make short-term trading a profitable strategy for amateur investors, taking into account the large brokerage commissions involved.

There are three main approaches to technical analysis that are not mutually exclusive. *One of them studies charts showing the past price behavior of a stock (or a market average); bars at the bottom of the chart represent the volume of trading. The second approach focuses on market indicators,* of which there are several dozen — for example, the mutual funds' cash/assets ratio, discussed in an earlier chapter. To those who know how to interpret market indicators, each of them gives a reading that is bullish, bearish, or "neutral"; taken together these readings are helpful in judging which way the market is headed. *The third approach focuses more directly than the others on supply and demand; it measures the flow of funds into or out of a stock or the market to determine whether greater pressure is being exerted by buyers or sellers.* The Lowry program, for example, measures

1. the total gains for all stocks closing at a higher price than the previous day's close and the total volume of transactions in those stocks, and
2. the total losses for all stocks closing lower than the previous day's close and the total volume of transactions. Out of these figures, Lowry's builds indexes from which it gets its buy and sell signals. (*Lowry's Weekly Market Trends Analysis Reports,* 701 North Federal Highway, North Palm Beach, FL 33408; $212 a year.)

The majority of technical analysts use charts (which show trading volume) together with market indicators. Here's a rundown on some of their basic concepts and tools, which — *used in conjunction with fundamental analysis* — could be of help to amateur investors, both in identifying market trends and in deciding when to buy and sell individual stocks.

☐ A Look at the Charts

Two of the key concepts underlying the chartist approach — "support" and "resistance" — are rooted in the plausible belief that the behavior of investors tends to repeat itself. If you look at a long-term chart of the Dow Jones Industrial Average, you will see clearly that, between 1966 and the close of 1981, the Dow backtracked when it approached, reached, or went slightly above the 1,000 level; that happened in 1966, 1968, 1973, 1976 (many times), 1980, and 1981. This tells us that throughout the 15-year period there was substantially more selling than buying whenever the Dow reached the area of 1,000. That's what is meant by resistance level; it is a level at which, in the past, supply has recurrently exceeded demand and pushed prices downward. Similarly, a "support level" is one at which previous declines have repeatedly been arrested because of more buying than selling. From 1976 through 1981, the 750 area was a major support level for the Dow.

In any given period, there are several support and resistance levels for the market average and for individual stocks — levels based on past turning points in long-term, intermediate-term, and short-term price movements. When a stock (or market average) falls below a support level on *large trading volume,* technicians expect it to go lower; when it breaks through a resistance level on large trading volume, they expect it to go higher. Their rationale: if demand fails to exceed supply at a price that has previously attracted buyers, it is a sign of trouble. And if demand is greater than supply at a price that has previously triggered selling, it is a sign of new-found strength. The breaking of support and resistance levels on a small volume isn't significant; *the amount of buying or selling accompanying the breakthrough is the decisive factor.*

The price zone between a support and resistance level is called a channel or trading range. A stock that in recent months has fluctuated within a channel of 24 to 30 may, over the past 12 months, have had a trading range of 18 to 35. If the stock drops below 24, its next support level will be 18, and if it rises above 30, its next resistance level will be 35. If it declines to 24 two or three times *without dropping below that level,* it is said to have successfully tested its support; technicians generally consider that an indication that, in due course, the price will start moving upward. On the other hand, if the stock rises to 30 two or three times, but fails to break through that resistance level, technicians would conclude that its price (at least temporarily) is likely to turn downward.

Take caution when minor and highly questionable support and resistance levels are used in so-called technical letters as the basis for near-term forecasts and recommendations. Such advice can only be described as drivel. For example, a technical letter will say that if a market average — let's use a hypothetical one standing at 1,000 — breaks through 1,018, the advance should "carry to" 1060; on the other hand, a drop below 988 would give "a downside reading to 940–950." This is a nonforecast couched in mumbo-jumbo: all it's saying is that if the market doesn't go up, it will go down, and the probable swing will be about 60 points in either direction. Another standard gambit of some technicians is to tell you that a stock, currently selling at 24, should be bought if it penetrates minor resistance at 24¾ "for a move to 29," but if the stock drops to 22½ after you have bought it, cut your losses and sell. It is hard to believe, but many investors follow that kind of trading advice, presumably out of a neurotic need to enrich their brokers and impoverish themselves.

There are, however, situations in which significant support and resistance levels offer guidance worth heeding, if only because so many people playing the market piously believe in technical analysis and act accordingly. Here are four simple precepts that could improve your investment performance. The information you will require about support and resistance levels and trading volume can usually be obtained from your broker; most brokers nowadays are technically oriented, and their firms supply them with reams of technical analysis.

1. If you are thinking of buying a stock or putting funds into the market, you would be well advised to hold off if that stock or the entire market has just broken a major support level — and trading volume was large.
2. If you are thinking of selling, act promptly when a major support level has been broken (on large volume).
3. If you are considering buying a stock which, after a sharp runup, has risen to a significant resistance level and has repeatedly failed to penetrate it, the prudent policy is to wait and watch. The probabilities are that the stock has risen too much too soon and that it will pull back as more investors sell it to cash in their profits. (A retreat equal to roughly one-third of the advance would provide a good buying opportunity.) But if the stock, instead of retreating, bounces up again and finally breaks through its resistance level, buy it without delay. The chances are good that now it will continue to rise.
4. If you like a stock for fundamental reasons but want to check on your chances of buying it at a somewhat lower price, find out where it stands within its trading channel. If it is somewhere in

the middle or below, buy it; if it is at the high end, there's a good chance it will backtrack — unless you know of a strong reason that could cause it to break through its resistance level or unless the market is rising sharply.

A final point about support and resistance levels. At any given moment, the only certainty about them is that sooner or later they will be broken. In severe bear markets, stock prices crash relentlessly through a succession of descending support levels, and in bull markets they surmount resistance levels with the greatest of ease.

□ Those Elusive Chart Formations

When the behavior of stock prices is recorded on charts, it assumes recurring patterns or formations, which technicians refer to as a head-and-shoulders, a flag, a pennant, a rounded top, a double bottom, and so on — one of the odder ones is known as a Prussian helmet. It would be pointless to discuss them here, because interpreting chart formations is not a game that amateurs should play. Even professionals, looking at the same formations, often read divergent conclusions.

□ Indicators and What They Indicate

Constant indicator-watching is neither practical nor necessary for the average investor. What he needs is to know which indicators to consult, and how to interpret them, when he is contemplating investment decisions or simply wants to sharpen his sense of the market's prospects. The technical indicators described below constitute a serviceable cross-section of the more than 50 tracked by market technicians. Although these indicators have been explained as simply as possible without lapsing into gross oversimplification, the pages that follow will be tough going for a novice. Rank beginners would be well advised to be guided by the fundamentals discussed in this book and not to try to decipher technical indicators, so we suggest that they skip the rest of this chapter. Investors who feel they could benefit from an elementary course in the use of technical indicators are urged to read on.

□ Moving Average

A moving average (MA) of stock prices is a trend indicator; its function is to smooth out day-to-day fluctuations and reveal a trend that could otherwise be masked. A ten-day moving average smooths out ripples and reveals small waves; a 30-day average smooths out small waves and reveals large ones; a 200-day average smooths out all waves and reveals ebbs and flows in the tide. A change of trend is indicated when a moving average that was declining has flattened and is turning upward, which is bullish; or when a moving average that was rising has flattened and is turning downward, which of course is bearish.

A simple moving average is composed by first adding up the daily (or weekly) closing prices of a market index or a stock and dividing the total by the number of days (or weeks) in the period. Then — if the average is a ten-day one — you add the eleventh day's closing price and subtract the first day's, and you go on repeating the procedure daily. A simple ten-day moving average is a crude indicator. It exposes traders to the risk of being whipsawed — buying just before prices drop and selling just before they rise. Most traders therefore use a weighted or an "exponential" moving average; these averages give considerably more weight to the latest than to the earliest prices, so they are quicker to reflect a change of trend. Since short-term moving averages are designed to reveal minor trends, investors who are not traders are best served by 90-day or even 200-day moving averages. Charts that show moving averages often appear in brokerage house technical reports, but investors who use technical analysis systematically usually subscribe to one of the chart services. (The weeklies typically cost anywhere from $200 to $500 a year.) Leading chart services include Chartcraft (One West Avenue, Larchmont, NY 10538); R. W. Mansfield Co. (26 Journal Square, Jersey City, NJ 07306); and Trendline Inc. (25 Broadway, New York, NY 10004).

Interpreting the behavior of a stock in relation to its moving average calls for considerable proficiency in technical analysis. In theory — to take a relatively simple example — when a stock rises above a declining moving average or drops below a rising moving average, its behavior indicates that the stock's trend may be reversing itself. The indication would be confirmed if the declining MA flattens and turns upward or if the rising MA flattens and turns downward. The former would be a signal to buy, the latter a signal to sell. It is advisable, however, to use a moving average in conjunction with other indicators and with fundamental data.

The Advance Decline Line — a moving average based on the ratio of stocks advancing to stocks declining — is a breadth indicator: it tells us whether the market is advancing or declining on a broad front or a narrow one. In its simplest form, the A/D Line is plotted by starting with an arbitrary number, say 10,000, and adding or subtracting the difference between the number of stocks advancing and declining; the difference is added to the base number if advances outnumber declines and subtracted if declines outnumber advances. (Advances and declines are reported on the next-to-last page of the *Wall Street Journal* and in other major newspapers.)

A weighted market index such as the Dow often rises even when a majority of stocks are declining or falls when a majority are rising, because (as explained in chapter 2) the Dow is strongly influenced by the behavior of its high-priced stocks. But the A/D Line, which reflects the cumulative difference between the number of stocks advancing and stocks declining, reveals whether the overall market is trending up or down. This indicator, which Joseph E. Granville has called "the single most important technical tool," has often been the first to show clearly a major change in the market's direction. For example, while the Dow Jones industrials were soaring to their 1972 peak of 1,052, the A/D Line was warning that the general market was in a menacing downturn — the downturn that eventually snowballed into the apalling crash of 1973–1974.

☐ **Volume Indicators**
▬▬▬▬▬▬▬▬▬▬▬▬▬▬▬▬ The volume of trading helps investors to identify trends in supply and demand, which price changes alone do not indicate reliably. The basic concepts are that it is bullish when volume tends to increase during price advances or decrease during declines; it is bearish when volume tends to decrease during advances or increase during declines. An important step forward in volume analysis was taken when Joseph E. Granville introduced the concept of on-balance volume (OBV) in his book, *Granville's New Strategy of Daily Stock Market Timing for Maximum Profit* (Englewood Cliffs: Prentice-Hall, 1976). The essence of Granville's contribution can be easily explained, but you need to have studied his book thoroughly to use OBV as an indicator of precisely when to buy and sell. Granville defines trading volume as "demand volume" on days when a stock or the market (depending on which you are tracking) advances; on declining days, volume is "supply volume"; when there is no price change, volume is ignored. On-balance volume is simply cumulative net supply or demand volume over a period of time. For example, XYZ stock rises on Monday on volume of 5,000 shares and declines Tuesday on volume of 20,000; OBV is 15,000 Down. Wednesday, XYZ rises on

volume of 4,000; OBV is now 11,000 Down. XYZ's price may have risen one point on each of the up days and declined two points on the down day, ending the period unchanged. But the OBV reading of 11,000 down indicates that supply was stronger than demand. Thus OBV is a refined way of using price changes coupled with trading volume to detect whether money is moving into stocks or out of them. Volume figures are given in newspaper stock market tables, so tracking OBV for an individual stock or the New York Stock Exchange index is a matter of simple arithmetic.

☐ Sentiment Indicators

These are indicators that reveal the expectations of different types of investors, in particular

1. the general public and the very small investors known as odd-lotters, who trade in units of less than 100 shares;
2. market insiders such as specialists (market makers on the exchanges) and exchange members trading for their own accounts.

When sentiment indicators show that the public is overwhelmingly bullish or bearish, they serve warning that it is time to take the contrary attitude. (The contrary opinion approach to investing is discussed in chapter 17.) And when sentiment indicators reveal a sharp divergence in the behavior of the general public and market insiders, it is sensible to take your cue from the insiders; the chances are they know more.

The Odd-Lot Short-Sales Ratio is one of the most widely watched contrary opinion indicators. (A short sale is a sale of borrowed stock made in the expectation that its price will decline. For a full explanation, see Appendix D.) The rationale of the odd-lot short-sales ratio is that odd-lot *short sellers* are the most unsophisticated of speculators. Indeed, the historical record shows them to have been *invariably* wrong: their selling has been greatest when bear markets were ending and smallest when bull markets were about to peak. (In contrast the ordinary odd-lotter, since the mid-1960s, has been among the savviest of investors; he has regularly been a buyer at market bottoms and has sold when prices were high.) The odd-lot short-sales ratio is generally computed by dividing odd-lot short sales by the average of odd-lot purchases and total sales (purchases and total sales divided by two). Over the past few decades the ratio has averaged 1.2 percent. Whenever it has soared above 4 percent — indicating that odd-lot short selling was exceptionally large — it has signaled a market advance;

when it has dropped to 0.5 percent, it has signaled a market decline. Over more than half a century, the odd-lot short-sales ratio has proved to be one of the best indicators for forecasting major turning points in the market.

The Specialists' Short-Sales Ratio is the ratio of short sales made by specialists to total short sales, calculated on a weekly basis. (The figures are published on Mondays in the *Wall Street Journal,* and they appear in *Barron's* on the Market Laboratory page.) As market makers, specialists are forced to do a lot of short selling to help bridge the gaps that occur when buyers outnumber sellers. Since they make their living in part by short selling — and specialists' earnings are so high that critics describe their function as "a license to steal" — it is almost axiomatic that specialists as a group are the most knowledgeable of short-sellers. Consequently, the greater the volume of their shorting in relation to total short sales, the likelier it is that prices will decline; the smaller their share of total short selling, the likelier it is that prices will rise. When the specialists' short-sales ratio rises above 60 percent, it is giving a bearish signal; when it falls below 45 percent, it is giving a bullish one. If it drops below 35 percent, the probability that stock prices will be higher a year later is 100 percent.

The Advisory Sentiment Indicator, which shows the percentage of advisory services that are bullish and bearish, is a contrary opinion indicator. It was explained in chapter 14 in the profile of the service that originated it, *Investors Intelligence.*

The Speculation Index compares the volume of trading on the American Stock Exchange with that on the New York Stock Exchange. Since there is a vastly larger proportion of speculative issues on the Amex than on the Big Board, the ratio of Amex volume to Big Board volume is a measure of speculative sentiment. Historically, the ratio has ranged between 10 percent and 60 percent and has averaged about 30 percent. When it rises above 40 percent, it is warning us that the speculative temperature is dangerously high, and a reading of 60 percent is a strong sell signal. A reading of 20 percent is bullish and one of 15 percent or less is a strong buy signal. This indicator has correctly foretold major peaks and bottoms in the market for more than 50 years.

☐ Seasonal Indicators

One of them merits attention because, though its rationale is vague, its predictive record has been phenomenally good. Its originator, Yale Hirsch, publisher of the *Stock Trader's Alma-*

nac, calls it the January Barometer. And what it indicates is that "as January goes, so goes the year as a whole." January was an up month for the S&P index in 23 of the 37 years from 1950 through 1986, and in all but one (1966) of those 23 years the index registered a gain. In 9 of the 15 years in which the market declined in January, the S&P index ended the year with a loss. On the basis of that record, the probabilities are 96 percent that a rise in January portends a rise for the year, and they are 60 percent that a decline in January portends a decline for the year. Overall, the January Barometer has proved prophetic 31 times out of 37, or 84 percent of the time.

Advisory services that track and interpret the leading indicators include five that were profiled in chapter 14: *Indicator Digest, Market Logic, The Professional Tape Reader, Systems and Forecasts,* and *The Zweig Forecast.*

▪17 The Psychological Approach: Profiting From Contrariness

When asked how he founded his great fortune, the nineteenth-century financier Russell Sage replied: "By buying straw hats in January." Buying summer hats in winter, when nobody wants them, is an example of the contrary opinion theory of investing, which holds that success comes from acting contrary to the herd. When panic prevails and the outlook for the stock market couldn't be darker, the theory says prices are close to a bottom and it is time to buy; when euphoria reigns, the market is approaching a peak and the time has come to sell.

But contrary opinion theory is much more than a psychological tool for anticipating market tops and bottoms. It is a mental discipline — a systematic way of thinking about investments — that can help investors to avoid the mistakes most commonly made by professionals as well as amateurs. Bernard Baruch said he saved himself millions of dollars by studying Charles Mackay's *Extraordinary Popular Delusions and the Madness of Crowds* (1841), one of the source books of contrary opinion theory.

The theory's modern formulator was Humphrey B. Neill, a successful stock market trader who died in 1977. After retiring on his profits to Vermont, Neill wrote essays and newspaper columns, which first appeared in book form in 1954 as *The Art of Contrary Thinking* (Caxton Printers, P.O. Box 700, Caldwell, ID 83605; $3.95 paperback). This small, chatty volume has become the bible of his disciples, who call themselves contrarians.

Neill credited the origin of his ideas to numerous writers on social psychology, but especially to Charles Mackay and Gustave Le Bon, whose classic, *The Crowd,* appeared in 1895. Neill's basic premise is that people acting as independent individuals are capable of rational thought and conduct, but people swayed by crowd psychology become totally irrational, succumbing to extremes of greed, fear, and gullibility. Said Neill, "A crowd thinks with its emotions, an individual thinks with his brain."

A celebrated example of mass folly in investing was the tulip mania that swept Holland from 1634 to 1636. When word got around that speculators were making fortunes in rare bulbs, ordinary people scrambled to sell their possessions, their land, even their houses, to invest in flowers, on the assumption that the boom would last indefinitely. At its peak, one rare bulb was paid for with 12 acres of choice building land. Another fetched a carriage and pair of horses. When tulip prices collapsed, the losses suffered were so great that the economy of Holland took years to recover.

Neill concluded that investors governed by crowd psychology cause the booms and busts, the fashions and fads of the stock market. "When everyone thinks alike, everyone is likely to be wrong" was his summation of his theory. It has a twofold rationale.

Since the future is largely unpredictable, an overwhelming consensus on where stock prices are heading usually ignores numerous uncertainties. Typically, consensus forecasts extrapolate current trends into the future and fail to take into account forces at work that could bring about change. Such consensus forecasts are therefore likely to be wrong. In addition, a market trend that nearly everyone expects isn't likely to occur, because investors act in anticipation of it, thereby changing the course of the market. By the time that an overwhelmingly bullish consensus (on the market or a stock) has taken shape, most investors have already done their buying and there isn't enough purchasing power left to sustain a further advance. Similarly, by the time pessimism is ubiquitous, scared investors have dumped their stocks and the selling pressure that has driven prices down is abating.

Contrary opinion theory teaches investors to be nonconformists. Its defensive function is to keep them from being led astray by popular sentiment; its positive function is to help them profit from the follies of the crowd. The principles are easy to grasp, but putting them into practice calls for discipline and guts — because for most people it is second nature to think and act as others do. *Contrary opinion theory requires investors to do what does not come naturally.*

For example, the natural impulse of investors is to buy stocks that are being widely recommended by leading analysts; contrarians argue that it is generally best to avoid such stocks and dig instead for unrecognized values among issues that are neglected or downright unpopular. Their reasoning: the highly touted stocks have already been widely bought and are usually up in price, so they are liable to decline on any disappointing news or as investors who got into them ahead of the pack cash in their profits. But the neglected stocks of sound companies with improving earnings will rise in price as investors gradually perceive their merits.

A leading exponent of contrary opinion theory is Humphrey Neill's former associate, James L. Fraser. An alumnus of Dartmouth college who served in army counterintelligence during the Korean War, Fraser worked at First National City Bank in New York and then at a Wall Street brokerage house before entering the investment counseling field in 1962. His firm, Fraser Management Associates (309 South Willard, Burlington, VT 05401), publishes two fortnightlies, *Contrary Investor* ($85 a year) and the *Fraser Opinion Letter* ($60), and it manages investment accounts for individuals and small corporations. Fraser thinks it is easier to be a contrarian if you are far removed from the swirling emotions of Wall Street; his combined home and business headquarters is an old New England stone house overlooking Lake Champlain. The following excerpts from interviews that we had with him in 1981 and 1986 provide a concise guide to using the contrarian approach.

Q. *What is the first step in applying contrary opinion theory to the stock market?*

A. Find out whether a powerful consensus exists — on the outlook for the market or certain types of stocks. You can learn this from the financial press and brokerage house reports; a shortcut is to subscribe to an investment advisory service that specializes in contrary opinion or keeps track of other services. For example, *Investors Intelligence* (see chapter 14) publishes a chart showing the percentage of services that are bullish and bearish.

When a powerful consensus exists, a contrarian acts on the opposite view. But it is only in the late stages of bull and bear markets that investors are overwhelmingly bullish or bearish. Most of the time you find a variety of conflicting views.

Q. *So what does a contrarian do then?*

A. He starts out by trying to determine what is the majority view. Mind you, contrary opinion theory does not — as many people mistakenly believe — assert that the majority is always wrong. Unlike a powerful consensus, which is the product of crowd psychology, a simple majority view may be rationally founded. [For example, a majority of investment strategists were extremely bullish on energy issues in 1978 for reasons that were entirely rational and proved to be correct. But two years later, the valuations of these issues had in many cases doubled, and to contrarians the continuing enthusiasm for them smacked of irrationality. Indeed, in the course of 1981, the prices of most energy issues peaked and turned sharply down.]

Q. *What does a contrarian do when he encounters a view that is held by a majority of analysts but is not an overwhelming consensus?*

A. He scans that view with rigorous scepticism to determine as best he can whether it is supported by reason and fact. Then he takes the antithetical view and subjects it to the same scrutiny. Suppose, for example, that a majority of year-end forecasters are predicting a market decline in the first half of the coming year and a rise in the second half. A contrarian would critically examine the pros and cons of that projection and also those of its opposite — that the market will rise in the first half and fall in the second. After then considering other possibilities — one being that throughout the year the market could trend upward or downward — a contrarian will finally reach his own conclusion. I should emphasize that contrary opinion's greatest value is to investors willing to take a longer-term view. Since a contrarian isn't a trend follower, he will nearly always do his buying and selling too early and have to wait some time before being proved right. But, as Neill said, "If you're not early, you'll probably be late."

Q. *What types of stock do contrarians tend to favor?*

A. It's risky to generalize. As a contrarian, I recommend stocks that fall into one of three main categories:

1. Unpopular stocks of large well-known companies that I consider turnaround situations — that is, I find the prevailing assessment of their problems overly pessimistic. For example, I bought Eastman Kodak at $44 in 1985, when pessimism about it was the prevailing sentiment. A year later Kodak was up to about $68.

2. Stocks of medium-size, usually regional, companies that have been around for decades and are currently unpopular with investors. Take Ransburg Corporation of Indianapolis, which makes industrial equipment and has been around for decades, making good products. The stock went from $37 in 1981 to around $10.50 in 1986. [In July, 1987, it was back to $15.]

3. Stocks of smaller, newer companies once hailed as emerging growth prospects but now out of favor. Triad Systems has been such a company, a maker of computer software for specialized users such as small businesses and dentists. Its stock in the past ten years has sold as high as $54 but in 1986 traded for as little as about $9. [In the next 12 months it ranged from $8 to $15.]

Q. *What guidelines do you, as a contrarian, follow for selling stocks?*

A. When I buy a stock, I project a price it will reach when it achieves popularity, which is my signal to sell. Since market psychology changes, I may have to readjust the stock's "popularity price." However, if something happens that spells sudden popularity for a stock, I sell it regardless of price. For example, my clients owned MCA stock when *Time* did a cover story in 1975 on the huge success of *Jaws,* an MCA movie. This prompted a surge of buying in MCA shares, which to me was a signal to sell. With all of the good news out, it was hard to see what could make the stock more popular. It was two years, in fact, before MCA again reached its $33.75 high of that week.

Q. *What would you do if the cover of a popular financial magazine featured a story on, say, the bright prospects for the aluminum industry?*

A. If I owned any aluminum stocks, I would sell them.

Q. *What is the toughest problem that faces investors who use contrary opinion theory?*

A. To persevere in a course you consider right when months go by and it continues to look wrong. It's awfully tough to hang on to a stock that is acting like a tortoise when the market is full of sprinters.

Q. *How widely is contrary opinion theory practiced by money managers?*

A. Its principles are widely accepted nowadays, but by its very nature the theory can never become popular — a crowd of money managers trying to act contrary to the crowd will simply become a different crowd. I would say, however, that every exceptionally successful money manager — and private investor — is a gifted contrarian. No one who has consistently beaten the market can possibly have done it by following the herd.

☐ The Case of the Contrarian Hog Raiser

In the October 2, 1978, issue of *Forbes* magazine, John Train, president of a New York investment counseling firm and the author of two fine books on investing, *Dance of the Money Bees* (Harper & Row, 1934) and *The Money Masters* (Penguin, 1981), recounted the beguiling saga of a Texas rice farmer and hog raiser who made a fortune in the stock market. This Mr. Womack had a simple system that he unswervingly followed for more than 40 years. Whenever a severe bear market had swept stock prices down to new lows, Womack would work his way through *Standard & Poor's Stock Guide* and pick about 30 stocks that had fallen below $10 a share — stocks of obscure, prosaic, profit-making companies in sound financial health and paying dividends. He would invest $25,000 in a package of these stocks and, if they declined much further, would buy another $25,000 worth. He would hold them — often for several years — until the next big boom in stocks was thundering along, and then sell all of his holdings. He would then stash away his gains until the bear was again clawing at the market. Mr. Womack, Train recounts, never seemed to buy a stock at its bottom or sell it at its top. But he never had a net loss on his round trips into and out of the market and he repeatedly made killings. Like Russell Sage, Mr. Womack bought straw hats in January, but his story reminds us to sell them in July. Train wrote this testimonial to Mr. Womack, who died in 1977: "He changed my investing lifestyle and I have made a profit ever since."

18 The Political Approach: Election Cycle Investing

In the August 1976 issue of *Money* magazine, an article by Charles Rolo started with the following forecast: "The stock market will end the year higher than it is on August 1. The Dow Jones Industrial Average will peak out early in 1977 and its subsequent decline will last about ten months. Then there will be a long and powerful recovery that should reach its high point after the 1980 elections." That forecast proved to be remarkably accurate. The Dow ended 1976 appreciably above its August 1 level. At the beginning of 1977, it went into a sustained downtrend that lasted 14 months. Then a long though erratic recovery got under way that lifted the Dow from its 1978 low of 742 to 1,000 on November 20, 1980. "Regrettably," Rolo wrote in the first edition of this book, "I can't claim credit for having displayed prophetic powers. The brilliant forecast wasn't made by me, nor did it come from Jeane Dixon, a supercomputer, or a wizard of Wall Street." Rolo's forecast was based on an abstraction — the average behavior of the stock market over all of the four-year presidential election cycles from 1948 through 1972.

Obviously, the market's behavior in any particular presidential election cycle has varied and will vary from the average pattern, to which it so closely conformed in the 1976–1980 cycle. Even so, the historical record clearly suggests which periods are apt to be best for buying stocks, for selling them, and for staying out of the market. Tests have shown that since 1961 an investment strategy based on these timing pointers has significantly outperformed the market. And the beauty of this strategy is that it couldn't be simpler: you buy a diversified portfolio of stocks on November 30 of the *second* year *after* a presidential election and you hold them for exactly two years. Then you sell your entire portfolio and invest the proceeds in Treasury Bills or money-market funds. On November 30, two years after the subsequent election, you go back into the market. That's all there is to it. We will give you specific figures showing the results of this strategy. But first let's look into the rationale of political cycle investing.

☐ Why Wall Street Dances to Washington's Tune

The connection between the election cycle and recurring tendencies of the stock market is rooted in the interaction of politics and economics. Francis H. M. Kelly, a prominent investment strategist, has summed up this interplay as follows: "The government's management of economic affairs naturally looms large in the electorate's estimate of its worthiness. Therefore, a great deal of orchestration goes into the fine art of making the economy sing appropriate melodies to the score of the quadrennial elections."

Hard data on how the economy has been orchestrated are presented in Edward R. Tufte's book *Political Control of the Economy* (Princeton: Princeton University Press, 1978.) Tufte's figures show, among other things, that increases in federal spending, Social Security, and real disposable income have been either larger or more frequent — and sometimes both — in presidential election years than in others. Then, some time after a President takes office, the economy usually has to pay the price for policies designed before the election to woo voters, and for the neglect of problems that require unpalatable remedies.

All this tends to create a correlation between the presidential cycle and the business cycle. According to figures published by the National Bureau of Economic Research, the average duration of business cycles has been about 48 months — the same length as the election cycle. Since 1948 the economy, on average, has peaked out seven months after election day and has sunk to its low point 11 months later. This has left the administration an average of 30 months before the next election to put through policies that will increase the public's sense of well-being.

The stock market's recovery phases have therefore tended to start about 30 months before the next presidential election. The market usually anticipates future developments — it is one of the so-called leading economic indicators — and its average lead time is about six months. For similar reasons, the market has tended to top out in the early part of postelection years. It is anticipating the contraction that is apt to begin some months later. Says Yale Hirsch, editor of the *Stock Trader's Almanac:* "Paying the piper after the making of Presidents induces the 'post-presidential year syndrome.' These are the years in which most of the big bear markets began — 1929, 1937, 1957, 1969, 1973, 1977, 1981."

From the end of World War II to the Reagan era, the Dow advanced after nine of the ten presidential elections. The exception was Harry Truman's surprise victory over Thomas E. Dewey in 1948. Five of those advances topped out within two months after the election; one lasted for eight months (under Eisenhower), one for 13 months (under Kennedy) and one for six months (under Reagan). Overall, the average length of the postelection advance was slightly more than four months. There's a warning in this for investors: after Election Day they should watch the market particularly closely for signs of an impending downturn.

The decline that has followed the market's postelection high has varied greatly in length — from six weeks under Lyndon Johnson to just over two years in Nixon's second term. On the average, this down phase has lasted ten to 11 months and the Dow has dropped about 22 percent. The ensuing recovery has almost invariably been long and substantial. It averaged slightly more than three years for the period 1948 through 1980, with the Dow posting an average advance of nearly 60 percent. The unprecedented bull market that got started in August 1982 — a premature 27 months before the landslide Reagan victory of 1984 — continued unabated into 1987, at which point the Dow was up more than 200 percent.

The political cycle timing strategy referred to earlier — buying stocks in November 30 of the second year after a presidential election and selling them on the November 30 following the next election — was formulated back in 1973 by David W. MacNeill, then a senior investment officer of the First National Bank of Boston. (He uses November 30 rather than November 5 as his selling date because the market usually continues to rise for a few weeks or months after Election Day.) MacNeill's research shows that between November 30,

1962, and November 30, 1980, Standard & Poor's 500-stock index had an average loss of 11.7 percent (taking into account dividends) in the two-year periods following presidential elections. In the two-year periods prior to presidential elections, the total return on the S&P index was a whopping 50 percent. Over the entire 18-year period, an investment in the S&P index managed in accordance with political cycle timing achieved a total return of 1,110 percent, or 14.6 percent compounded annually — more than three times the total return of 341 percent on an investment in the S&P index that was simply held throughout the period.

A study by Fred C. Allvine and Daniel E. O'Neill published in the *Financial Analysts Journal* (September-October 1980) amplifies MacNeill's findings by taking into account the brokerage commissions and capital gains taxes incurred in a political cycle timing program. Allvine and O'Neill covered a slightly different period, 1961 to 1978, and they used the S&P 400-stock index rather than the 500-stock index as their stock portfolio. *They found that the political cycle timing program outperformed a buy-and-hold strategy by a margin of 3½ to 1.*

There's an extraordinarily easy and economical way for the individual investor to use the political cycle strategy. You simply put your money into a no-load, common stock mutual fund that emulates the S&P 500 (the Vanguard Index Trust is the oldest such fund open to individual investors; see Appendix B) on November 30 two years before a presidential election; two years later, you switch into a money-market fund; and you continue to switch, back and forth, once every two years. It's that simple; you don't have to worry about stock selection and you don't pay any brokerage commissions.

If large numbers of investors were to adopt the political cycle timing strategy, they would, of course, alter the quadrennial pattern of market behavior — and the strategy would cease to work. But it seems unlikely that political cycle timing will achieve wide popularity. To date relatively few people know about it, and it is not something the brokerage houses will promote; it would be suicidal for them to tell their clients to stay totally out of stocks two years out of four. Second, for many people it goes against the grain to act like a rigidly programmed robot; following a formula takes the challenge and the fun out of investing. Third and most important, political cycle investing isn't a strategy that institutions with billion-dollar portfolios can practice; they could not swing their huge assets into and out of stocks once every two years without altering the course of the market.

To anyone tempted to adopt a political cycle timing strategy, let us proffer two *caveats:*

1. Large market advances are not *invariably* confined to the two years preceding presidential elections, so you may find yourself out of stocks at a time when you would dearly like to be in them. The first two years of Ronald Reagan's second term was such a time. The S&P index shot up 52 percent in those historically bearish years, propelled by a prolonged period of low inflation, low interest rates, and heavy foreign investment in a relatively inexpensive U.S. stock market. Even so, the MacNeill study, if extended through 1986, still gave the presidential cycle investor considerably more than a two-to-one advantage over the investor who held the S&P all those years.

2. If you tinker with the timetable or shoot for better results by, say, investing in a handful of speculative stocks instead of a mutual fund or a broadly diversified portfolio, then you are strictly on your own. When you invest according to the political-cycle timing formula, or any other formula, you must adhere to it faithfully.

☐ A Postscript

The evidence that recurring tendencies in the stock market are related to the presidential election cycle refutes — or at least runs counter to — the Random walk and efficient market hypotheses (discussed in chapter 12). The well-defined four-year pattern of market behavior just described shows that, over the long term, stocks don't move randomly; they move in trends. And the discovery that, over a 24-year period, a political cycle timing strategy achieved significantly higher returns than those on the S&P index punctures the efficient market doctrine that no investment strategy can consistently outperform the market.

Managing Your Money: Strategy and Tactics

19 Choosing a Portfolio Strategy That Fits Your Stance

Many of the mistakes that people make in managing their investments result from acting haphazardly. The top priority in investing is to develop and follow a coherent, reasoned approach — an overall battle plan or portfolio strategy. The main steps are these:

1. **Select your investment objective,** which will hinge on the degree of risk you are willing to assume.
2. **Decide on a timing policy.** Will you hold stocks for the long pull or try to anticipate swings in the market?
3. **From time to time, evaluate the investment outlook** — the prospects for the economy, individual industries, and the stock and bond markets.
4. **In light of the investment outlook, decide on a portfolio mix that fits your investment objective.** (The mix is the apportioning of your capital among different types of investments — stocks, corporate and municipal bonds, money market securities, precious metals and so on.)
5. **Select the specific securities for your portfolio.**
6. Once a year, **review your performance.**

☐ Setting the Objective

Most people's definition of their investment objective will correspond, more or less, to one of the following designations, which in principle imply descending level of risk:

1. maximum capital gains;
2. high growth with minimal concern for income;
3. average growth combined with income (for example, the growth and dividend yield of the S&P 500 index);
4. income with some growth, but with the emphasis mainly on income;
5. the highest possible income compatible with safety of principal.

An investor's objective reflects the degree of risk he is willing to assume. And that, as you have probably heard all too often, should be determined by his age, family situation, current and prospective earning power, net worth, tax bracket, and temperament. A single person of 30 with excellent career prospects and expectations of a sizable inheritance can obviously take much larger risks than a middle-aged couple with young children, moderate earning power, and no hopes of inheriting a nest egg. It's obvious, too, that retired people living on a modest pension and income from their savings must keep their exposure to risk low. What the homilies about risk taking usually fail to mention is that *it is as foolish not to take risks that you can reasonably afford as it is to run risks that you can't afford.* In the long run, taking above-average risks should bring larger than average rewards.

Risk can be measured, not with certainty but in terms of probabilities. And risk can be managed — that is to say, kept within reasonable bounds. So let's take a closer look at the different types of risk and how to handle them.

☐ **Market Risk**
■■■■■ This is the risk related to the overall behavior of any securities market. Nowadays, the standard yardstick of a stock's market risk is its volatility — the extent of its fluctuations in relation to the S&P index. The academics who developed Modern Portfolio Theory chose beta, the second letter of the Greek alphabet, to express the volatility of a stock as shown by its price history. Since the S&P index was taken as representing the market as a whole, it was assigned a beta of 1. Thus a stock whose beta is 1.5 can be expected to rise and fall one-and-a-half times as much as the index; such a stock is considered 50 percent riskier than average.

You can try to protect yourself against market risk in a variety of ways. One is to put a portion of your assets into gold investments — bullion, coins, or gold mining stocks — whose prices tend to move *counter* to the stock market, though not as consistently as they used to. (See chapter 25, "Gold Isn't Just for Goldbugs.") Another way is to use hedging tactics. You hedge the stocks you own — your "long positions," in Wall Street's lingo — by taking "short positions." One way to do this is by making short sales — that is, borrowing from your broker the stocks you think are likeliest to go down, and then selling them. (Short selling is more fully explained in Appendix D.) If the market drops, you will presumably make profits on your shorts, which will offset, partially or wholly, the losses on your longs. The danger is that, if the market moves sideways, you may wind up making the worst of both worlds — your shorts go up and your longs go down. A vastly preferable way of hedging is through the use of options, which are discussed in chapter 26.

Brokerage house strategists still prescribe an old-fashioned way of reducing market risk when the outlook seems threatening; they tell you to switch out of the stocks with above-average risks into so-called defensive ones — for example, food, cosmetics, and retailing issues — whose earnings hold up well in recessions. This tactic may have made sense in bygone days when defensive stocks yielded substantially more than Treasury Bills, and there were no money-market funds. But nowadays switching into defensive issues will do no more for you in a market slump than add to your brokerage commissions; only 1 percent of all stocks move counter to a major bear (or bull) market, and that 1 percent includes the golds. In fact, a defensive issue might aptly be defined as a stock in which you will lose less money than in other stocks when the market is in a slump. So if you are bearish, why settle for a probable loss when you can move into the safe haven of a money-market fund? Defensive stocks certainly have a place in conservative, income-oriented portfolios. *But the best way to cope with mounting market risk is to decrease the proportion of your assets invested in the stock market.*

☐ Unique or Diversifiable Risk

A stock's risk is, of course, only partly contingent on the behavior of the market — stock prices also rise and fall because of industry and company developments. This type of risk, which is not reflected in beta, is known as unique or diversifiable risk; it can be minimized by proper diversification, because price fluctuations caused by factors other than the market's behavior vary from industry to industry and company to company. For example, high-beta stocks in the data processing industry will at times perform better and at times worse than high-beta issues in the airline industry. Consequently, an efficiently diversified portfolio with an average beta of, say, 1.2 is considerably less risky than a couple of stocks with the same beta. Studies of the behavior of stock prices suggest that diversifiable risk accounts for anywhere from 30 percent to 70 percent of a stock's total risk (depending on the industry and the company).

How many stocks are needed to achieve good diversification? The answer provided by scholarly research is that, if you put an equal amount of money into ten stocks in different industries exposed to different types of risk, you will eliminate about 90 percent of the diversifiable risk involved in owning one stock; you can eliminate 80 percent of that risk by owning only five stocks, similarly chosen. So even small investors who don't choose to use mutual funds can easily achieve good diversification, provided they are willing to buy some stocks in less than 100-share lots.

Remember, though, that diversification depends far less on the number of stocks you own than on choosing stocks whose risks are related to different economic, social, and political factors; without this qualitative diversification, a portfolio of 100 stocks can offer less protection against diversifiable risk than a 15-stock portfolio. Many brokers seem not to understand this. Their conventional "widows' and orphans' portfolio" — supposedly an ultraconservative portfolio designed to provide safety and high income — tends to be heavily invested in public utility stocks and bonds, all of which will decline simultaneously whenever interest rates rise. Even a portfolio of 50 or more stocks in the airline, auto, rubber, textile, and steel industries would offer very little diversification; all of those industries are highly cyclical, and most if not all of the stocks will take a beating whenever a serious recession is expected. A list of a dozen industries with differing types of risk might include airlines, banks, computers, cosmetics, drugs, electronics, energy exploration, fertilizers, financial printing and publishing, gold mining, hospital management, and telecommunications. But whether you are building a portfolio from scratch or tinkering with an existing one, your choice of industries must depend on the general outlook for the economy and the stock market.

☐ **Interest Rate Risk**
■■■■■■■■■■■■■■■■ The risk stemming from changes in interest rates applies primarily to bonds; precisely how it affects them will be shown in chapter 22, "Investing for Income." But it also applies to the stocks of companies whose earnings are significantly affected by the trend of interest rates — favorably by a downtrend and unfavorably by an uptrend. The groups that Wall Street categorizes as "interest-sensitive" include utilities, banks, savings and loans, finance companies, and housing and building materials. When interest rates rise, utilities incur higher costs for the heavy long-term borrowing they do to finance expansion; banks and finance companies pay more for lendable funds; S & Ls have a weaker mortgage market; and home building slackens because of the rising cost of mortgage money. Clearly, it is unwise to stay invested in these groups if you expect an upward spiral in interest

rates. And you can make good profits in the interest-sensitive stocks when rates peak and start heading down.

□ Deciding on a Timing Policy

Excluding in-and-out trading — a dumb policy for the average investor — there are three basic approaches to market timing.

1. You adopt a buy-and-hold strategy, which means that you invest for the long haul and ignore swings in the market. It doesn't mean, however, that you just put away the stocks you buy and plan to hold them indefinitely. Even issues bought as long-term holdings need to be watched, and a time may come when they should be sold — either because they have risen to levels at which they offer less potential than other stocks or because they have been stagnating.

2. You adopt a market timing approach, which involves buying or selling when you anticipate major turning points in the market.

3. You use dollar cost averaging, a timing system that eliminates timing decisions: you automatically invest a fixed amount monthly in the same selected stocks or mutual funds. Your money will buy fewer shares when prices are high and more shares when prices are low; so your average cost over a period of 12 months or longer will approximate the average price of the shares you have been buying.

There's no reason you can't combine two or all of these approaches except that it requires more time, effort, and discipline. You might, for example, invest part of your capital for the long term and manage some of your money in accordance with a market timing system. When you sell, you park the proceeds in a money fund until you get your next strong buy signal.

An important consideration in your choice of a timing strategy used to be income taxes. Gains taken on investments held long enough to qualify as long-term gains were taxed, until 1987, less than half as severely as ordinary income. So to maximize his returns in the stock market, an investor had to aim at long-term gains. With the distinction between long- and short-term gains eliminated by the Tax Reform Act of 1986, you may be tempted to trade whenever a profit can be made on a stock you hold. However, most investors still must give at least 28 percent and some as much as 33 percent of each gain to the Internal Revenue Service.

What remains true is that it is a mistaken policy to let your investment decisions be dictated at all times by tax considerations. For example, you may buy a stock and see it shoot up 50 percent or more because it belongs to an ultrafashionable group. In such cases, your stock could be dangerously overpriced, and you might well be wise to grab your splendid profit regardless of the tax bite. Stocks that skyrocket can drop sharply, whether because of a change in investment fashions, a disappointing company development, or a sinking spell in the market. Paying 28 percent in income taxes on a gain of $2,000 leaves you considerably better off than paying the same rate on a profit that has dwindled to $500. While there's no truth in the adage "you can't go wrong by taking a profit," it is sometimes true that you can go wrong by *not* taking a profit.

☐ Evaluating the Investment Outlook

The main factors to consider are the trend of corporate profits, inflation, and interest rates; the policies of the Federal Reserve Board; and the current stage of the economy — whether it is in the early, middle, or late phase of an uptrend or a recession. How these factors affect stock prices was discussed in earlier chapters (6 through 8). Ideally, your evaluation would also include a scrutiny of the leading technical indicators discussed in chapter 16. And if you detect a strong consensus about the market outlook, you should give some thought to the contrary opinion view. A handy forecasting system that combines all of these approaches is described in the following chapter.

☐ Deciding on the Portfolio Mix

Whether you are starting from scratch or reviewing your existing holdings, you have to ask yourself from time to time what types of investment you should be in and what proportion of your assets you should have in each of them. For most people, the main choices are common stocks, including high-risk and medium-risk stocks and conservative stocks that pay high dividends; options; convertible issues; government, municipal, and corporate bonds; short-term fixed-income securities (which are highly liquid and essentially risk-free); and precious metals. The mix you choose at a given point reflects the overall degree of risk you are willing to assume; then you manage your risk by modifying the portfolio mix in response to significant changes in the investment outlook.

Let's consider the case of an investor with $50,000 whose goal is average growth combined with income. Assuming that he is on the whole positive about the investment outlook but not extremely bullish, he might distribute his assets as follows, using no-load mutual funds rather than individual securities: 50 percent in a common stock fund (such as Neuberger & Berman Guardian) whose goal is growth and income; 20 percent in a high-growth fund; 25 percent in a money-market fund; and 5 percent in a gold fund. If this investor later turns bearish, he should switch the assets in the high-growth fund and all or most of those in the growth-and-income fund into the money fund. If he becomes decidedly bullish, he might cut back to 15 percent in the money fund, and to 35 percent in the growth and income fund, and switch the proceeds into the high-growth fund. Switching between mutual funds is discussed more fully in chapter 23.

Whatever your investment objective, any number of possible portfolio mixes will give you the desired *overall* level of risk — and it is the overall risk of the portfolio that counts, not the risk or safety of its individual components. An investor aggressively seeking very high growth might invest all of his funds in high-growth, high-risk issues, or he could choose medium-risk growth stocks and leverage his risk and potential return by buying on margin with funds borrowed from his broker. In this way, he could invest twice as much money in the market. A leveraged portfolio of medium-risk growth stocks would have about the same beta as one invested in riskier growth stocks (and an amount of the interest on the broker's loan equal to your dividends, interest, and capital gains in a given calendar year would be tax-deductible). Yet another possible portfolio strategy for this same high-risk investor would be to put most of his capital into medium-risk stocks and to shoot for large speculative gains with the balance by buying options.

An investor whose objective is income and some growth also has a variety of possible portfolio mixes. He might put 40 percent in high-yielding blue-chip stocks with low betas, 30 percent in convertible bonds, and 30 percent in a money-market fund. Or he might use a combination of blue-chip stocks, closed-end bond funds (which are traded on the stock exchanges — see chapter 22), and money-market funds. Whether your portfolio is an aggressive or middle-of-the-road one, the principles of managing risk remain the same. *When you turn bearish you cut back on the securities that represent your tier of maximum risk (relative to the overall character of the portfolio) and switch the proceeds into your minimum-risk tier. When you turn bullish, you do the opposite.* For all but the more conservative investors, good judgment about when to lessen exposure to risk and when to increase it and push for higher returns is possibly the most important determinant of investment success.

☐ Selecting the Securities

The selection of individual securities will be covered in two separate chapters. One will focus on methods of stock picking that seek to beat the market. The other will discuss security selection for investors whose primary objective is income.

☐ Reviewing Your Performance

Investors who are trying to beat, or at least match, the results of the S&P 500-stock index should measure the total return on their stock portfolios at least once a year; the total return is dividends received plus capital gains (or minus losses) actually realized and those still on paper. Divide this figure for the previous year by the market value of the portfolio at the beginning of the year, and you will get your percentage return. If you have done significantly worse than the S&P index, try to find out where you went wrong; you can learn a lot from your mistakes. Some sources of error: acting on unreliable tips from friends or a broker; not keeping abreast of your investments, with the result that you are slow to act when one of them turns sour; buying hot stocks after they already have had a spectacular run-up; or selling your winners too soon and hanging on to your losers in the vague hope that they will eventually recover. A Wall Street maxim says, "Cut your losses and let your profits run." And a savvy trader observes, "Never hesitate to quit while you're behind — you could be farther behind."

20 Predicting Major Market Movements

A buy-and-hold approach was hard to beat during the period of fairly stable economic expansion that followed World War II; from 1949 through 1959, there were only two significant market declines — one of 19 percent and one of 17 percent in the Dow Jones Industrial Average — and the Dow rose from 177 to 679, a gain of 284 percent. But between 1960 and 1986 investors were hit by eight landslides in stock prices in which the average loss of the Dow Jones industrials was 28.6 percent. Staying fully invested throughout a market slump has become a brutally punishing experience. It is even worse, of course, if you finally panic, sell out near the bottom, and then fail to get in again until stock prices have had a big rebound.

To avoid such disasters, you don't need uncannily good foresight. You can substantially improve your investment results if your timing is only partially right — that is, if you sell some or all of your stocks within a few months of the peak of a bull market and then move back into stocks not too long before or after prices have hit bottom. This doesn't entail frequent trading and heavy commission expense. In fact, if you invest in no-load or low-load mutual funds, the cost of making switches is negligible.

From 1960 through 1986, there were only six ideal occasions to buy stocks — in mid-1962, late 1966, mid-1970, late 1974, early 1978, and mid-1982. And there were six ideal occasions to sell — in December 1961, early 1966, late 1968, early January 1973, the fall of 1976, and April 1980. *That averages out at one buy or sell decision every couple of years.* If your timing had been partially right on those occasions — if you had caught, say, 70 percent of each uptrend — you would have done better than twice as well as by following a buy-and-hold policy (assuming your portfolio matched the behavior of the Dow, your tax rate on capital gains was 20 percent, and you did not reinvest dividends). However, haphazard attempts at market forecasting can do more harm than good. And buying or selling because you feel confident or nervous is almost certain to lead you astray, since your feelings are likely to reflect the predominant mood among investors. To use market timing with any hope of success, you need to develop a system that isn't too complex and time-consuming — and stick with it.

Possibly the best system devised for the layman — one that neatly combines the fundamental, technical, and psychological approaches — was presented in a book entitled *Stock Market Strategy* by Richard A. Crowell, senior vice president of the Boston Company, an investment management firm. The market-timing strategy described in the rest of this chapter is a slightly modified version of Crowell's system; its main goal is to help investors to anticipate the turning points in *major market* cycles.

The system simply requires you to answer two parallel sets of questions on "Time to Buy" and "Time to Sell" checklists. Investors should keep their answers current by updating them, ideally once a month. If all or most of the answers on the "Time to Buy" questionnaire are "yes," then the chances are strong that it's an excellent time to buy, and similarly for the "Time to Sell" checklist.

☐ The Time-to-Buy Checklist*

("Yes" answers are favorable.)

The Business Cycle
1. Is business activity nationally in a downtrend, and if so, do you foresee the end of that downtrend?
2. Is inflation decelerating?
3. Have corporate profits declined from their previous peak, and if so, do you expect them to start moving up soon?
4. Is the economic news largely negative and are most forecasters pessimistic?

Monetary Policy and Interest Rates
5. Have short-term interest rates started to decline?
6. Has the Federal Reserve Board given indications that there will be an easing of monetary policy?

---

* From *Stock Market Strategy* by Richard A. Crowell. Copyright © 1977 by Richard A. Crowell. Used with the permission of the author.

Stock Valuations

7. What is the P/E ratio of the S&P 500-stock index or the Dow Jones Industrial Average? Is it approaching or below the P/E ratio at the last previous cyclical low point of the market?

Sentiment Indicators

8. Are the mutual funds heavily in cash? (Chapter 9 told you how to interpret the mutual funds' cash/assets ratio.)

9. Is the odd-lot short sales ratio exceptionally high?

10. Is the specialists' short sales ratio exceptionally low?

11. Are your friends and business associates pessimistic or apathetic about the market?

State of the Market

12. Has the market been declining for many months since its previous cyclical high?

13. Has the market registered a large drop from its previous cyclical high? (Since 1960, bear market declines have averaged about 29 percent, but a decline of 20 percent could be considered large.)

14. Has the market recently accelerated its rate of decline, which is typical of the final stages of bear markets?

15. Does the market appear to have bottomed? Has it rebounded from its low point, then tested that low a couple of times without falling below it, and then started to advance?

☐ The Time-to-Sell Checklist*

("Yes" answers are worrisome or bearish.)

The Business Cycle

1. Is there growing evidence of a business cycle peak?

2. Is inflation accelerating?

3. Has the rate of gain of corporate profits slowed or is the current rate too strong to last?

4. Are most of the economic forecasts optimistic?

---

*From *Stock Market Strategy* by Richard A. Crowell. Copyright © 1977 by Richard A. Crowell. Used with the permission of the author.

Monetary Policy and Interest Rates

5. Are short-term interest rates rising and are they as high as they were at the corresponding stage of the last previous business upturn?

6. Has the Federal Reserve Board started to tighten monetary policy?

Stock Valuations

7. What is the market's P/E ratio? Has it approached or risen above the P/E at the last cyclical peak of the market?

Sentiment Indicators

8. Are the cash reserves of the mutual funds low?

9. Is the odd-lot short sales ratio exceptionally low?

10. Is the specialists' short sales ratio exceptionally high?

11. Are your friends and business associates talking about winners they've bought and feeling euphoric about the market?

State of the Market

12. Has the market been advancing for many months since its previous cyclical low?

13. Has the market registered a large percentage gain from its previous cyclical low?

14. Is the advance/decline line underperforming the popular averages? (This would be an indication that fewer stocks are advancing and the market's condition is deteriorating even though the averages are still rising.)

15. Does the market appear to have peaked? Has the Dow dropped below its recent high and climbed back to it a couple of times or more, but only to retreat again?

You will notice that the questionnaires are designed to give you a sell signal when the economy is still booming, the market is still rising (or close to a peak), and public sentiment is optimistic. And they will give you a buy signal when the economy is in the doldrums, when the market seems to be in deep trouble, and when public sentiment is pessimistic. But most of the time neither checklist will give a clear-cut go-ahead signal, since major market turning points occur infrequently. So what should an investor do who finds it impractical to wait for the ideal moment, which may be far distant? Crowell doesn't say so himself, but the questionnaires can be of considerable help even when they are not giving a decisive signal. If "yes" answers substantially outnumber "no" answers on the time-to-buy checklist, you might consider doing some buying and increasing your portfolio's exposure to risk. By the same token, if "yeses" substantially outnumber "noes" on the sell checklist, it might be prudent to lessen somewhat your exposure to risk. But what if you come up with a majority of "no" answers to *both* questionnaires, which can happen? That would be a strong indication that you should stay put until the answers provide a less ambiguous reading. If you are in the market, hang on to your stocks until you get a sell signal; if you are out of the market, stay out and wait for a buy signal.

21 Stock Strategies to Beat the Market

Most if not all of the mutual fund managers and investment advisers who have dazzling performance records owe their success to astute stock selection rather than to brilliant market timing. Each of these superpros has a distinctive investment style. But their methods in most cases are based on one of four basic approaches to stock selection: (1) the asset-oriented, or Benjamin Graham, approach, whose progenitor was the founder of modern security analysis, (2) the contrarian strategy, which consists of buying unpopular stocks with low price/earnings ratios, (3) the emerging-growth-company approach, which surfaced in the early 1960s, though it had been pioneered more than two decades earlier by the great mutual fund manager T. Rowe Price, (4) the wonderful business approach, which John Train, in his admirable book *The Money Masters,* associates with the fabulously successful money manager Warren Buffett. A fifth strategy available to individuals might be called the discount store approach: you invest in closed-end common-stock mutual funds whose shares are selling at appreciable discounts from their asset value. Each of these strategies has its special merits and its drawbacks. And there's no reason an investor trying to beat the market should limit himself to one method of stock selection.

☐ Loaded Laggards

Benjamin Graham's asset-oriented methods of stock selection and his rules for when to sell were described in chapter 15. A disciple of Graham's, Mark Boyar, president of a Manhattan brokerage firm that bears his name, has developed an asset-oriented system of his own, which combines three complementary approaches. Boyar hunts for stocks whose market price is less than their "net net" working capital per share — current assets minus all current and long-term liabilities (including preferred stock, lease obligations, and certain pension liabilities), divided by the number of shares outstanding. Boyar also probes for hidden assets — assets such as real estate or natural resources that are carried on the balance sheet at less than their current value. For example, in 1986 Boyar concluded that Playboy Enterprises stock, then selling at $8 a share, was on the bargain counter; the magazine's California real estate, chairman Hugh Hefner's art collection, a pay TV operation, licensed use of the Playboy logo, and cash on hand added up to assets worth $30 a share. A year later, the stock was selling at $14.

Boyar's third approach is to look for what he calls business value. Essentially, this is the value that a company would have to a knowledgeable acquirer, and it is based on the company's historical earning power, its product line and market penetration, and its financial condition. The stocks featured in Boyar's $20,000-a-year monthly advisory service, *Asset Focus Analysis,* have had an impressive performance record, partly because a substantial number of the bargain-priced issues that he discovers are eventually acquired by other companies at very much higher prices.

The virtue of rigorous, asset-oriented approaches like Boyar's and Graham's is that they more or less ensure that the price you pay for a stock will represent bedrock value. One research study found that over a six-year period in the 1970s, several portfolios of stocks priced at less than their net net asset value per share (see chapter 15) outperformed the market by two to one (without exposure to above-average risk). The drawback of investing in net net asset plays is that you very seldom find one with the glamour of a Playboy; typically, they are the stocks of drab-looking companies or troubled companies with depressed earnings, and it often takes a long time for their lode of value to win recognition.

Discovering asset-rich stocks on your own calls for an awful lot of statistical drudgery. But a list of them, which you can get from your broker, appears weekly in the *Value Line Investment Survey,* and when stock prices have fallen steeply, *Forbes* sometimes catalogues such stocks under the heading "Loaded Laggards." Some loaded laggards may be losing money or may have such serious problems that you wouldn't want to own them, so you have to be carefully selective.

If an asset-oriented approach appeals to you but seems too tough to handle, you can let a mutual fund do the work for you. Fidelity Value Fund, a no-load fund in the Fidelity group, specializes in stocks selling below their book value.

☐ Low Price/Earnings Ratios

The strategy that we referred to earlier as contrarian — actually, it is just one of several approaches to contrarian investing — focuses on large, well-known companies paying liberal dividends, whose stocks are selling at P/E ratios well below the average for the market. Such stocks are at the low end of the popularity spectrum. If stocks in general are valued at, say, eight times earnings, a stock priced at 25 times earnings is obviously a popular favorite and one valued at four times earnings is in the doghouse.

Research studies carried out by Francis Nicholson, Paul F. Miller, Jr., William Avera, and others found that low P/E stocks — the unpopular ones — consistently produced larger long-term returns than high P/E stocks; indeed, a grouping of stocks into five categories based on their P/E ratios revealed that returns diminished as one proceeded up the scale of P/E ratios. Richard J. Dowen and W. Scott Bauman of Northern Illinois University updated these studies by tracking the performance of as many as 660 New York and American exchange stocks over the 14 years 1969 to 1983. The compound annual return for the high P/E group was 10.66 percent, for the medium P/E group 13.67 percent, and for the low P/E group 17.79 percent. Since low P/E stocks produce higher returns, modern portfolio theory would lead one to conclude that they are riskier than high P/E issues. But insofar as market risk is concerned the contrary is true; the betas of stocks decline as one goes from the highest to the lowest P/E groupings. And the risks of low P/E stocks not reflected in their betas can be largely eliminated by proper diversification.

Why are unpopular stocks more rewarding in the long run than popular issues? The leading proponent of the large-company, low-P/E approach, David Dreman, proffers the following explanation in his book *The Contrarian Investment Strategy*. The "visibility" of companies' future earnings is much less clear than analysts and investors like to think; forecasts frequently go wrong because, among other things, they tend to assume that current trends will continue. Moreover, analysts and investors give too much credence to these fallible forecasts. They become overenthusiastic about companies whose future growth seems to be highly visible and overly pessimistic about companies whose prospects look murky or drab. The historical record, Dreman argues, shows that in the aggregate the companies for which the strongest growth is projected don't do as well as is expected, and the companies with supposedly the worst prospects don't do as badly as investors anticipate. Thus disappointments occur frequently enough in the universe of high P/E stocks to cause them to underperform the market. On the other hand, there are enough favorable surprises in the unpopular universe to cause low P/E stocks to outperform the market. Dreman wisely qualifies this argument with the following observation: "It is true, of course, that there are excellent companies that will continue to chalk up above-average growth for many years or even decades . . . and there are especially talented investors who find them at reasonable prices."

Investors who opt for the low P/E strategy that Dreman advocates should observe the following guidelines.

1. Select the stocks of large, well-established companies that provide liberal yields and preferably have a good record of dividend growth. Large companies offer more stability than smaller ones, and a high yield lessens downside risk and increases your total return.
2. Make sure that the company's financial condition is strong. The ratios and other factors you should consider were discussed in the chapters on annual reports and fundamental stock analysis.
3. Look for companies with a respectable record of earnings growth.
4. If a company is highly cyclical, check into whether its current P/E ratio is low simply because earnings are at a cyclical peak. For example, when Ford was selling above 50 in 1978, it was valued at only about four times that year's earnings, which up to then were the second highest in Ford's history; in 1980, Ford reported a loss of $12.83 a share and the stock fell to just above 18. For a cyclical company, a genuinely low P/E is one that is low on the basis of average earnings over the previous four or five years.

5. Sell when the stock's P/E rises to the same level as that of the S&P index.
6. Diversify widely. Your portfolio should contain at least a dozen stocks in eight or nine different industries. If you can't afford to do this, put your money into a no-load fund that takes the contrarian, low P/E approach. John Neff's Windsor Fund, which is part of the Vanguard group, would be an excellent choice. It concentrates on stocks that Neff describes as "the downtrodden, the pummeled, the overlooked," and it returned an average of 18.8 percent per year, compounded, in the ten years through 1986. By comparison, the S&P 500 returned 13.7 percent. In 1985, Windsor stopped accepting new investors, but its sponsors at Vanguard started a similar fund called Windsor II under a different manager. While this Windsor clone is too new to have proved itself, it actually did a little better than its role model in 1968.

In mid-1987, stocks that met the requirements mentioned in the guidelines above included half a dozen leading electric utilities; several international banks such as Bank of America, Chemical, Chase Manhattan, and Citicorp; and Boeing and Lockheed in the defense industry group. A broker in the Westlake, California, office of Sutro & Co., Josef Ben-Porat, has long specialized in managing individual and pension fund accounts in accordance with the large-company, low P/E strategy; his fully documented performance record over the 15 years 1972 to 1987 was remarkably good.

☐ Think Small: The Emerging Growth Stock Approach

Dramatic evidence that small companies significantly outperformed larger ones during the 1960s and 1970s emerged from scholarly research published in the early 1980s. These findings don't invalidate the Dreman approach as a strategy that can produce better than average long-term gains with below average risks. But they do indicate that to make it big investors sometimes should think small.

Small firms listed on the New York and American stock exchanges produced annual returns 20 percent greater than those of large firms during the period 1963 to 1977, according to a study published in the March-April 1981 issue of *The Financial Analysts Journal* by Marc Reinganum, a professor at the University of California. Computations made for *Fortune* by Rolf W. Banz, then a finance professor at the University of Chicago, also show that portfolios of the smallest stocks — those with market capitalizations of $50 million or less — outperformed portfolios of large stocks. From 1975 to 1979, a period that became known for its "hidden bull market," the total return on the midgets was more than double that of the S&P index. This small-stock phenomenon continued until mid-1983, when the price/earnings ratio of these stocks reached a peak and then retreated. Until then, the little stocks had beaten the market fairly consistently for at least 50 years, even on a risk-adjusted basis. As *Fortune* commented, "The implication is obvious: 'buy little.' " But if you buy little, you must diversify much, hold fast against temporary reversals and hang in for the long term. In 1986, with the stock market in an exuberant rise, mutual funds and other institutional investors began buying small companies almost indiscriminately by letting computer programs create their shopping lists. As you would expect, this caused the prices of small stocks to lose their bargain appeal, so much so that the gain achieved by stocks began running inversely to their size. The small-stock advantage showed no sign of revival in the first half of 1987, even though the 30 giant companies represented in the Dow Jones Industrial Average added 27 percent to their value. Wall Streeters began calling the little companies "submerging growth stocks."

Even when they behave more traditionally, small companies have greater chances both of going down the drain and of soaring into the stratosphere. So you have to own a lot of them to avoid getting massacred by the failures or missing the wild successes. The best way for most investors to get sufficient diversification is, of course, through a mutual fund. And the most diversified of the small company funds with at least five years of results under their belt is Over-the-Counter Securities, which is sold through brokers at a sales charge of 8.5 percent at the maximum; OTC Securities owns more than 350 stocks and has had a first-rate performance record; in the ten years to April 1987, it returned a total, including dividends and capital gains, of 670 percent. Several no-load funds with long track records also concentrate on small stocks. Among them are the Evergreen Fund, up 925 percent in ten years; Acorn, up 570 percent; and T. Rowe Price New Horizons, up 487 percent.

A number of technical and fundamental advantages account for the superior performance of little stocks. The earnings of small companies grow faster than those of larger ones, because they are starting from a far smaller base. Then, too, the managers of small companies have greater flexibility and freedom to exploit the opportunities created by social and economic change. They are not hobbled by obsolescent facilities, and the small scale of their operations gives them an edge over the giants of industry in introducing new techniques. Most important of all, they are run by owner-entrepreneurs whose investment in the company gives them a significant stake in the success of their own efforts.

The stars that shine brightest in the small company universe are generally known as emerging or junior growth companies. A growth company — senior as well as junior — might be defined as one that is in a growth market and has a leading position in it or in a rapidly growing subsector of that market. In the mid-1980s, for example, time-release medication was a dynamic sector of the pharmaceuticals industry, and Health-Chem was one of the companies leading the way in a subsector, adhesive patches. Different analysts have different criteria for a growth company in regard to earnings and profitability, but the following would be widely acceptable:

1. The company should have shown an increase in earnings in each of the past five years and an annually compounded growth rate over the period of at least 15 percent.
2. It should have strong prospects of maintaining or increasing its established growth rate.
3. It should have a high return on equity — preferably 20 percent or more — to provide the capital for future growth without often having to borrow heavily or issue new stock.

Historically, the average price/earnings ratio of junior growth stocks has been about the same as the P/E of the S&P index at the bottom of bear markets and twice the P/E of the index at the peak of bull markets. Thus, in principle, junior growth stocks tend to be relatively undervalued when their average P/E is appreciably less than 1.5 times that of the index and relatively overvalued when their average P/E is appreciably more than 1.5 times the S&P multiple. To invest successfully in such stocks, you need the patience to wait at least three years and perhaps as long as five years for large gains. You should also have the fortitude to hang on through severe market declines.

Adventurous devotees of emerging growth do not shrink from

buying stocks in the business frontier category that have lofty price/earnings ratios. Success is also possible, though, with a conservative, value-conscious approach. For example, Charles Allmon, a money manager in Bethesda, Maryland, tends to avoid glamorous high-tech companies because he believes their valuations are usually excessive. His policy is to ferret out small growth companies that have not yet achieved recognition and are selling at relatively low price/earnings ratios. He requires a five-year growth record of 15 percent to 20 percent compounded annually and a strong balance sheet. He also attaches great importance to the man who runs the company, and he especially likes the inner-directed entrepreneurial type who doggedly hews to his own course. Allmon has displayed an astonishing flair for discovering successful small companies, often in prosaic industries. In the heyday of emerging growth companies, 1976 to 1982, his advisory service recommended 69 issues; only seven of them were losers, and 37 of them more than doubled in price. His record stood up pretty well even when updated through the rough weather of 1986: from January 1977 to January 1987, 34 of his 118 recommendations doubled and 12 rose more than 500%. And his advisory service newsletter, *Growth Stock Outlook,* ranked third among major letters tracked by *Hulbert Financial Digest* from 1982 through 1986 (see chapter 14).

In the portfolios he manages, Allmon does some selling when he thinks the market is dangerously high, and he parks the proceeds in money-market securities until he sees a buying opportunity. In March 1987, for example, with stocks bouncing near their record highs, he had 70 percent of his clients' assets into cash. He also cuts his losses, as a rule, in stocks that perform poorly; he tends to sell his Big Board stocks if they drop 10 percent to 15 percent, Amex stocks (they are usually more volatile) if they drop 15 percent to 20 percent and OTC stocks (they are still more volatile) if they drop 20 percent to 25 percent. He has no hard-and-fast rules for selling stocks that have made big gains. But he is generally reluctant to stay in a stock when its valuation has climbed to 30 times earnings. Allmon is one of the relatively few successful money managers who will accept an account of less than $200,000; his minimum requirement is $125,000; his annual fee is 1.65 percent of the first $200,000 of assets under management, declining in increments to 1 percent for amounts above $700,000. You can also buy Allmon's investment management services through a closed-end mutual fund, GSO Trust, which trades on the New York Stock Exchange. (Closed-ends are described later in this chapter.)

□ The Wonderful Business Approach

The achievement of Warren Buffett, writes John Train in *The Money Masters,* "stands alone in modern portfolio management." An investment of $10,000 in the partnership that Buffett founded in 1956 was worth $300,000 when the partnership was dissolved in 1969, and its portfolio never had a down year in spite of the bear markets of 1957, 1962, 1966, and 1969. Buffett has continued his brilliant investment career as president of a holding company, Berkshire-Hathaway, where an investment of $10,000 in its first year, 1965, would have been worth $2.4 million in 1986. Buffett's philosophy has been to invest only in the stocks of companies that he considers "wonderful businesses" and to buy them when they are out of favor. The key to a wonderful business is that it has a privileged or oligopolistic position — for example, that of broadcasters and newspapers (particularly newspaper chains such as Harte-Hanks and Gannett operating largely in single-paper towns). Other examples of companies with virtually unassailable business franchises would include Dun & Bradstreet and American Express (which has a premier position in the credit card and traveler's check businesses). Another kind of wonderful business in the Buffett sense is a major advertising agency, because its profit growth stems from the investments of others. Corporations invest to increase their sales; and as their sales grow, so do their advertising expenditures and hence the profits of the ad agencies.

Some of the other characteristics of wonderful businesses are that they have a good return on equity; they are "cash-generating machines" — that is, they don't have to keep plowing back their profits in new plant and development or in research and development; they are easy to understand; and their earnings are fairly predictable.

The companies that Buffett is drawn to are for the most part large and well known; to practice his style of investing successfully you have to buy the stocks when they are out of favor or the market is weak. You can own a piece of Buffett's portfolio by investing in his holding company, Berkshire-Hathaway, which is traded over the counter; in July 1987, however, the stock was selling at $3,750 a share. There are several no-load and low-load mutual funds whose investment philosphies are similar to Buffett's: Evergreen, Lindner, Mutual Shares, Royce Value, Sequoia, and Windsor; as this goes to press, only Evergreen, Mutual Shares, and Royce Value are accepting new shareholders.

☐ The Discount Store Approach: Buying Closed-End Funds

Closed-end funds, in contrast to open-end mutual funds, don't issue shares after the original offering, nor do they redeem them. Closed-end fund shares of broadly diversified investment companies are traded, in most cases, on the New York Stock Exchange, in the same way as stocks. In other words, the price of the shares depends on what investors are willing to pay for them, which may be more or less than their net asset value per share (the market value of all stocks in the portfolio divided by the number of shares outstanding).

Throughout most of the 1970s and early 1980s, the shares of closed-end common-stock funds sold at substantial discounts from their net asset value. Discounts provide leverage. When you buy $100 worth of stock at a 20 percent discount, you have the profit potential of $100 working for you, and you have put up only $80. Second, discounts mean higher yields; if for $80 you get $100 worth of stock paying $8 in dividends, your yield is not 8 percent but 10 percent. Third, discounts can improve capital gains potential and provide protection in declining markets; large discounts often narrow when stock prices are rising — they all but disappeared during the mid-1980s — and, surprisingly, they often narrow, too, when prices decline sharply. In sum, if you can buy shares of broadly invested closed-end funds at a discount from their asset value, you will be getting a diversified portfolio of stocks at less than their current market price, and that, of course, improves your chances of beating the market.

Why do the discounts exist? Many explanations have been put forward. The most plausible one is given by Burton Malkiel in *Winning Investment Strategies* (New York: W. W. Norton Co., 1982). The closed-end funds, Malkiel argues, are not supported by an active marketing campaign. Once the fund has been brought out, there's no payoff for the investment manager in promoting it, and brokers generally prefer to sell open-end load funds, on which they earn much larger commissions. The major closed-end stock funds, including specialized funds, are listed in the following table.

□ Closed-End Stock Funds

Fund	Stock exchange	% change in net asset value, 4/1/86 to 3/31/87	Expenses as % of net assets	Net income as % of net assets	Range of discount/ premium 1st quarter of 1987
Diversified funds with assets above $100 million					
Adams Express	NYSE	+16.7	0.53	2.81	−5 to +4
Baker Fentress	OTC	+9.8	0.53	2.33	−19 to −13
Central Securities	ASE	+10.3	0.84	1.61	−16 to −8
Gabelli Equity Trust	NYSE	+0.5	1.24	2.89	−11 to 0
General American Investors	NYSE	+9.5	1.09	1.86	−14 to −5
Growth Stock Outlook Trust[a]	NYSE	+1.8	1.50	4.10	−10 to −1
Lehman Corp	NYSE	+13.3	0.43	0.58	−11 to +3
Liberty All-Star Equity	NYSE	−2.0	2.77	1.81	−14 to +4
MassMutual Corporate Investors	NYSE	+2.5	2.10	8.64	+27 to +42
Niagara Shares Corp.	NYSE	+10.2	1.09	1.20	−15 to −4
Petroleum & Resources	NYSE	+10.7	0.46	3.64	−1 to +12
Royce Value Trust	NYSE	+9.1	1.79	3.45	−8 to +16
Source Capital	NYSE	+9.1	0.97	4.70	−1 to +11
Tri-Continental	NYSE	+20.4	0.53	3.14	−3 to +10
Foreign Funds					
ASA Ltd.[b]	NYSE	+43.0	0.31	5.55	−53 to −15
First Australia Fund	ASE	+34.0	3.05	6.78	−25 to −12
France Fund	NYSE	+29.4	1.93	0.25	−26 to −12
Germany Fund	NYSE	+18.0	1.52	loss	−9 to +3
Italy Fund	NYSE	+25.0	1.46	2.46	−27 to −5
Korea Fund	NYSE	+10.1	1.47	1.50	+30 to +123
Mexico Fund	NYSE	+33.8	1.70	5.84	−36 to −19
Scandinavia Fund	ASE	+3.5	1.34	4.15	−14 to −5
Taiwan Fund[c]	ASE	—	—	—	+45 to +230

[a] New fund with a large cash position in March 1987.
[b] Specializes in South African gold mining shares.
[c] New issue in 1987.

(Source: Thomas J. Herzfeld Advisors, Inc. *The Investor's Guide to Closed-End Funds*)

☐ WHAT TO AVOID: WHEN TO SELL

Many people prefer not to commit themselves to a single style of investing; they look for undervalued stocks of different types that could outperform the market. They might, for example, own some junior growth companies, some low P/E stocks selling below book value, some stocks in Buffett's wonderful business category, and so on. To prevent an eclectic approach from becoming disorderly, you need to develop certain principles of your own in regard to stock selection and the timing of sales. Here — stated without elaboration — are some organizing precepts.

Stay away from certain types of companies as long-term investments if you are trying to beat the market. Our list of undesirables includes:

1. companies that are labor-intensive and employ blue-collar, strongly unionized labor; they have relatively little control over a large portion of their costs, and wage increases often outstrip gains in productivity;

2. companies that are capital-intensive and are handicapped by obsolescent plant and equipment — some giants of the tire industry, for example;

3. companies whose sales growth has been coming more from price increases than from growth in unit sales — the number of cars, books, or refrigerators they sell (such companies are either losing market share to competitors or are operating in markets where there is little or no growth).

There are, to be sure, times when large trading profits can be made in the stocks of companies in the above categories; for example, Goodyear bounced from its 1986 low of 29 to 50 in November of that year on a takeover threat by James Goldsmith, a British financier. But from a long-term standpoint, stocks with the characteristics just described are fundamentally unattractive.

Be careful not to overpay for expectations of high growth. As pointed out earlier, future earnings growth is not nearly so visible as analysts like to think it is. And stratospheric valuations make stocks highly vulnerable to any disappointment. As a rule, it is advisable to stay away from stocks whose price/earnings ratios — based on their estimated earnings for the current year — are more than four-fifths of their projected growth rate; if earnings are expected to grow 25 percent annually, a P/E of more than 20 would be on the high side for a value-conscious investor. And a P/E of 30 or more for any stock might reasonably be considered prohibitive.

Stay away from fashionable "concept" stocks with no earnings and no prospects of showing appreciable earnings for some time. Genetic engineering is "such stuff as dreams are made on," but even dreams can be overvalued; when Genentech went public in 1980, the prices that starry-eyed investors initially paid for its stock discounted the hereafter.

Decide on certain yardsticks that will tell you when to sell and do your best to act on them. The yardsticks will be different for different investors, but one injunction applies to all: forget about buying at the bottom and selling at the top. Some investors who try to get good returns by minimizing losses make it a practice to sell automatically when a stock has declined a certain amount from their purchase price — the amount might be 10 percent, 15 percent, or 20 percent. If you buy a stock in the expectation of a specific development — for example, huge success for a new product — and the development doesn't occur, sell promptly. When to sell your winners is always a tough decision. Here are some rules worth considering.

1. Sell a stock whose price has quickly shot up 50 percent. (This rule would not apply if some development has dramatically improved the company's prospects.)

2. Sell a stock when its price/earnings ratio — based on estimated earnings for the current year — is one-and-a-half times the P/E ratio at which you bought it.

3. Ben Graham's rule — sell if the stock hasn't risen 50 percent in three years — may be overexacting, but it is a sound principle not to stay wedded to stocks that aren't producing respectable returns.

4. Sell any stock that appears to offer substantially less potential than other stocks that you could buy if you had funds available.

·22 Investing for Income

There are many people who firmly believe that, for them, the risks of investing for growth are too high and the rewards too uncertain. Their attitude is summed up in the remark an investor made to his stock-broker: "I want income, not if-come." But when inflation is rampant, the conventional wisdom that investing for income is a safe policy that brings assured returns has been shot full of holes. Two of the staples of income-oriented portfolios — bonds and public utility stocks — were rotten investments to own throughout most of the 1970s and the first two years of the 1980s. Indeed, in that era, when the consumer price index rose an average of 9.4 percent a year, the only certainty about investing strictly for income was that you would have been a loser in the battle against inflation. If, for example, you had put your savings into risk-free short-term investments such as money funds, the yield you would have earned would seldom have been much above the rate of inflation before taxes and never after taxes. Meanwhile, the purchasing power of your capital would have shrunk each year by an amount equal to the rise in consumer prices. What the 1970s taught us is that most if not all income-oriented investors should include in their portfolios securities that provide some possibility of capital appreciation — for example, high-yielding common stocks, convertible securities, and, when they are available, deep discount bonds (which are discussed later in this chapter).

Income-oriented investors should also get a firm handle on the four main types of risk that apply to fixed-income securities. And they should familiarize themselves with timing tactics that can significantly improve the returns on their investments. By selecting the proper portfolio mix and using timing tactics that reduce risk and exploit opportunities, income-oriented investors can do much to protect themselves against any new and severe onset of inflation.

☐ The Four Types of Risk

☐ Credit Risk
This is the risk of default by the bond issuer on interest payments or repayment of principal when the bond reaches maturity. The bond quality ratings issued by Standard & Poor's and Moody's

evaluate credit risk. Bonds rated AAA or AA by Standard & Poor's (Aaa or Aa by Moody's) are of the highest quality. An A rating stands for upper-medium quality; interest and principal are regarded as safe. The BBB, or medium-grade, category represents "adequate" quality; it is the lowest category in which commercial banks are allowed to invest. Any bond with a lower rating — or no rating at all — falls in a category widely referred to as junk bonds. A BB rating signifies "lower medium grade," and B, CCC, and CC are speculative ratings that reflect increasing degrees of risk. Remember that bond ratings are relative yardsticks; a B-rated bond is riskier than an A-rated one, but that doesn't mean its chances of default are high. During the Great Depression of the 1930s, only 1/2 percent of all bond issues defaulted on repayment of principal. Even in the lower grades — the so-called junk bonds — the historical rate of default in this country has been low. From 1974 through 1985, the rate averaged 1.5 percent. However, flimsy financing used in takeovers and leveraged buyouts, in which corporate executives backed by investment bankers take their companies off the stock market, contributed to a doubling of junk bond defaults in 1986 to a 3 percent rate.

☐ **Market Risk**
This risk that bonds will decline in price hinges mainly on changes in interest rates. When interest rates rise, bond prices fall (and conversely when rates fall, prices rise). A bond's price can also decline because investors expect its rating to be lowered or because the supply of new bond offerings is abnormally large.

A bond's rate of interest, known as its coupon rate, is a fixed percentage of its face, or par, value of $1,000; for example, the American Telephone bond maturing in 2005 with an 8.80 percent rate offers a fixed annual return of $88. Clearly nobody would pay the same price for a bond already on the market as for a newly issued bond of comparable quality with a higher return. So when interest rates rise, the prices of bonds with coupon rates below the prevailing rates fall sufficiently to make their yields competitive with those of newly issued bonds.

There is, however, a minor complication that needs to be explained. A bond's yield is measured in two ways. Its current yield is its interest rate divided by its market price; if the rate is 9 percent and the bond is selling at $900,* the current yield is 10 percent. But when that

---

* Bond prices are quoted as a percentage of par. A price of 85 means that the bond is selling at $850.

bond reaches maturity, its owner will receive not $900 but $1,000. *So the proper measure of a bond's return is its annual yield to maturity, a figure that takes into account the gain or loss on the bond's current price when the bond is eventually redeemed.* For example, if a bond with a 9 percent coupon selling at $900 matures in ten years, the bondholder's total return to maturity will be ten times $90 plus $100, or $1,000. The easiest way to get a bond's annual yield to maturity is to ask your broker to look it up for you in a yield table. But there's a rough-and-ready way of calculating yield to maturity: you simply divide the average annual return by the average price of the bond (the midpoint between its current price and its redemption value). Thus for a bond with a ten-year maturity, a 9 percent coupon, and a current price of $900, the arithmetic is as follows:

$$\frac{\$900 \ (\text{interest}) + \$100 \ (\text{gain}) \ \text{divided by 10 years}}{\$900 + \$1,000 \ \text{divided by 2 (average price of the bond)}}$$

That equals 100/950, or 10.53 percent.

Since the true measure of a bond's return is its yield to maturity, bond prices tend to rise or fall to the extent necessary to make their yield to maturity competitive with those of newly issued bonds. A theoretical illustration: if long-term interest rates were to rise overnight from 10 percent to 11 percent (which, of course, couldn't happen), the price of a bond with a 10 percent coupon, selling at $1,000 and maturing in 10 years, would drop to around $936; at that price its annual yield to maturity (taking into account the eventual $64 gain) would be 11 percent.

In the 1970s and 1980s, recurrent sharp swings in interest rates resulted in unprecedented volatility in the bond market. In 1980, for example, drops or rises of more than 20 percent in bond prices occurred within periods of a few months. When the underlying trend of long-term interest rates was upward, many bondholders suffered severe losses. From January 1977 to October 1981, long-term Treasury bonds plunged in price nearly 54 percent, top-quality bonds 53.6 percent, and municipals 54.4 percent. Later, as inflation subsided, the Federal Reserve Board slacked its reins on the money supply, dropping interest rates from double digits to below 8 percent for Treasuries. The ensuing bull market in bonds rivaled the one in stocks.

Nonetheless, inflation remains the bondholder's chief bugbear. Investors who intend to hold a bond to maturity sometimes argue that a drop in the bond's price is "only a paper loss" because eventually they will receive $1,000. This reasoning is specious. Consider the case of an investor who bought at par the AT&T bond mentioned above and owned it in the spring of 1981, when top-quality corporate bonds offered yields to maturity of 13½ percent. By holding the bond — then quoted at around $695 — for redemption in 2005, he might lose for as long as 24 years the difference between his annual return of $88 and the available return of $135, a total of $1,128.* And if he sold the bond at $695 (less commission) and reinvested the proceeds in a bond yielding 13½ percent, his annual return would still be only about $92. Either way, he suffers a very real loss.

These figures underscore a vital point: the old concept of bonds as a relatively safe long-term investment is thoroughly obsolete. One disconsolate bondholder dourly observed in 1981, "Bonds have been my hedge against prosperity." Interest rate risk has grown large, and the longer the bond's maturity, the greater is the risk. If long-term rates rise, a bond maturing in 30 years will have to drop much more than one maturing in 12 years for its yield to maturity to make it competitive with newly issued bonds. Because of their greater risk, long-term bonds normally offer higher yields than bonds with shorter maturities. But if you think that interest rates may rise and you still wish to own bonds because of the assured high yields that they provide, you should switch out of long-term bonds into intermediate bonds — preferably those with maturities of not more than ten years. Another way of lessening somewhat your exposure to interest rate risk is to shun long-term bonds at all times and stick with intermediate maturities.

There is, of course, a case for owning long-term bonds; it hinges on the possibility that inflation will remain in check and that long-term interest rates will decline and not climb back to (or above) their levels when you bought the bonds. If that were to happen, owners of long-term bonds would profit in one of two ways:

1. holders of bonds issued when interest rates were at or close to peak levels would have assured themselves of much higher yields than those available in the future;

---

* In reality, this risk is likely to be negated by another, call risk, which is explained later.

2. investors who own "deep discount" bonds — old bonds with low coupon rates, purchased when they were selling at large discounts from their par value — would make hefty capital gains, because the prices of such bonds rise sharply when interest rates fall.

In mid-November 1981, an AT&T bond with an interest rate of 7⅛ percent maturing in 2003 was selling at $580. If long-term rates were to drop back to 7⅛ percent — a level they indeed approached in 1986 — a buyer of that bond at $580 might well make a profit of about $420 (before commissions), or 72 percent.

☐ Call Risk
A bond selling above par (because interest rates have dropped) may be called away from you by the issuer and redeemed at below its market price. If interest rates fall sharply, a company will invoke the call provision in its high-coupon bonds as soon as the bondholders' protection lapses. So much for the hope of earning high yields for many years after a decline in rates on the open market. The only bonds with long-term call protection are U.S. Treasury bonds. Most industrial and utility bonds are protected for no more than five to ten years. And there may be loopholes in even that modest call protection. So before buying a bond, don't forget to ask your broker to check out its call provisions.

☐ Purchasing Power Risk
This has to do with the amount of *purchasing power* you will lose through inflation. Since the prospects of actual deflation appear to be virtually nil, loss of purchasing power in fixed-income securities is a near certainty. And the longer a bond's maturity, the greater the prospective loss, because your real capital will be shrinking each year. The bond you buy today for $1,000 will return $1,000 when it comes due. If inflation averages 5 percent annually, the $1,000 you receive 10 years hence will be worth only $614 in today's purchasing power; if inflation averages 7 percent and a bond matures in 15 years, the $1,000 you receive then will be worth, in today's money, $362.

☐ Timing Matters

Timing tactics are just about as important for income-oriented investors as they are for those seeking growth. If you stay in a money market fund when interest rates are declining, you will

1. get diminishing yields,
2. miss out on opportunities for profit in bonds or interest-sensitive stocks.

Conversely, if you sit tight in bonds and interest-sensitive stocks throughout an upward spiral in interest rates, you will suffer punishing losses and miss out on the high returns available from short-term securities. Ideally, you would buy long-term bonds or interest-sensitive stocks when an up cycle in interest rates is close to its peak, hold them throughout the down cycle, and switch into short-term securities before the next up spiral begins. Calling the turns in interest rates that accurately is an impossible dream, but being partially right can make a big difference in your investment results. Chapter 8 explained how watching the weekly changes in the money supply and the actions of the Federal Reserve can help you to anticipate the trend of interest rates.

☐ Shopping in a Supermarket

Investing for income has been made easier and more economic for the average investor by the emergence of no-load mutual funds that specialize in various types of income investments (see Appendix B). In addition, there are brokerage-house unit trusts that invest in bonds and then simply hold them to their maturity, thereby eliminating management fees. Indeed, so many choices are now readily available to income-oriented investors that investing for income has changed from shopping in a delicatessen to shopping in a supermarket. Here's a closer look at the main types of income investments.

☐ U.S. Government Securities

Treasury securities — bills, notes, and bonds — are guaranteed by the U.S. government and have the world's highest credit rating; there has never ever been a default. Treasury Bills are short-term securities with maturities of up to one year, but most commonly 13 and 26 weeks. The interest is paid up front — that is, the bills are issued at a discount and redeemed at their par value; their minimum denomination is $10,000. Treasury notes have maturities of one to ten years, and bond maturities range from ten to 30 years; both are available in denominations of $1,000, and they pay interest semiannually. Treasury securities also come in the form of zero coupon bonds, which pay no semi-annual interest. You buy them at a huge discount and collect par value at maturity, which you can time to suit your need for the money. That makes zeros useful investments for a child's college fund. For example, a $1,000 ten-year zero paying 8.5 percent would cost $435. The unpaid interest translates to a compound rate of return that is guaranteed for the life of the bond at a rate that could not be duplicated if you had to reinvest the interest in small amounts. The interest payments are, in effect, deferred, and the IRS recognizes this by taxing it currently, as though it had been paid out. The locked-in compounding feature makes zero bond prices more volatile than interest-paying bonds. Zero-coupon bonds called STRIPS (for separate trading of registered interest and principal of securities) are issued by the Treasury. Brokerage houses market zeros under such names as TIGER (Treasury interest growth receipt) and CATS (certificates of accrual on Treasury securities).

Treasury securities can be bought and sold through commercial banks and brokerage houses. The income from them is exempt from state and local but not from federal taxes. Because they have the highest credit rating, Treasury Bills, notes, and bonds normally offer somewhat lower yields than those provided by other fixed-income securities with comparable maturities.

Of the numerous other government securities, the most interesting to individual investors are Government National Mortgage Association certificates, familiarly known as Ginnie Maes. These certificates, whose average life span is 9 to 12 years, represent shares in a government-guaranteed pool of home mortgages. Holders of Ginnie Maes receive monthly checks that include, in addition to interest, repayment of principal on their shares of the mortgages in the pool. The minimum denomination for Ginnie Maes is $25,000, but investors can own them through brokerage house unit trusts and specialized no-load mutual funds such as Fidelity Mortgage Securities, Lexington GNMA Income and Vanguard Fixed Income — GNMA (see Appendix B). Ginnie Maes are unique in that they offer government-guaranteed face value, high yields, and gradual return of principal. You can expect, however, to get back large slabs of principal when mortgage rates take a dive, because homeowners then refinance their loans just as corporations do to cut their borrowing costs. A second pitfall at such times awaits holders of Ginnie Maes bought at premium prices. They risk losing not only the high yields they expected to get for many years but also some of their principal. Furthermore, interest payments from all Ginnie Maes are subject to state and local as well as federal income taxes.

☐ Tax-Exempt Bonds

State and local government bonds — generically known as municipals or tax-exempts — have long ceased to be an investment only for the very rich. You don't have to be earning megabucks to find yourself in a tax bracket of 28 percent, and if you are taxed 28 percent on every dollar of incremental income, a 7 percent yield on a municipal bond is equivalent to a taxable yield of 9.72 percent. Moreover, *the interest on municipals is exempt from state and city taxes in the state in which the bond is issued,* an important consideration to residents of California, Massachusetts, New York, and other states where the tax bite is large. Most investors can reach for somewhat higher tax-free yields in a new class of municipal bonds created under the 1986 Tax Reform Act. Congress, while preserving the tax exemption, laid down some limits on private-purpose financing such as airport and student loan bonds. People who load up on too many tax-sheltered investments risk having to pay tax on the interest from private-purpose municipals, because that interest has to be reported on the form for figuring the alternative minimum tax. Thus, such issues have become known as AMT bonds. Only about one in a hundred taxpayers gets hooked by the AMT. The other 99 percent could earn an extra one-half to one percentage point of tax-free yield on AMT bonds.

There are three ways of investing in tax-exempt bonds:

1. you can buy them individually through brokers or commercial banks;
2. you can buy units in one of the unit investment trusts that are regularly marketed by major brokerage firms and by bond houses such as John Nuveen & Co. in Manhattan;
3. you can buy shares in a tax-exempt bond fund — more than 50 no-loads are listed in Appendix B.

You will have to decide for yourself which of these ways suits you best. Here's what you need to know about them.

Tax-exempt mutual funds have the following points in their favor. The minimum investment required can be as low as $1,000. The funds offer professional management, diversification, and other benefits —

you can have your dividends automatically reinvested; you can make additional investments of as little as $100; and you can switch at little or no cost into another type of fund within the same sponsoring group.

The chief liability of tax-exempt bond funds is that management fees and operating expenses together reduce the portfolio's annual yield by 33 to 90 cents per $100 invested, depending on the fund; Vanguard's municipal portfolios are at the low end of that range. If the yield earned is 8 percent, fund shareholders receive somewhere between 7.1 and 7.67 percent. For some investors a loss of one-third of a percentage point of interest is a reasonable price to pay for the benefits the fund offers; for others, it is an undue sacrifice of income, since the fund manager has not been sufficiently adept at risk management to mitigate appreciably the portfolio losses caused by upward spirals in interest rates.

Unit investment trusts are unmanaged portfolios of bonds; the bonds are assembled and then simply held to maturity. Some trusts require an investment of at least $5,000, others accept $1,000. The initial sales charge is 3½ percent to 4½ percent, but subsequent administrative expenses are small — they reduce the portfolio's yield by only 0.2 percent a year. If an investor wants out, his broker can usually arrange for his units to be redeemed by the trust at their current net asset value, or the investor can deal directly with the trust. The annual return remains more or less fixed throughout the life of the trust. For people who live in states where income taxes are high, there are mutual funds and unit trusts with portfolios composed entirely of bonds that are issued in their states and are therefore exempt from all taxes.

Conventional wisdom has it that small investors should not buy municipal bonds individually. The reasons: first, most municipals come in denominations of $5,000 and up, so an investor who has earmarked $10,000 or less for tax-exempts can't obtain diversification. Second, when you buy only one or two bonds, you usually pay more than the quoted price, and you get less than the quoted price when you sell.

These drawbacks aren't quite as bad as they may sound. The price differentials when you buy and sell, plus brokerage commissions, can amount to less than the management fees of a mutual fund or the sales charge on a unit trust. And if you buy a bond rated A or better, the risk you run by not diversifying is small.

☐ Corporate Bonds

If you are buying bonds individually, it's prudent to stick to issues rated A or better. But with the diversification that a mutual fund provides, the risk of owning so-called junk bonds — those rated no higher than BB — is small; contrary to what you might imagine, defaults on low-grade bonds have been rare, and studies show that their long-term returns have been much larger than those on high-grade issues. Funds that specialize in low-grade bonds include American Investors Income, Financial Bond Shares — High Yield, and Fidelity High Income (see Appendix B).

In the recent past, bond prices have taken such a drubbing during upward spirals in interest rates and have reaped such handsome gains when rates cycled down that a good case can be made for trading bonds rather than buying them as a long-term investment. You buy when you think interest rates are close to a peak and you sell when you think they won't go much lower — or else when you have made a satisfactory profit and consider other investments more attractive. For investors of limited means, the simplest and most economical way of trading bonds is through a closed-end bond fund. These funds offer little-known advantages over buying bonds individually. They sometimes sell at discounts of 5 percent or more from their net asset value; and when bond prices have rallied, investors have usually made an extra profit from a narrowing of the discount. Moreover, you can invest small amounts in the closed-end funds; in mid-1987, most of them were selling at less than $20 a share. Thirty-two closed-end bond funds are traded on the New York Stock Exchange. Among them are American Capital Bond, Bunker Hill Income Securities, Drexel Bond Debenture, Excelsior Income Shares, Fort Dearborn Income Securities, Global Yield, Intercapital Income Securities, John Hancock Income Trust, and Transamerica Income.

☐ It's a Bond, It's a Stock, It's a Convertible

Convertible bonds and convertible preferred stocks are hybrids. Like bonds, they offer fixed returns; but they are also equities, since they can be swapped for a specified number of shares of the issuing company's stock. *The value of a convertible is therefore a composite of its value as a fixed-income security and as a stock.* Consider, first, the equity value of a hypothetical bond issued with a 6 percent coupon and convertible into 40 shares of common stock; the bond is currently priced at $900 and the common is selling at $18. The bond's *conversion value* is 40 times $18, or $720, so it is selling at a premium of 25 percent over its conversion value. Its *conversion parity* — the share price at which an investor who bought at $900 would break even by converting into the common — is $22.50. Any rise in the stock above $22.50 would be accompanied by at least an equal percentage rise in the price of the convertible. If, for example, the stock were to go to $25, the bond would be worth $1,000 and would probably sell for more than that because of the value of the conversion feature.

Now let's look at what the same convertible might be worth as a straight bond. This is known as its *investment value*; it is the price at which the convertible's yield to maturity equals the yield to maturity offered by straight bonds of similar quality with comparable maturities. If our hypothetical convertible bond matures in 10 years, and if yields to maturity on comparable straight bonds are 9.5 percent, a glance at the bond yield tables will tell us that the convertible would have an investment value of about $775.

A convertible's investment value limits its downside risk; regardless of how much the common stock drops, the convertible won't decline below its investment value unless interest rates rise. On the other hand, the conversion feature, or "equity kicker," endows well-chosen convertibles with large profit potential. That's why it is sometimes said that there is a floor, but no ceiling, on the price of convertibles. There is, however, a danger that the bondholder will be, so to speak, evicted; since most convertibles are callable, the company may force you to convert — at a price somewhat above par — by calling the issue. Moreover, the convertibility of some bonds diminishes or even vanishes after a time. Consequently, a convertible buyer should get his broker to look up the call and conversion provisions.

The dual character of convertibles makes them complicated to evaluate. The ideal convertible would have the following characteristics:

1. the common stock appears to have excellent prospects of advancing;
2. the current price of the common is not more than 15 percent to 20 percent below the conversion parity price;
3. the convertible provides a higher yield than the common stock;

4. the convertible's value as a straight bond is not more than 15 percent to 20 percent below its current price;

5. the price of the bond is not more than 20 percent above the current call price — this minimizes the risk of forced conversion.

It is unlikely that you will find a convertible that meets all of those requirements. Although convertibles are, in principle, a middle-of-the-road species, there are some that will act more like stocks than bonds and some that will act more like bonds than stocks. The former are selling 'way above their investment value, the latter 'way above their conversion value. Your choice must depend on how much risk you are willing to assume. If you are seeking some growth, make sure you pick a convertible that stands a decent chance of scoring extra points with its equity kicker.

For inexperienced investors, the best way of investing in convertibles is to buy shares in a convertible bond mutual fund or closed-end fund. Four closed-ends are traded on the New York Stock Exchange: American Capital Convertible Securities, Convertible Holdings, Lincoln National Convertible Securities, and TCW Convertible Securities. Three others are available on the American Stock Exchange: Bancroft Convertible, Castle Convertible, and Ellsworth Convertible Growth and Income. In mid-1987, four of these funds were selling at discounts above 5 percent: Ellsworth (−15.1 percent), Lincoln National (−9.6), Castle (−7.7), and TCW (−5.7). Five no-load convertible-bond mutual funds also were operating: Dreyfus Convertible Securities, Noddings Calamos Growth and Income funds, Value Line Convertible, and Vanguard Convertible.

☐ Love that Discount

Deep discount bonds are old bonds with low coupon rates that are selling substantially below their face value; they may be Treasury bonds, municipals, corporates, or convertibles. When you buy a deep discount bond, your current yield is a lot lower than the prevailing rate, but a profit awaits you when the bond matures. A sound strategy is to buy deep discount bonds maturing within five years or less. When this book first appeared, you could hit such bonds by throwing darts at the bond table in the New York Times. At the present writing, deep discounts are scarce and are limited largely to issues of shaky companies. For example, a 5.4 percent coupon Bethlehem Steel bond due in 1992 is selling at $699. A buyer is assured of a $301 profit — 43 percent — in about five years and he doesn't have to worry about rising interest rates; as bonds approach maturity they become relatively insensitive to interest rate changes. To be sure, a buyer of the Bethlehem Steel bond sacrifices current income. But unless the company goes down the tubes, his *annual return to maturity* will amount to nearly 14 percent.

□ Preferred Stocks

Preferred stocks, like bonds, are fixed-income securities; they pay a fixed dividend that must be met before any dividends may be paid on the common. Preferred stocks that aren't convertible have little appeal for the individual investor. They don't have the growth potential of common stocks and, if a company gets into a financial bind, the interest due to its bondholders takes precedence over the dividend claims of the holders of preferred stock.

□ Common Stocks

To give their portfolios some possibility of growth, even income-oriented investors should have a portion of their assets in common stocks. The equities traditionally favored for such investors have been public utilities. The trouble is that anyone who allocates most of his resources to bonds and utility stocks will have virtually no real diversification; when interest rates rise, both his bonds and his utilities will come tumbling down.

A stock selection strategy suitable for income-oriented investors was described in chapter 21 — investing in large, well-established companies whose stocks are out of favor, are selling at low price/ earnings ratios, and pay liberal dividends. Another sound strategy is to invest in a diversified package of companies whose dividend growth has outpaced inflation.

When this chapter was written, nine companies of the 1,700 followed by Value Line had increased their dividends by at least 15 percent a year for the previous five years and were currently yielded at least 2.5 percent, the median yield of all dividend-paying stocks in the

Value Line Universe. They were Bristol-Myers (with average annual dividend growth of 17.5 percent), First Wachovia Corp. (17.5 percent), H. J. Heinz (17 percent), Lee Enterprises (17.5 percent), Maryland National Bank (15 percent), Pfizer (15 percent), Philip Morris (20.5 percent), RJR Nabisco (16.5 percent), and U.S. Tobacco (18.5 percent). The *Value Line Investment Survey* periodically publishes lists of high-yielding stocks with good prospects of continued payout growth. Major brokerage houses also generate such lists for their clients. These are usually excellent sources of leads for income-oriented investors. The New York Stock Exchange's annual *Fact Book,* available from the Exchange for $3.70, lists companies that have paid uninterrupted dividends since the 19th century. In 1985 there were 63 names on the list. Since people investing for income are highly vulnerable to the inroads of inflation, they should try to include in their portfolios issues that are inflation-proof and still offer high yields — oil stocks such as Exxon, Mobil, or Standard Oil and electric utilities with little need of additional debt in the next few years.

As a rule, the risks and potential rewards of investing for income are smaller than those of investing for growth. But you would be wrong to conclude that the approach you take doesn't much matter. Far too many income-oriented investors simply reach out for the highest obtainable current yields. Except for elderly retired people, that's a shortsighted strategy; over the years, it will ensure that the purchasing power of your capital is seriously eroded by inflation. In an inflationary age, you can't afford to give up on growth or to be a passive investor. You have to try, as best you can, to manage your portfolio. That means staying alert to changes in interest rates and in the relative attraction of different types of securities. It means choosing the stocks of companies that have consistently raised their dividend, because stock prices and payouts go up hand in hand. Or it means letting a professional investor man the financial watch. Many no-load and low-load mutual funds pursue a cautious strategy of growth and income by seeking out stocks they believe will produce a strong *total return* from a combination of rising dividends and price appreciation. Among funds with ten or more years of steady if unspectacular results are Fidelity Equity-Income, Mutual Shares, Neuberger & Berman Guardian, and Selected American Shares. A younger fund that has turned in six very impressive years of steady growth is Strong Total Return, which charges a modest 1 percent sales charge.

23 The Manifold Merits of Mutual Funds

There is hardly any type of investment mentioned in this book that can't be made through mutual funds, and nearly always more economically than if you were to buy the securities individually. Such a burst of new mutual funds was set off by, first, high interest rates, then high taxes, and finally the mighty bull market of the 1980s, that the number of funds grew beyond 1,800 — more than the number of stocks listed on the New York Stock Exchange. In terms of money under management, this country's mutual funds were responsible as 1987 began for investing $716.3 billion, compared with $100 billion ten years earlier.

The existing types of funds include money-market, tax-exempt money-market, government bond, corporate bond, junk bond, and municipal bond funds; income funds that invest mainly in high-yielding stocks; so-called balanced funds, which maintain a balance between stocks and bonds; growth-and-income funds; quality growth, aggressive growth, and maximum gains funds; funds that specialize in foreign stocks or bonds; and sector funds, which invest in single industries, from the frontiers of high tech to the ancient enterprise of gold mining. Funds with sales charges (usually 4 to 8½ percent) can be bought through brokers and personal financial planners, who will help you to choose among those that fit your objectives. No-load funds and low-load funds, with sales charges of 1 to 3.5 percent, sell directly to investors; you have to telephone the fund, usually toll-free, or write for a prospectus and order form. You will find a classified directory of no-load and low-load funds, with a description of each fund's investment policy, in Appendix B.

If you see more no-load than load funds on a list of the top performers, it is simply because there are more of the former among the growth funds; no evidence exists that either type outperforms the other. For some investors, the convenience of buying through a broker or financial planner and the guidance he provides may be well worth the commission. Or you may be so dazzled by a particular load fund's record that you feel you have to be in it, and the sales charge be damned. The big argument in favor of the no-loads is that when you invest $1,000, you get $1,000 of stock; in a load fund, you typically start out with $915, and the fund's net asset value has to rise nearly 11 percent before you break even.

Here is a fast rundown of other basic facts that you need to know about mutual funds. The minimum initial investment is commonly $500 or $1,000, but a number of funds accept as little as $200 and a few require $2,500 or more. Subsequent minimum purchases are typically $25 or $50, though a minority of funds won't take less than $100 or even $250. Almost all funds offer automatic reinvestment of dividends and capital gains, and most accept Keogh Plan and Individual Retirement Accounts. Money-market funds and some bond funds allow you to write checks (provided by the fund), usually for amounts not less than $500; to do this — or to make withdrawals by telephone — you must first have filed an authorization form with the fund. When a withdrawal request is made in writing, many funds require a guarantee of your signature by a bank or a brokerage firm. Chekcs drawn on mutual funds ordinarily take as long as two weeks to clear the banking system, delaying your access to those funds. For ready cash, which you may need in the form of a certified check drawn on your bank account to buy a car or close a real estate deal, you can authorize most funds to wire money directly to your checking account in amounts of $1,000 or more. And when you decide to retire or to start living off your investments, many mutual funds will send a check for a set amount each month to your bank account or your home.

☐ Switching to Beat the Market

In addition to eliminating the problems of security selection and diversification, investing through mutual funds provides fantastic flexibility: you can switch from one type of fund to another within the same family of funds — in most cases, by telephone — and save yourself the brokerage commissions you would have to pay if you bought and sold individual securities. Some fund groups have even eliminated the need for a telephone call. Holders of shares in their growth fund can place stop-loss orders at a specific price; if the shares decline to that level, they are sold automatically and the proceeds are transferred to the money fund. Investors can also specify the price at which they want to get back into the growth fund, and when that price is reached, their order will be executed automatically. A switch or exchange, as it is known, costs either nothing or a trifling $5. Most fund families set no limit on the number of switches a shareholder may make, but some do restrict the frequency — to four a year, for example. Fund-switching has caught on in a big way among individual investors. In 1975, the amount of money involved in exchanges was $700 million; in 1986, it was $108 *billion* and rising.

There are two basic approaches to fund-switching. Most aggressive investors take the all-or-nothing approach; they keep all of their assets in high-growth or maximum-gains funds when they are bullish and move completely into a money-market fund when they anticipate a market decline. The second, or risk adjustment, approach, which consists in modifying the portfolio mix, was illustrated in chapter 19. In the example used there, an investor with $40,000 seeking growth and income and feeling moderately bullish starts out with 50 percent of his assets in a growth-and-income fund, 20 percent in a high-growth fund, 25 percent in a money fund, and 5 percent in a gold fund. If he turns bearish, he would switch the assets in the stock funds into the money fund, or, if inflation is on the rise, he might use 5 percent of these assets to increase his investment in gold. If he becomes decidedly bullish, he could take a more aggressive stance by reducing his investment in the money fund or the growth-and-income fund or both and funneling the proceeds into the high-growth fund. A different investor might prefer simply to keep a portion of his assets in a growth fund and the balance in a money fund, and modify the percentages in accordance with his state of confidence.

Investors who take the risk modification approach can get the timing guidance they need from the system described in chapter 20. A preponderance of "yes" answers to the "Time to Buy" or "Time to Sell" checklist will indicate whether they should become more aggressive or more defensive. All-or-nothing fund switchers, too, can use that system, provided their goal is simply to try to anticipate major turning points in the market and they are willing to ignore secondary swings. But they should switch only when the system gives a decisive buy or sell signal.

A great many all-or-nothing fund-switchers are market timing buffs who are out to catch secondary and even minor swings in stock prices. They usually get their signals from a weighted or exponential moving average (see page 122) of the price behavior of the growth fund they are using. The available evidence suggests that short-term fund-switching doesn't produce alluring results even when it is done by pros. The all-or-nothing approach works best when it is used to avoid getting pummeled by major declines and to make the most of major advances.

☐ Finding the Right Family

Investors who plan to use the switch privilege can choose among no fewer than 123 fund families, plus independent stock funds that have exchange arrangements with a money-market fund. If you are an aggressive investor you should look for a family with a growth fund that has an outstanding performance record or else select a top-performing independent with a tie-up to a money fund. Don't pick a fund simply because it has been the number one over the past one-year, five-year, or ten-year period. Pick one that has a consistently excellent record; you will find at the end of this chapter a list of funds that have been outstanding performers. Anyone who plans to buy and hold fund shares should check the fund's yearly records to find out how much it has dropped in bear markets. Some of the best-performing funds over the past 15 years were down 60 percent to 70 percent from 1973 through 1974. A shareholder losing that much might understandably get so nervous that he would sell at a tremendous loss and be discouraged from going back in again.

Investors whose objective calls for a balanced portfolio will want to be in a fund group that offers a wide variety of funds; but they, too, should select a group that has a high-performance growth fund that they could switch into when they are bullish. Some of the families that meet these criteria are ABT Midwest, Dreyfus Corp., Fidelity Group, GIT Investment, Hutton Group, Legg Mason, Merrill Lynch, Neuberger & Berman, T. Rowe Price, Stein Roe & Farnham, and Vanguard.

The mutual fund industry is constantly broadening the range of funds and services offered to investors. Here's a sampling of innovative "products" introduced in recent years. In combination with life insurance companies, mutual fund groups have begun managing special stock and bond portfolios for investors in variable annuities and variable life insurance companies. This enables the customer to invest in any of several funds and to switch from one type to another as market conditions change. Monarch Life, for example, has assigned the management of its single-premium variable life portfolios to Merrill Lynch. As with traditional annuities and insurance policies, taxes on the earnings of an investment inside the plan are deferred. With an annuity you pay no taxes until you either cash it in or start receiving lifetime income, usually after retirement. With single-premium and other types of variable life insurance, you or your beneficiaries may be able to escape taxes on the investment earnings forever. Massachusetts Financial Services is the sponsor of an innovation in investing overseas: its Massachusetts Financial International Trust-Bond Portfolio, established in 1981, invests in foreign bonds, which can be attractive to bond buyers when the dollar is weakening against foreign currencies or when the U.S. bond market looks endangered (see chapter 24). In its first six years, the fund had an average annual total return of 18 percent. The fall of the dollar in 1985 and 1986 inspired the creation of similar bond funds by T. Rowe Price, Merrill Lynch, and others. The 1980s brought forth a great outpouring of other fund ideas, such as sector funds for investing in individual industries or segments of industries, bond funds that use call options and financial futures to try for "enhanced yields," and market timing funds, whose prospectuses authorize them to liquidate all or most of their long-term securities and hold the money in Treasury Bills — in other words, funds that do your switching for you.

☐ Advice for Fund-Switchers

Two advisory services that give timing advice to fund-switchers were profiled in chapter 14 — James Schabacker's *Switch Fund Advisory* and Gerald Appel's *Systems and Forecasts.* Dick Fabian's *Telephone Switch Newsletter* (P.O. Box 2538, Huntington Beach, CA 92647; $117 a year) and *Professional Timing Service* (P.O. Box 7483, Missoula, MT 59801; $185 a year) also have yielded good results. In a study of buy and sell recommendations from 1980 to 1985, the *Hulbert Financial Digest* singled out one model portfolio in *Switch Fund Advisory* that would have more than doubled the market's performance and found that the other two services' recommendations would have nearly doubled the market. Services that track fund performance include *Switch Fund Advisory, Growth Fund Guide, The No-Load Fund Investor* (see chapter 14), and Burton Berry's *NoLoad Fund*X* (DAL Investment Co., 235 Montgomery Street, San Francisco, CA 94104; $95 a year). Norman Fosback's *Mutual Fund Forecaster* (3471 North Federal Highway, Fort Lauderdale, FL 33306; $100 a year) recommends specific funds for various investment strategies.

About 50 money managers specialize in handling fund-switching accounts. Some have already been mentioned (their addresses are given in chapter 14 or above): Gerald Appel, Burton Berry, Dick Fabian, and James Schabacker. *Money* magazine identified a number of others whose actual client statements for 62 months through September 1986 proved that the manager had outperformed the average untimed stock fund: J. D. Reynolds & Co. (706 Indian Hill Rd., Terrace Park, OH 45174), Portfolio Management Services (27001 East La Paz Rd., Suite 148, Mission Viejo, CA 92691), R. M. Leary & Co. (3300 East First Ave., Suite 380, Denver, CO 80206), Lincoln Investment Planning (Benson East, Suite 1000, Jenkintown, PA 19046), Portfolio Timing Inc. (402 Ranier Bank Building, 11th and Broadway, Tacoma, WA 98402), and R. Meeder & Associates (6000 Memorial Dr., Dublin, OH 43017). Annual fees usually start at 2 percent or 3 percent of the amount under management and step down on assets above $500,000. Some managers accept as little as $10,000; others require $100,000 and up. Anyone thinking of entrusting his money to a switch-fund manager should write to several of them for information about their investment strategy, performance record, and fee schedule; inclusion in the list we have given should not be construed as an endorsement.

☐ The Twenty-Five Top Performing Mutual Funds Over Three Time Periods

Percentage increase in net asset value assuming reinvestment of dividends and capital gains

(Source: *Lipper Analytical Services*)

15 YEARS: 3/31/72 TO 3/31/87

1. International Investors	1,776%
2. Twentieth Century Select	1,650
3. Fidelity Magellan	1,645
4. Twentieth Century Growth	1,559
5. Mutual Shares Corporation	1,413
6. Evergreen Fund	1,325
7. Templeton Growth	1,193
8. Sequoia Fund	1,186
9. Pioneer II	1,112
10. Fidelity Destiny I	1,111
11. Quasar Associates	1,061
12. American Capital Comstock	1,010
13. Over-the-Counter Securities	997

14. Fidelity Equity-Income	967
15. Oppenheimer Equity	929
16. Loomis-Sayles Capital	918
17. Windsor Fund	880
18. Amev Growth Fund	843
19. American Capital Pace	838
20. Weingarten Equity	816
21. New England Growth Fund	816
22. IDS Growth Fund	781
23. Charter Fund	766
24. Financial Industrial Income	765
25. Guardian Mutual	729

5 YEARS: 3/31/82 TO 3/31/87

1. Merrill Lynch Pacific	445
2. Fidelity Magellan	381
3. BBK International	379
4. Loomis-Sayles Capital	374
5. Vanguard World International Growth	355
6. Alliance Technology	348
7. Fidelity Select-Health	328
8. Putnam International Equities	324
9. New England Growth Fund	285
10. Vanguard Qualified Dividend I	284
11. Fidelity Destiny I	284
12. Weingarten Equity	283
13. Fairmont Fund	278
14. Guardian Park Avenue	278
15. T. Rowe Price International	277
16. Scudder International	273
17. Twentieth Century Select	269
18. Phoenix Growth	265
19. Phoenix Stock	265
20. Quasar Associates	262
21. United Income	261
22. Manhattan Fund	261
23. Alliance International	260
24. Investors Research	257
25. Lehman Opportunity	255

1 YEAR: 3/31/86 TO 3/31/87

1. New England Zenith Capital Growth	142
2. USAA Gold	120
3. Van Eck Gold/Resources	114
4. US New Prospector	106
5. Financial Portfolio-Gold	97
6. United Services Prospector	96

7.	IDS Precious Metals	94%
8.	Colonial Advanced Strategies Gold	93
9.	Vanguard Special-Gold	90
10.	Hutton Investors Series-Precious Metals	90
11.	Keystone Precious Metals	89
12.	United Services Gold Shares	89
13.	Midas Gold Shares and Bullion	88
14.	International Investors	85
15.	Franklin Gold Fund	83
16.	U.S. Boston International	82
17.	Strategic Investments	80
18.	Fidelity Select-Precious Metals	78
19.	Golconda Investors Ltd.	77
20.	Oppenheimer Gold and Specialty Minerals	76
21.	Merrill Lynch Pacific	74
22.	Lexington Goldfund	73
23.	Financial Portfolio-Pacific	71
24.	Fidelity Select-American Gold	70
25.	United Gold and Government	69

▪24 Going Global

For 30 years, master investor John Templeton preached the gospel of global investing. Why limit yourself to the American stock markets when prices were rising faster in foreign markets, he asked, or when other economies were growing faster than ours? To Templeton, investing abroad was just one more essential form of diversification. The performance of his Templeton Growth Fund supports his point. In the 15 years from 1972 through the first quarter of 1987, it compiled a total return of about 1,200 percent, seventh-best among all equity funds with that long a history. Most other American investors did not awaken to the benefits of global prospecting until much later, but by 1986 $45 billion dollars of American money was sitting in foreign stocks and bonds. That was a meteoric rise from $1 billion in 1980.

No portfolio can be considered adequately diversified these days unless some portion of it is invested in nondollar securities. Besides broadening your stock-picking horizon, foreign investing guards against one risk that Americans can no longer afford to ignore — sharp declines in the value of the dollar against other major currencies. The illusion of an almighty dollar blew apart when the United States became a debtor nation in 1985. That was the year in which the federal deficit reached the trillion-dollar mark and the year in which this country's obligations to foreign investors outgrew their obligations to us.

When a country becomes that dependent on overseas creditors, they gain the power to set — or at least strongly influence — the debtor nation's interest rates. It must bend its monetary policy to keep rates attractive to those creditors. That handicaps the debtor nation in its efforts to fend off inflation, which, in turn, makes its creditors uneasy and weakens its currency in foreign exchange markets. From 1985 to 1987, the dollar declined 37 percent against a market basket of major foreign currencies.

For American investors with assets abroad, a sagging dollar becomes a windfall. To buy shares on foreign stock exchanges, they had to convert dollars to the currencies used in those markets. If the dollar later falls in relation to those currencies, Americans can repatriate their money at a pretty profit. For example, a dollar bought 250 Japanese yen in 1985. About 15 months later, those 250 yen were worth $1.79. By repatriating their money at that point, American investors brought home 79 percent more money than they had sent to Tokyo. Furthermore, if the dollars they sent abroad were used to buy stocks representative of the Nikkae Average, Japan's equivalent of the Dow Jones Industrial Average, their winnings were much further enhanced. The Nikkae rose about 90 percent in those 15 months, fattening the Americans' repatriated take to $3.40 per dollar invested — a total gain of 240 percent.

Making money on foreign investments is seldom that easy, of course; world markets follow the same unpredictable turns that our markets do: *The dollar can strengthen as suddenly as it can weaken* even though the U.S. government, in concert with its major international trading partners, does everything in its power to stabilize this key currency.

Foreign stock markets are even harder to forecast than our own. Only Japan's total market capitalization, at $1.7 trillion in 1987, comes close to America's $2.2 trillion. By contrast, all the shares traded on the Copenhagen stock exchange were worth about $11 billion in 1987; Korean stocks were worth $13 billion; Spain's, $47 billion; West

Germany's, $246 billion; and England's, $440 billion. Huge international flows of funds in and out of small markets like those makes them extremely vulnerable to price shocks.

Information on foreign companies can be hard to come by and tricky to interpret. U.S. securities regulations require full and prompt disclosure of corporate income statements and balance sheets; few other countries try as hard to put all investors on an equal footing. Moreover, accounting and financial reporting rules in other countries do not always produce data comparable with ours. For example, by Dutch calculations of depreciation, the earnings of Heineken, Holland's largest brewery, are understated by nearly 40 percent in comparison with those of Anheuser-Busch; Heineken and many other Dutch companies therefore have misleadingly high price-earnings ratios.

It can be downright sticky executing trades on some foreign markets. At the extreme, some Americans have been kept waiting six months for confirmation of orders placed on the Milan stock exchange.

Struggling against all these handicaps, professional money managers on Wall Street have a tough time matching foreign stock performance indexes with their overseas portfolios. When *Barron's* measured the results of international mutual fund managers against Morgan Stanley's comprehensive Europe, Australia, Far East Index (EAFE) at the end of the first quarter of 1987, the financial weekly found most fund managers lacking. The world is, nonetheless, full of small and not-so-small companies with tantalizing growth potential. Their hunger for capital is propelling international financial reporting toward uniformity, while communication by space satellite is making instant transmission of this information a reality in the farthest corners of earth. The modern investor needs to know these global ropes. He can buy foreign securities on their own markets, though that takes wealth and first-rate brokerage connections. He can buy hundreds of foreign companies in the form of American Depositary Receipts, always referred to as ADRs, which are traded on U.S. exchanges. And he can invest abroad through American-based mutual funds.

☐ Mutual Funds

As with domestic markets for common stocks, mutual funds make foreign markets accessible to investors with little time to study them and insufficient assets to achieve diversification. Richard Murray, a senior vice president at the multinational investment firm of S. G. Warburg & Co., is not condescending when he says, "Small investors are wise to buy whole markets instead of individual foreign stocks — and this can be done only through a mutual fund." Even if your results fall short of world stock indexes, they will give you a piece of the action. In 1986, international funds as a group returned an average of 53.3 percent, nearly triple the total return on the S&P 500.

The minimum investment in a foreign-stock fund is often as little as $250 and seldom more than $2,500. With modest capital, therefore, anybody can take his first step into world investing. Foreign mutual funds can be roughly divided into three categories: *global funds,* whose franchise lets them mix foreign and domestic stocks in their portfolio; *international funds,* which invest only in foreign securities; and *single-country funds,* which usually operate as closed-end funds and are described in chapter 21. (A table of single-country closed-ends appears there.) Without labeling themselves global, many diversified growth funds began adding foreign stocks to their holdings in the mid-1980s. The global funds with the best long-term records, Putnam International Equities and Oppenheimer Global, showed total returns of 647 percent in the ten years through the first quarter of 1987, before adjustment for 8.5 percent sales charges.

Instead of letting a fund manager decide for you how much of your money to invest overseas, you can control that decision by investing in international funds. The international fund with the best ten-year return through March 31, 1987, was Merrill Lynch Pacific, which gained 878 percent before adjustment for a 6.5 percent sales charge. Four younger international funds with strong records and no sales charges are Vanguard World-International Growth, Financial Strategic-Pacific Basin, T. Rowe Price International, and Scudder International. An even younger fund — and the one with the most spectacular performance for the 12 months through March 31, 1987 — was Fidelity Overseas (3 percent load), with a 62 percent return. The no-load Nomura Pacific Basic fund ran a close second, returning 57 percent. An investor who wants to have a say in the parts of the world where his money will go can pick a Pacific Basin fund like Nomura's, Merrill Lynch's, or Financial Strategic's, which concentrate in the stock markets of Japan, Korea, Hong Kong, Singapore, Malasia, and Australia. Or he can assemble a portfolio of funds specializing in a single country. G. T. Japan Growth, for example, is a single-country no-load fund.

☐ American Depositary Receipts

The next step for investors beginning to feel at home abroad is to pick their own stocks. Many major Canadian, Israeli, and Philippine companies trade directly on U.S. stock markets; more than 600 other foreign companies trade as American Depositary Receipts, which are receipts issued by U.S. banks for one or more shares held by the bank (or a fraction of a share when the price of one share is higher than customary here). Among them are many South African gold mining stocks, which we discuss in the next chapter, and a goodly selection of large and small companies from many countries, representing a full range of industries.

Brokerage commissions on ADRs are the same as on U.S. stocks, and ADRs pay dividends, if any, in U.S. dollars. But in other respects you are on your own, without the rich flow of analysts' reports and quick financial information that is available about domestic companies. The most informative companies trading as ADRs are the 120 or so listed on the New York and American stock exchanges or registered with NASDAQ, the National Association of Securities Dealers Automated Quotations system, for over-the-counter trading. Most such companies must follow strict SEC financial reporting requirements. More important, you can find the prices of these ADRs in the newspapers, and you can buy and sell them as readily as domestic issues. With some 500 other ADRs, that cannot always be said. Like thousands of small American companies, their trading is managed by a few brokerage house market makers, and their prices are reported only in the Pink Sheets, a publication that circulates among brokers. Don't buy these ADRs before finding out how many brokers make a market in them. Unless at least eight do, you cannot count on sufficient liquidity to assure you of a ready market at a realistic price.

☐ Trading Abroad

Whether they are heavily or thinly traded, ADRs represent only two thirds of the companies on Morgan Stanley's Europe, Australia, Far East Index and less than 5 percent of the world's stocks. If you are determined to scout the far corners of the globe for undiscovered gems, you will need allies abroad. Don't try unless you have at least $50,000 to invest in the safari, and then look first for a special kind of broker. The big wirehouses have people here and there who are knowledgeable in international arenas. To find them, draw up a list of companies you might want to invest in, take it around to some of the major brokerage firms, and ask for someone who can help you with stocks like those. When you find someone who wants to work with you, make sure his firm has a trading office in each country you expect to invest in. Also discuss commissions and fees, which will be much higher than in the domestic markets. You will be paying an overseas broker as well as your local person, and there will be stiff costs of currency conversion.

25 Gold Isn't Just for Goldbugs

To John Maynard Keynes, gold was "the barbarous relic"; for Charles de Gaulle, it remained "the fiduciary value *par excellence.*" Embracing Lord Keynes's view, the U.S. Treasury — under Presidents Nixon and Carter — campaigned to downgrade gold's role in the international monetary sphere. And the Treasury conducted a series of gold auctions, which, it hoped, would be a depressant on the market — a curiously perverse policy for a nation that is by far the world's largest holder of gold; with every $10 swing in the gold price, the U.S. Treasury gains or loses more than two-and-a-half billion dollars. Fortunately for the United States, its antigold crusade flopped. The barbarous relic retained its fiduciary value; gold accounts for an overwhelming portion of the reserves of the world's central banks. And in the private sector, loss of faith in paper currencies has greatly enlarged the constituency whose motto is "In gold we trust."

Some members of the global gold Mafia are certainly not a lovable lot — the money men whose only allegiance is to their wealth, the oil sheikhs, and the American doomsayers promoting fear and paranoia for profit. But investors in gold now also include large numbers of Main Street Americans, who are simply looking for a trustworthy hedge against inflation. Ownership of gold bullion was made legal again for U.S. citizens at the close of 1974. And from that time to 1980, gold was indeed a good inflation hedge; its price rose 2½ times as much as the Consumer Price Index. But it didn't rise steadily. Like any other investment, gold has had severe setbacks. It declined from $187.50 an ounce at the end of 1974 to $103 in the fall of 1976, and at the close of 1978 its average annual gain over the previous four years was a puny 5 percent. Gold then soared in 1979 and early 1980, but in November 1981 its price was back to where it had stood about two years earlier, $399. From there it sank to a low of $284 in 1985 but took off again as the specter of inflation reappeared. By mid-1987, with the U.S. dollar in full retreat against major foreign currencies and the Consumer Price Index pointing skyward, gold again approached $500. Gold mining stocks were rising even faster, as evidenced by the one-year mutual fund performance table in chapter 23: for the 12 months that ended on March 31, 1987, gold funds dominated the top ranks. But as a *Fortune* study shows, just buying gold and holding it gives you no great talisman against the inflationary devil. From the time that gold ownership became legal in 1975 until May 1, 1987 — a period that encompassed some of the worst price inflation in American history, when consumer prices rose 120 percent — gold barely kept pace, rising 143 percent, while U.S. Treasury Bills produced a return of 171 percent and Standard & Poor's 500-stock index returned 646%. In short, gold is an inflation hedge only if you buy it when the price is right and sell it at profitable moments. So let's take a closer look at the anatomy and dynamics of the gold price.

Gold has a dual personality. It is what economists call a "store of value" and it is an industrial commodity used mainly in jewelry but also in dentistry and electronics. The industrial use of gold declines whenever the price rises; it was much lower in 1980 than in 1970. On the basis of an index of the price history of other nonferrous metals, gold, valued strictly as an industrial commodity, was probably worth about $325 an ounce in 1981. At that time, several leading gold analysts estimated that a likely floor for the gold price was about $350. Their principal reasons:

1. a price below $350 would probably induce strong buying from the central banks;
2. new production was shrinking: the non-Communist world's gold output of 943 metric tons in 1980 was 26 percent lower than in 1970.

Nearly three-quarters of this output came from South Africa,* where

---

* The Soviet Union is the world's second largest producer of gold, with an estimated annual output of 360 tons.

most of the mines have a remaining life expectancy of less than 20 years. So by the end of this century, gold in the ground may be in short supply.

While there is a basis for estimating the floor for the gold price, there's no telling what might be its ceiling. Some goldbugs predicted in 1980 that we would see a price of $3,000 before 1990. And we may — if some of the things that could go wrong for mankind do go wrong. The gold price, at least in the short run, can be a barometer of world anxiety. For example, fears triggered by the cutoff of Iranian oil, the taking of American hostages, and the Russian invasion of Afghanistan sent the gold price rocketing from below $400 to a peak of $850 on January 21, 1981. But after the price had slid back into the $300 range, even the prolonged war between Iran and Iraq, with its daily threats to oil tankers negotiating the Strait of Hormuz, did not set off a new flight to bullion. With oil selling below $20 a barrel, the sheikhs kept their billions in U.S. and Japanese treasury securities rather than entrust their riches to bullion. Nevertheless, bad news for humanity is usually good news for gold, and the converse holds true. An outbreak of peace and goodwill on this planet would cause a crash in the gold price.

Aside from the ebb and flow of political anxiety, the major determinant of the goal price is inflation — more specifically, the extent to which inflation prompts a flight from paper money (and investments such as bonds). Gold performs best when inflationary expectations are rising but interest rates are not yet in the stratosphere. Extremely high interest rates tend to depress gold because borrowing costs then become a deterrent to speculators who buy gold futures on margin. Moreover, gold, which produces no income, becomes less attractive to some investors when the yields on money-market securities are exceptionally high.

Since the inflation rate is strongly influenced by increases in energy costs, there exists at least a shaky correlation between the price of gold and the cost of a barrel of oil. In the first 12 years after gold ownership became legal again, the metal sold most of the time at 12 to 30 times the oil price. During placid periods in the gold markets, a gold/oil ratio of about 15 is considered normal. That ratio can be helpful in judging whether, at a given moment, gold seems to be significantly overpriced or underpriced. The problem is that the gold price has become so volatile that the ratio has tended to rise as high as 20 in times that previously would have been thought normal.

☐ Bullion vs. Stocks

The conventional wisdom is that most investors should consider putting 5 percent of their assets into gold and 15 percent or more when inflation looks particularly threatening. In addition to being a hedge against high inflation, gold investments usually hold up or rise in price when there is a big slump in the stock market; they are, in effect, a form of disaster insurance. The types of gold investment that best serve the purpose are the metal itself and bullion coins (which sell for about 4 percent to 10 percent more than the value of their gold content), gold mining stocks, and certain U.S. mutual funds. That list leaves out gold futures and collectors' coins. Trading in futures is a fast-track game, suitable only for experienced speculators with plenty of money. The leverage is tremendous; initial margin requirements for the standard 100-ounce contract are not more than 5 percent. Anyone speculating with less than $10,000 has sharply increased chances of loss, because he won't have sufficient reserves to ride out short-term fluctuations in the market. Collectors' coins — which have been one of the strongest hedges against inflation — have an altogether different drawback: they are valued for their rarity and condition more than for their gold content, so buying them calls for a high degree of expertise. If you don't have it, you should let yourself be guided by a reputable firm that specializes in numismatics. (Some are listed later in this chapter.) Commissions on rare coins are rather high but negotiable, ranging from 10 to 20 percent. And if the commission rate is abnormally small, the firm is probably making an extra large profit on the price of the coins.

The pros and cons of investing in gold through the metal or through mining stocks can be summed up as follows. Bullion and bullion coins produce no income, and their safekeeping may involve you in storage or insurance costs. Western Hemisphere mining stocks pay only trifling dividends, and the share prices have a tendency to exaggerate wildly the changes in bullion price. That leaves the ethically and financially difficult choice of whether or not to invest in South African mines. Most of the trusts that hold these shares used to pay annual dividend yields of 9 percent to as high as 20 percent, but in the mid-1980s they were paying in the 3 to 10 percent range. These payments are in effect a taxable return of capital, since a gold mine is a depleting asset. A conservative investor might prefer to own bullion or coins, because the risks in the stocks are significantly larger. So, too, are their potential rewards, however — especially when unrest or uprisings by the black majority in South Africa force the mines to shut down, depressing share prices. To an aggressive investor, the combination of high dividends and fear-driven share prices makes South African mines much more attractive than bullion. Gold mutual funds, along with a couple of closed-end funds, have most or all of their assets in mining stocks. Like other investment companies, they provide diversification and professional management — significant benefits for an inexperienced person investing in gold. Here are the specifics you need to know about each of these forms of gold investment.

☐ "Wafers" and Bullion Coins

The standard gold bar is one kilogram, 32.15 troy ounces. But bullion can be bought in smaller forms called "wafers," which come in a variety of sizes; those of one ounce and upward are better value than the smaller ones. Alternatively, for as little as $1,000, investors can own gold without taking possession of it. For example, Deak International, a dealer in currencies and precious metals, offers small investors the chance to buy gold or silver at regular intervals as a means of dollar-cost averaging (a strategy described in chapter 19). Under Deak's Precious Metals Storage Program, you make a minimum initial investment of $1,000 and then can add as little as $100 once every month, three months or year. Deak buys the metal on fixed dates — the second Wednesday of each month. Sales commissions are typically 3 percent or less, and there is an annual administrative charge of half of one percent of the value of your holdings. You also pay a fee to sell your gold: typically $10 plus a 1 percent commission. Similar programs are available at Dreyfus Gold Deposits Inc. and Citibank. And Richard C. Young, an investment adviser in Newport, Rhode Island, with a keen interest in precious metals, reports that small investors can apply to the Rhode Island Hospital Trust (401-278-7595) for certificates representing one ounce of gold or 50 ounces of silver tucked safely in a bank vault.

Bullion coins are official coins that typically sell for 4 percent or 5 percent more than the current value of their gold content, not including state sales tax. The most widely owned, until they were banned from the United States in 1986 as a protest against apartheid, was the

South African Krugerrand, which contains one troy ounce of gold. That same year the U.S. Treasury introduced its own one-ounce gold coin, the American Eagle, along with other sizes ranging from one-tenth of an ounce to 1.2 ounces. The Eagle became an immediate sellout. Other bullion coins include the Canadian Maple Leaf (1 ounce), the Mexican 50-peso (1.2056 ounces), the Chinese Panda (1 ounce), and the Austrian 100-corona (.9886 ounce). Bullion coins are traded by dealers in all major cities. Reputable dealers include Deak International, which has about 65 offices throughout North America (for information call the Washington, D.C., office, 800-424-1186), Numisco (1423 Fullerton Avenue, Chicago, IL 60614, 312-528-8000), Sinclair de Marinis (90 Broad Street, New York, NY 10004, 212-558-1037), and Dreyfus Precious Metals, Inc. (666 Old Country Road, Garden City, NY 11530, 800-544-4424/718-895-1330 in NY), an affiliate of Dreyfus Corp. Some major brokerage houses, including Prudential-Bache and Merrill Lynch, handle gold purchases. The commission rates on bullion and coins depend on the size of the order and vary somewhat from firm to firm; they range from slightly less to slightly more than commissions on stock trades. Deak, Numisco, and Sinclair de Marinis are also specialists in numismatics.

☐ The North American Golds

If you feel that the potential rewards of gold shares are worth the extra volatility of their market price in comparison with that of gold, most analysts wisely counsel choosing possible price appreciation over the higher but potentially unstable dividends from the mines of South Africa in troubled times there. In North America, the centerpiece operation of Newmont Gold, a 1986 spinoff from Newmont Mining, is Nevada's Carlin mine. The company, which trades on the New York Stock Exchange, has the potential to extract and process 30 or more tons of gold a year by 1990, according to Brad Heaston, manager of the no-load United Services New Prospector, a mutual fund specializing in North American mining. Another Nevada operation with lively prospects, Battle Mountain Gold, an over-the-counter company spun off by Penzoil in 1985, is producing more than eight tons of gold a year there and in Australia. And Echo Bay Mines, with producing mines near the Arctic Circle as well as in Nevada, was prospecting for gold in Washington State in 1987. Homestake Mining (New York Stock Exchange) operates a large high-cost mine in South Dakota; it has major production in California and joint ventures in Australia with Kalgoorli Mining Associates. But Homestake is not purely an investment in gold mining; a sizable chunk of its earnings comes from silver, lead, zinc, uranium, oil, and gas.

☐ South African Mines

The South African gold mining stocks are traded in the over-the-counter market through American Depositary Receipts (ADRs); their prices are quoted in the *Wall Street Journal.* A South African with-holding tax of 15 percent is deducted from the semiannual dividend, but U.S. residents can subtract the full amount of the tax from their U.S. income taxes. Because of the political risks in South Africa, its gold-mining shares sell at much lower valuations than North American gold stocks; they were priced at 10 to 15 times earnings in mid-1987 as against 30 to 50 times earnings for the Western Hemisphere golds. That makes South African mines extremely undervalued if you can overlook the political instability that besets this racially riven country and the hardening polarization of whites against blacks. To some Americans, no valuation could be low enough to overcome their ab-horrence for the white government's racial segregation policies.

The South African mines are generally grouped in three categories on the basis of the life expectancy of their proven reserves, their ore grade, and their extraction costs. Analyst Brad Heaston classifies them as follows:

☐ The Top-Quality Group
This group is made up of long-life (20 years and over) or medium-life (10 to 20 years) mines with low to moderate extraction costs; life expectancy is indicated by (L) or (M), and an asterisk signifies substantial production of uranium: Driefontein Consolidated (L), Hartebeestfontein (M*), Kloof (L), Freestate Con-solidated (L), Southvaal (L), Vaal Reefs (L*), Western Deep Levels (L*). Dr. Joseph Collender, a leading mining geologist, has called Vaal Reefs "without doubt the world's best mine."

☐ The Medium-Quality Group
Mines with a medium life expectancy and low to moderate costs, unless otherwise indicated, belong to the medium-quality group: Deelkraal, Doornfontein, Harmony* (high cost), Kinross, Libanon, Randfontein, Winkelhaak.

□ The Speculative Group

"Marginal" mines with a short life expectancy (less than ten years) and high extraction costs, unless otherwise indicated, belong to the speculative group: Blyvooruitzicht (medium cost), Bracken, Buffelsfontein,* Grootvlei, Leslie, Stilfontein (medium cost), Venterspost, Western Areas (M).

Long-term investors should stick to the top-quality group. The medium-quality issues tend to be somewhat more volatile and therefore offer larger profit potential in a bull market for gold. The earnings of the marginal mines are so leveraged that you make a killing in their stocks when gold stages a large advance and you will be killed in them when gold settles into a downtrend. Here's an example of how a stock in each of these groups performed in a strong up market — their gains are measured from their August 1986 lows to April 1987: Southvaal, 236 percent; Deelkraal, 246 percent; Venterpost, 221 percent.

□ Mutual Funds and Investment Companies

When you invest in gold mining, there is an added need for diversification; a mine's earnings can be slashed by natural disasters — fires, floods, cave-ins, but even a not-so-small investor putting 10 percent of his assets into gold stocks may not have enough money to diversify. So for many people the best way of owning these stocks is through a U.S. mutual fund or a South African investment company. Eight gold funds can be bought through brokers for a sales charge of 4 percent to 8½ percent; one low-load fund, the gold portfolio of the Fidelity Select group of sector funds, has a 2 percent sales charge; and ten others are no-loads (see Appendix B, Speciality Funds). In the ten-year period that ended March 31, 1987, Franklin Gold Fund (4 percent load) and US Gold Shares (no load) were the 13th and 14th best performers among all mutual funds.

Shares in South African closed-end investment companies are traded in the same way as stocks. For an investor who wants to own gold stocks and likes to keep things simple, ASA Ltd. is an unbeatable choice. It is listed on the New York Stock Exchange; it often sells at a discount from asset value; it pays hefty dividends when the gold price is high; and its put and call options are traded on the Amex. (Puts and calls on Homestake Mining trade on the Chicago Board Options Exchange.) Anglo-American Gold Investment Company, known as Amgold, has all the investment merits of ASA, except that it is a foreign company that is traded over the counter as an American Depositary Receipt (see chapter 24) and has no options. Both Amgold and ASA have been terrific performers during bull markets in gold. So if you want to speculate on a big advance in gold, just buy a call or two on ASA. (The use of puts and calls is discussed in chapter 26.)

□ A Side Glance at Silver

Buying silver rather than gold as an inflation hedge makes sense only when silver is sharply undervalued. There's a rough-and-ready way of determining this, according to Leroy S. Brenna, chairman of the Strategic Family of Funds in Dallas. In the recent past, the normal ratio of gold's price to silver's has been 32 to 1. When the ratio climbs to 37 to 1, silver is probably the better buy; when the ratio sinks to 24 to 1, silver is overpriced in relation to gold.

A popular though cumbersome silver investment has been bags containing $1,000 face value of U.S. silver coins (90 percent silver content) minted before 1965. These bags are available from bullion dealers, and they usually sell at a 25 percent premium over the market price of their silver content because the coins have some scarcity value. When silver bullion was selling for $7.80 an ounce in 1987, dealers were asking a bit less than $7,000 plus commission for a bag containing 720 ounces. A typical commission is 4 percent. A more convenient way of investing in silver is through bullion buying programs, which are similar to the gold programs described earlier; they are issued by Citibank, Deak, and others.

All silver mines also produce zinc, lead, and copper, so there are no pure silver investments in mining stocks. Three North American mining companies with major stakes in silver are Callahan Mining Corp. (New York Stock Exchange), Hecla Mining Co. (New York Stock Exchange), and Coeur d'Alene Mines (traded over the counter).

□ Precious Metals Options

No legitimate investment has been worse abused by charlatans than precious metals futures. Bucket shop operators, working the telephone circuits over long-distance WATTs lines from bases in Florida, Utah, and wherever else local regulators are lax, regularly dupe naive people out of their money. Never entrust money to a telephone salesperson, no matter how persuasive his pitch or how sincere his manner. The only way to venture into gold futures or other sophisticated speculations is through a broker you have met face to face who works for a well-established firm in good standing with the Better Business Bureau and the securities department in the state where the firm has its offices.

Options on futures contracts in gold and silver are traded on the Comex (short for the Commodity Exchange, Inc., in New York). They can be bought and sold through stockbrokers. Metals options are as complex as stock options and even more alluring to speculators prepared to blow their stake, because wide price swings have multiplied the potential for profit. *As with stock options (but not commodity futures themselves), you can't lose more than your initial investment. But you can occasionally double or even triple your money in a short time.*

26 The Uses and Abuses of Options

Option buying is a game in which incredible profits have been made; a Conoco option contract, in 1981, soared in value 5,000 percent in the space of a few months as a result of the bidding war for Conoco, eventually won by Du Pont. Despite scores of sensational episodes like that one, it is a near certainty that any option buyer reckless enough to keep all of his money in play all of the time will eventually wind up broke. What prudent investors should remember is that options are by no means simply an instrument for speculators shooting for maximum gains. They have a variety of uses in portfolio strategies; in particular, they can be a versatile and economical tool for managing risk.

The options market is an arcane world. An uninitiated reader who plunged into it without a map and a dictionary would soon find himself in a state of total confusion. So it is necessary to begin this chapter with a rundown of the basics — the terminology and mechanics of option trading.

An option is a contract, and there are just two kinds of option — a call and a put. A *call* gives its holder the right to *buy* — a *put* gives its holder the right to *sell* — exactly 100 shares of a particular stock (or 100 units of a stock index) at a specified price during the stated lifetime of the option. The stock named in the contract is referred to as the *underlying stock* — a term that will be used throughout this chapter. The price specified is known as the *exercise* or *strike* price. Throughout most of the 1980s, no specific stock underlay most option trades; instead, action focused on whole indexes of stocks representing the market as a whole. With index options, contracts give the holders a stake in the rise or fall of equities worth 100 times the present or anticipated level of an index such as the S&P 500 or an abbreviated representation of that index, the S&P 100, designed exclusively for option trading.*

The life of an option on a stock is never more than nine months, but it may be a few weeks or even days.† The price that an option buyer pays, and a seller receives, is called the *premium,* and it is quoted in newspaper option tables on a per-share basis; if the premium is $4, the cost of a contract is $400, plus the broker's commission of about $25. (The commission rates on option transactions vary greatly. They depend on the size of the premium, the number of contracts traded, and the tariff scale of the particular brokerage house.)

Every option contract bought is a contract sold by another investor, who is known as the option writer. An option writer profits when the option he has sold expires worthless or worth less than the premium he received. For example, the writer of a call with a strike price of $45 and a premium of $3 per share ($300 per contract) will

---

* In April, 1987, for example, 18.7 million option contracts changed hands on the nation's biggest options exchange, the CBOE, about 12 million were puts and calls on the S&P 100 or S&P 500.

† The options on some bonds extend for 11 months.

pocket $300 if the price of the underlying stock is $45 or less at the option's expiration date. The put writer makes his profit in the same way, except that a put becomes worthless when the price of the underlying stock is at or *above* the strike price at the expiration date. A call *buyer* is betting that the underlying stock or stock index will rise; if it does, he exercises his option by requiring the writer of an identical call to sell him the stock at the predetermined (lower) strike price. A put *buyer* is betting that the underlying stock will go down; if it does, he exercises his option by requiring a writer of that particular put to buy the stock from him at the predetermined (higher) strike price. *But in most option transactions, stock does not actually change hands.* Buyers (and often writers) simply trade their contracts on an options exchange.

Before 1973, options trading was a small-scale business, handled by over-the-counter dealers. This situation was revolutionized when, on April 26, 1973, the Chicago Board Options Exchange opened the first formal public options market in history. Later, the American, Pacific, and Philadelphia exchanges introduced options trading, and even the New York Stock Exchange now lists options on a handful of stocks. In 1987, puts and calls were available on about 500 stocks, including nearly 60 over-the-counter issues.

The options exchanges bring together buyers and sellers in the same way a stock exchange does. An option buyer can, at any time before the expiration date, sell his contract to another investor on the exchange on which it is traded. Similarly, an option writer can "close out" his contract — at a profit or a loss, depending on the price behavior of the underlying stock — by buying an identical contract at its current market price from another investor. (This process is similar to "covering" a short sale of stock. See the definition of short sale in Appendix D.) However, there is a fundamental difference between the stock and options markets. The stock market is not a finite universe; when stock prices rise, investors collectively get richer. In the options market, *gains made by buyers represent losses for writers, and vice versa.* * In fact, option trading is not a zero sum but a minus sum game;

---

* A call writer who owns the underlying stock may — even though he loses money on the option transaction — make a net profit if the stock rises sharply; his gain on the stock can be larger than his loss on the option.

out of every $100 that enters the market, $97 or less is returned to investors — the balance is siphoned off in commissions collected by the brokerage firms. In short, when you play the options game, you are pitting your judgment and your luck against those of the other participants.

An option is a wasting asset — the closer it approaches its expiration date, the lower is its time value. On any given day, the options traded on a particular stock have three different expiration dates, each of them three months away from the next. Some stocks have options that expire in January, April, July, and October; others have options that expire in February, May, August, and November; and for others, the cycle is March, June, September, and December. The longest possible expiration time is nine months. So in March, an investor buying an option with a January-April-July-October cycle has the choice of options expiring in April, July, and October. When an option expires — say, the April one — trading in a new option with a nine-month life begins; in this case, it would be the January one.

The actual day on which options expire is the Saturday following the third Friday of the month named in the contract. But the Friday (or, if it's a holiday, the day before) is the deadline for exercising your option — that is, using it to buy or sell the underlying stock. On four Fridays each year, contracts for stock index futures expire, along with options on individual stocks and the S&P 500 stock index. During the first and last 60 minutes of such days, arbitrageurs and managers of huge institutional portfolios take their profits on hedged positions and sell their unprofitable contracts. So chaotic is trading at such times and so volatile do stock prices become that Wall Streeters call these *triple witching hours.*

As we have already noted, the majority of options are not exercised. Except in cases where an investor owns the stock on which he has sold an option, exercising an option requires two transactions and costs the investor two brokerage commissions. To cash in his profit by exercising, a call buyer has to purchase the underlying stock from the option writer and then turn around and sell it on the stock market. And a put buyer has to purchase the underlying stock on the stock market and then sell it to the option writer. It is far more convenient, and usually more economical, for option buyers to take their profit simply by selling their contract on an options exchange. For option writers, too, it may be advantageous to close out a contract by buying the same contract (at its current market price) instead of waiting for its expiration date. A case in point: a call writer who is losing money because the underlying stock has risen substantially above the strike price. By closing out his contract on an options exchange, this writer can avoid the potentially greater loss he might suffer by waiting until just before the option expires, at which point it will be exercised against him. However, an option writer cannot close out a contract once he has received notice from his broker that the option has been exercised by its holder; when that happens, a call writer is forced to deliver the stock itself and a put writer is forced to take delivery of the stock.

When you buy or write an option, you usually have the choice of several strike prices. The intervals between them are $2.50 for stocks selling below 25, $5 for stocks selling from 25 to 200, and $10 for stocks above 200. When trading in a new option is introduced, the initial strike prices will be somewhat above and below the price of the underlying stock; if the stock's price is 32, the strike prices will be 30 and 35. But if the stock is selling at or very close to a round multiple of 5 — say, 30 — there will be three strike prices; 25, 30, and 35.

As the stock's price rises or falls, new strike prices are created by the options exchanges. Thus, on June 4, 1987, when Allegis, the holding company for United Air Lines and other travel-related businesses, was the target for rival takeover offers from an outside bidding syndicate and its own pilots, the stock closed at 87⅝, after having traded as low as 60 in mid-May. On that June day, there were Allegis call options with strike prices of $55, $60, $65, $70, $75, $80, $85, $90, and $95. A call option whose exercise price is below the market price of the stock is said to be "in the money" because it has an intrinsic cash value; with Allegis selling at 87⅝, the $80 call had a cash value of $7.67, and the $75 call had a cash value of $12.67. Similarly a put option is "in the money" when its exercise price is above the market price of the stock. An "at-the-money" option is one whose strike price is the same as the price of the stock.

The principal factors that determine options premiums are five.

1. **The current price of the underlying stock or index in relation to the strike price of the option, together with the length of time remaining until the option expires.** The farther the strike price is in the money, the greater is the option's cash value; in addition, the

option has a time value, which depends on its remaining life span. If an option is out of the money, it has no cash value, but it has a time value. For options with the same expiration date, the farther out of the money the strike price, the lower will be the premium; if a stock is selling at $42, you would obviously pay less for the right to buy it at $50 within the next six months than you would for the right to buy it at $45 within the same period. And for out-of-the-money options with the same strike price, the closer the expiration date, the lower will be the premium.

2. **The volatility of the underlying stock or index.** The options of stocks with large price swings command high premiums because they offer greater profit potential within a given period than the options of more stable stocks.

3. **Crowd psychology.** When investors are predominantly bullish, the demand for calls increases, causing premiums to rise. When pessimism prevails, premiums on calls decline and those on puts rise.

4. **The level of interest rates.** In principle, high interest rates strengthen the incentive for buying calls rather than buying the stocks itself, because the option ties up less money; consequently, premiums tend to be larger when interest rates are high. Conversely, higher interest rates depress the price of puts.

5. **The level of dividends.** As dividend yields increase, the value of a call is likely to fall and the value of a put is likely to rise. That's because dividend payments tend to reduce stock prices temporarily when the stock goes ex-dividend.

There are complicated formulas for determining whether a particular option is overpriced, underpriced, or fairly priced, but fortunately amateur investors have no need to master them. The options departments of major brokerage houses provide option valuations, which are usually based on the Black-Scholes Model (developed by Fischer Black and Myron Scholes) or are read off a computer terminal of the Options Monitor Service, a service sold to brokers by Standard & Poor's.

Now that you have a handle on the basics, you should have no trouble understanding the options tables in your daily newspaper. In the table below, the price under the name of the stock is its last closing price on the New York Stock Exchange; the several prices in the first column are the available strike prices; the headings "Calls-

Chicago Board

Option & NY Close	Strike Price	Calls-Last Aug	Calls-Last Nov	Calls-Last Feb	Puts-Last Aug	Puts-Last Nov	Puts-Last Feb
AlexAl	22½	2½	r	r	r	¾	r
24¾	25	⅝	r	r	r	2¼	r
24¾	30	⅛	r	1	r	r	r
Allegis	55	r	r	s	r	⅛	s
94	60	r	r	s	1/16	r	s
94	65	30½	r	r	1/16	r	r
94	70	24	27	r	r	r	r
94	75	20	r	r	1/16	r	r
94	80	14¾	17	19¼	3/16	11/16	1
94	85	10	14	r	⅜	1	2¼
94	90	5½	9½	r	1 1/16	2½	r
94	95	2 1/16	5¼	r	2½	4½	r
94	100	¾	3⅝	5½	r	7¼	7½
Amdahl	30	9½	r	r	r	r	r
38⅞	35	5¼	r	r	7/16	1½	r
38⅞	40	1⅞	3¼	4½	2½	r	r
38⅞	45	7/16	r	r	r	r	r
AlnGrp	65	3¾	r	r	9/16	r	r
67¾	70	1½	4	r	r	r	r
67¾	75	r	2½	3¾	7	r	8¼
67¾	80	r	1	s	r	r	s
Amoco	75	12¾	13½	s	r	r	s
87½	80	r	r	11	¼	r	2
87½	85	4	6½	r	1 5/16	2¾	3¾
87½	90	1¼	3½	5	3¾	5½	r
87½	95	r	1⅝	2⅞	r	r	r
AMP	50	r	r	r	1/16	r	r
59⅞	55	5¾	7¼	r	r	1⅞	r
59⅞	60	2⅛	4¼	r	2¼	r	r
59⅞	65	9/16	r	r	r	r	r
Anadrk	25	r	r	r	r	½	r
30¼	30	r	3	r	r	r	r
Baxter	15	9¾	s	s	r	s	s
24½	20	4¾	5	5¾	r	3/16	r
24½	22½	2½	3	4	r	½	⅞
24½	25	⅝	1⅝	2 5/16	1	1½	1⅞
24½	30	1/16	7/16	15/16	r	r	r
Blk Dk	20	5	r	r	r	r	r
25	22½	2⅝	3¼	r	⅛	r	r
25	25	⅞	2	3	1⅛	1⅝	r
25	30	3/16	⅝	1⅛	r	r	r
Boeing	40	r	r	r	r	⅜	r
47½	45	3¼	4¼	6	9/16	1½	1⅞
47½	50	⅝	2⅛	3¼	3⅜	3¾	4½
47½	55	⅛	¾	s	r	r	s

Source: Wall Street Journal, July 21, 1987

Last" and "Puts-Last" refer to the last closing prices of the options expiring in the months named in the next bank of headings. The letter r means that the option was not traded that day; s indicates that no option is available for that exercise price.

☐ Opening an Options Account

A prospectus of the Options Clearing Corporation, an excellent manual on options trading, cautions that "both the purchase and writing of options involve a high degree of risk and are not suitable for many investors." Brokerage firms are required by the SEC to send this prospectus to an investor who wishes to open an options account. With it the brokerage house must mail a "qualification form," on which the investor states his objectives, age, income, and net worth. To qualify for options trading you must not only be willing to take risks, you must also indicate that you are able to afford them. If you plan to write so-called uncovered or naked options — that is, to sell calls and puts without owning the underlying stock — you will be required to maintain at all times a minimum equity in a margin account; the amount typically ranges from $10,000 to $25,000, depending on the brokerage house. The reason for this is that, if a naked call is exercised, the writer has to buy the stock in order to sell it (at the strike price) to the call owner — and there's no telling how much the writer stands to lose. Suppose, for example, that you write two naked at-the-money calls on a stock selling at $40, the stock then soars to $60, and the option is exercised. You have to cough up 50 percent of $12,000 (plus a commission of $190) to buy the stock on margin, and your loss on your sale price of $8,000 is $4,190, minus the option premium of perhaps $900.

☐ Options for Offense and Defense

There are literally dozens of option strategies, some of them highly esoteric. In program trading, a strategy used by arbitrageurs at major investment banking firms, traders using computers try to profit from price discrepancies between option and future contracts on stock market indexes and the individual stocks that make up those indexes.

We will confine this discussion to relatively uncomplicated strategies that can help to improve the performance of an investor actively involved in managing his portfolio. The greatest value of options is their convenience and their versatility as a tool for increasing or decreasing your exposure to risk, in accordance with your state of confidence about the market. Here is a closer look at some of the ways in which options can be used aggressively and defensively.

☐ Buying Calls

You usually buy a call when you expect a stock to rise sharply but wish to limit the amount you could lose if you are wrong. For example, instead of investing $5,925 (plus a commission of $140) in 300 shares of a stock selling at $19.75, you might buy eight calls with a strike price of $20 for $800, plus a $50 commission. (In this example, the premium is $1, so the cost of one contract is $100.) If the stock rises from $19.75 to $22, your eight option contracts with a strike price of 20 would be worth about $1,600,* whether you exercise them or sell them on the options exchange on which they are traded. Your profit (before brokerage commissions) would be $750: 88 percent on your investment of $850. That's eight times the percentage gain you would have made by owning the stock. Moreover, the most you could have lost on the options was $850; had the stock dropped to $14.75, a holder of 300 shares would have had a $1,640 loss ($1,500 plus the original $140 commission). The big drawback is that you lose all of the money invested in an option premium unless the stock rises above the strike price, and you don't break even until the stock rises above the strike price plus the price per share of the option. In the example above, that adds up to $12.75, a price at which an investor who has bought the stock itself at $19.75 has a gain of 5 percent.

The lure of buying options is leverage; when the underlying stock rises, the price of its calls goes up much faster in percentage terms. In one seven-week period in which Texas Instruments stock rose 36

---

* We have assumed that the options are about to expire. They would be worth more than $2,700 if they had some time remaining.

percent, the price of its April $90 call shot up 850 percent. While that kind of gain is exceptional, it is not exceptional for a call on a stock that goes up 30 percent to rise in value 200 percent. Nonetheless, you should buy a call for speculative profit only when you strongly believe the underlying stock will soon rise sharply. And however confident you are, remind yourself before you act that the odds are against call buyers. The average premium on at-the-money, six-month calls has ranged from roughly 7 percent to 11 percent of the prices of the underlying stocks. Since stock prices often don't rise that much in half a year or less, a large majority of calls expire valueless or at a lower price than the buyer paid for them. However, call buyers can signifi-cantly improve their chances of making money by observing the fol-lowing precepts:

1. Buy when you think a market decline appears to have bottomed or when there has been a setback in what you believe to be a genuine bull market; in the latter case, pick stocks that have come down sharply but were previously among the strongest per-formers.
2. Don't pay exorbitant premiums; ask your broker whether his valuation model shows the premium to be fairly priced.
3. Don't place at-the-market orders, which will result in your paying whatever premium is currently being asked. Place a "limit" order; the limit you set might be the price of the last sale or else the current bid price.
4. Select a strike price that is the same as, or not more than slightly above, the market price of the stock. Buying calls that are far out of the money is like betting on rank outsiders at the racetrack; your losses are likely to be so frequent that they won't be offset by the occasional bonanza.
5. Don't buy deep-in-the-money calls — for example, a call exercis-able at 40 on a stock selling at 49. Deep-in-the-money options are expensive, because you are paying for the intrinsic cash value of the call, and they offer limited profit potential. *There's an excep-tion to this rule:* deep-in-the-money calls make sense if your policy is to invest in large, well-established companies whose stocks are out of favor and are selling at low price/earnings ratios. Since such stocks tend to be relatively stable, the risk of losing all of the option premium is slight, and any rise in the price of the

stock will be matched, dollar for dollar, in the value of the option. Buying deep-in-the-money calls on unpopular, low P/E stocks is a preferable alternative to buying those stocks on margin; the advantage is that you put up less money for an option contract than for 100 shares bought on margin and you don't incur the high interest charges on money borrowed from your broker.

There's a simple strategy involving the purchase of calls that might appeal to a conservative investor with upward of $25,000. Instead of putting, say, 65 percent of his assets into a money-market fund and 35 percent into stocks, he would keep 90 percent of his assets in a money fund and use the balance to buy calls on a stock index. This would provide him with a high degree of security at all times, plus the possibility of handsome profits in a rising market. According to one scholarly study covering a 12-year period through December 1975, a hypothetical portfolio with 90 percent of its funds in money-market securities and 10 percent invested in calls on the 30 Dow Jones industrials achieved a significantly higher total return than a portfolio fully invested in the Dow stocks. Dow Jones refuses to let options exchanges base contracts on its averages, but the S&P 100 option makes a perfectly adequate substitute.

Calls can also be used for protective reasons — for example, in the following situation: You have large gains in a stock and you are uncertain whether it is due for a fall or whether it could climb substantially higher. By selling the stock and simultaneously buying a call on it, you can realize your gain without sacrificing the possibility of further profit. If the stock continues to rise, you make money on the call; if the stock drops sharply, your loss — the call premium — is likely to be smaller than the loss you would have suffered by holding the stock.

☐ Buying Puts

A put, let us remind you, is the opposite of a call; it gives you the right to *sell* 100 shares of a particular stock — or 100 times the value of a stock index — at a specified strike price within the life of the option. You buy a put for speculative profit when you are confident the price of the underlying stock or market of stocks will drop. As a bearish strategy, buying puts is generally preferable to selling short; the put buyer's risk is limited to the option premium, whereas a short seller's losses can be catastrophic (and he must pay dividends to the owner of the borrowed stock). Except when sentiment is emphatically bearish, puts are cheaper than calls for several reasons, one being that, historically, stock prices have risen about two-thirds of the time. Aside from the fact that you are seeking to anticipate declines instead of advances, the precepts for buying puts are the same as those for buying calls.

Puts have a variety of defensive uses. For example, puts can be helpful if you have become apprehensive but have reasons for being reluctant to sell: You may own stocks bought or inherited long ago at such low prices that the capital gains tax on your profits would be huge; or you may simply be holding stocks that you consider attractive for the long haul. In such situations, buying puts on your stocks can be a relatively inexpensive form of insurance. If the stocks take a tumble, your losses will be partially offset by the gains on your puts. And if the stocks rise, your portfolio gains are likely to be larger than your losses on the option premiums. Institutional money managers with large portfolios to protect habitually buy puts on a stock index and call them "portfolio insurance."

Buying puts on stocks you don't own is another defensive strategy worth considering when you are turning bearish but are not bearish enough to want to sell. The big advantage is that you can either select issues you consider particularly vulnerable should the market decline, or you offset losses on the market as a whole by purchasing puts on the S&P 100.

□ Selling Naked Options

Since the odds are against option buyers, it follows that they are favorable to option writers. Nonetheless, writing options on stocks you don't own is a high-risk strategy, because it exposes you to potentially catastrophic losses. For example, on February 24, 1981, when Ford Motor stock was selling at 19½, the premium on the Ford March call with a strike price of 20 was 62½ cents. At the expiration date Ford stock had jumped to $25 and the March contracts were worth $5 a share, or $500 each. So a speculator who had sold 50 naked calls for a total premium of $3,125 had to cover them at a cost of $25,000.

An option writer may at any time have the option exercised

against him. Consequently, writers of naked options, in addition to maintaining a minimum equity of $10,000 to $25,000 in a margin account, must deposit in the account as much as 25 percent of the price of the underlying stock, plus (if the option is in the money) or minus (if the option is out of the money) an amount based on the difference between the market price and the strike price. Any marginable security may be used to meet this requirement.

The risks of writing naked options can be substantially reduced by closing out a losing contract as soon as the premium goes to a predetermined price. But, all in all, the writing of naked options is a strategy best left to highly sophisticated traders. There is, however, one fairly common situation in which any investor might find it advantageous to write a naked put. You have decided to buy XYZ stock, selling at 63, if it drops to 60. Instead of just waiting, watching, and hoping, you sell for $200 a naked put exercisable at 60. If XYZ doesn't drop to 60, you pocket the $200, presumably with no regrets because 60 was the most you wanted to pay for the stock. On the other hand, if XYZ declines to, say, 58, the shares will be sold to you by the put buyer at 60, and your actual purchase price, taking into account the premium, will be only $58. Even if XYZ sinks as low as 54, the option ploy has been successful; it has saved you $200 because your original intention was to buy at 60. Selling a naked put is an effective way to bid on a stock that you want to buy at less than its current market price.

☐ Selling Covered Calls

Writing calls on stocks you own is a conservative strategy widely used by institutions and also by income-oriented investors. Covered call writing is often wrongly touted as a strategy that both lessens risk *and* produces increased income. Clearly, the premium that a writer collects must be regarded *either* as a reduction in the cost of his investment, and therefore a protection against loss, *or* as an addition to income; it can't be both. The effect of writing covered calls is either to reduce risk *and* lessen potential reward, or to increase income and leave risk unchanged.

Amateurs who plan to write covered options should own or buy stable, blue-chip stocks with relatively low price/earnings ratios. The losses they could suffer on volatile, high P/E issues could greatly exceed the option premiums, and the possibility of large rewards has been forfeited by writing the call. Indeed, if the stock price soars, a covered-call writer finds himself in a distressing situation; either he must close out the contract at a substantial loss, or the call will be exercised and he will have to part with his stock at the strike price. With low-beta, blue-chip stocks, there's relatively little risk of a quick, dramatic runup in the price.

At times when stock prices are moving sideways or are not advancing rapidly, a call writer can get an annual return (including dividends) of 18 percent to 20 percent and sometimes more on a portfolio of blue-chip stocks. And under those market conditions, he may not have to part with any of his holdings, because relatively few calls will be exercised. But those numbers tell only one side of the story; they focus on yields and ignore the overall long-term performance of the portfolio. While mutual funds that write covered calls have sometimes done relatively well when the market was sluggish, their records over the long haul have generally been uninspiring. One scholarly study of the results of writing covered calls over a 12-year period found that the total return on the portfolio — income plus net gains or minus net losses — was 4 percent lower than the return the stocks would have provided had the options not been written, even without considering the commissions involved in the options transactions. That shouldn't be surprising; writing covered calls provides protection, which doesn't come free — the price you pay for it over the long term is diminished performance. For conservative investors who are strongly income-oriented, the writing of covered calls makes sense, though it should probably be avoided after stock prices have suffered a serious decline. It is not, however, the panacea that it is sometimes represented to be.

☐ Ploys for the Pros

Expert players in the options game trade combinations of options in which they like to think the odds are in their favor whether the stock rises or falls. "Straps" and "strips" are combinations of puts and calls on the same stock with the same strike price and expiration date. A "straddle" combines a put and a call on the same stock, each exercisable or salable separately and both having the same strike price. A "spread" involves the purchase of one option and the sale of another on the same stock, each having a different strike price or expiration date. A certain type of spread is derisively known as an alligator spread, because the commissions involved will eat you alive. The same can be said for most option combinations, if they are used regularly. So leave these ploys to the option buffs, who play around with complex valuation formulas and enjoy doing things the hard way.

□ Sources of Information

A neophyte who plans to engage in options trading would be well advised to do some further study before laying his money on the line. By far the best book on options for the amateur investor is *The New Options Market* (New York: Walker and Company, 1987, paperback $14.95) by Max G. Ansbacher, a top authority on options and an associate director in the New York City office of the Bear, Stearns & Company brokerage firm. A beginner can also learn a lot from the literature on options trading that is available free of charge. Booklets issued by the Chicago Board Options Exchange include *Understanding Options* and *S&P 100 Index Options: The Index Edge.* They are obtainable free from the CBOE (Marketing Services Department, 400 South LaSalle St., Chicago, IL 60605). You can also get a booklet called *Characteristics and Risks of Standardized Options,* prepared jointly by the options exchanges and the Options Clearing Corporation and distributed free by the Options Clearing Corporation (200 South Wacker Drive, Chicago, IL 60606). A similar assortment of pamphlets is published and distributed free by the American Stock Exchange (86 Trinity Place, New York, NY 10006). Your broker may hand out one or more of these useful guides.

Some brokerage houses put out explanatory reports on options strategies with current trading recommendations. In addition, there are any number of options advisory services, some of them garbage but some of them excellent. You can get sample copies of 20 options advisory services for $18 from Select Information Exchange, 2095 Broadway, New York, NY 10023.

27 Playing the New Issues Game

The market in new issues — companies making their first public offering of stock — is the most speculative sector of the stock market. It booms when speculative fever rises, slumps when investors turn cautious, and collapses when bearishness prevails. In 1969, 1972, and again in 1983, runaway speculation in new issues culminated in crashes that inflicted murderous losses on investors and cast a pall on the underwriting business. The new-issues market became a wasteland, but it was reborn in 1985, and in 1987 it remained a speculator's paradise. Investors fortunate enough to pick front-runners among the newcomers make handsome profits literally overnight and gains of 50 percent or more in months. *Money* magazine followed the course of all 360 initial public offerings (IPOs in Street parlance) underwritten by brokerage houses in 1985; it identified seven issues that had doubled or tripled by the end of the year. So spectacular was the new issues market that 71 percent of 1985's IPOs were selling above their initial offering price on December 31.

Over longer periods, however, most who speculate in new issues are not adequately rewarded for the extra risk they take. When the 1,577 IPOs launched from 1980 through 1985 were lumped together in the *Money* study, their average six-year gain was only 27.5 percent, while the S&P stocks over the same time spans appreciated by 35.1 percent.* Expressed in terms of annual growth, IPOs rose 9.8 percent to the S&P's 14.6 percent. Since new issues are by definition the riskiest of stocks, investors in them were actually penalized over time for taking the added risk.

Furthermore, in 1986 the Reagan administration reneged on a commitment to foster the revival of American industries through tax incentives for business expansion and private investment. The Tax

---

* *Money* limited its study to IPOs whose sales were underwritten, or brought to market, by the investment banking arms of brokerage houses. Excluded were so-called best-efforts offerings, in which the underwriter does not risk its own capital, and unit offerings consisting of common stock plus warrants, which are difficult to value accurately over time.

Reform Act of 1986 ended, with Ronald Reagan's approval, the tax-favored treatment of long-term capital gains and new investments in plant, equipment, research, and development. Thus died a public policy of helping new ventures to survive their infancy and inducing people to invest in them when they are ready to go public. Even so, the forward sweep of technology and social change has continued to vitalize the new-issues market by providing a flow of offerings by enterprises that are trailblazers in the new technologies and needed services. Such firms have the kind of dramatic growth potential that puts stars into investors' eyes.

Make no mistake about it: buying new issues is a speculative game. From time to time, the owners of a large and long-established private company finally decide to go public, as did the owners of Ford Motor in 1956 and Fireman's Fund Insurance in 1985. But the majority of newcomers to the public market are young firms with a brief history of profitability. Indeed, some of them have not yet turned a profit and some never will. When new issues are booming, companies too questionable for blue-ribbon underwriters to touch have little trouble finding unexacting sponsors.

Even IPOs of genuine substance — an impressive record of business performance, a respectable balance sheet, and well-defined prospects — tend to be overvalued in relation to comparable companies in the same industry that have been publicly traded for some time. The price/earnings ratios of the stocks in *Money*'s six-year survey averaged 35 on offering day as against 10 for the S&P. Remember, too, that about 7 percent of the offering price doesn't wind up in the company's coffers; it goes to the underwriters and to the brokerage firms that join the syndicate formed to market the issue.

So much for the necessary caveats. Here, now, is a short guide to how to handle yourself in this treacherous, intriguing, and sometimes enormously profitable sector of the market.

When investors learn of a new issue that the Wall Street grapevine says is hot — typically a classy high-tech company — the demand for shares usually runs way ahead of supply. For most investors, getting stock in the original offering is considerably tougher than securing choice seats to a new Broadway hit at short notice. Even huge financial institutions have to be satisfied with a modest number of shares. If you do business regularly with a broker, he may be able to scrounge some shares for you provided that

1. he does enough business to have pull with his branch-office manager;
2. the branch is important enough to have pull with the firm's syndicate department, which allots new issues;
3. the firm is a member of the selling group that has teamed up to market the issue.

If those provisos are not met, your chances of getting in on a ballyhooed offering are nil. When Genentech, the highly publicized genetic-engineering company, was marketed in October 1980, one medium-sized New York brokerage house was allotted just 100 shares; two customers, selected by lot, received 50 shares each. Offered at $35, Genentech started trading over the counter at $80, up 129 percent.

If you miss out on a sought-after offering, you can still buy it in the aftermarket — that is, when the shares start trading over the counter. And at times when the general market is weak, the price you pay may be no higher than when the stock first came out. Avantek, a high-growth electronics firm, hit the market at $14 a share during the market slump of October 1978 and traded at or below $14 for some time; two years later it was selling at $47 after a two-for-one split ($94 on the original basis).

But when the stock market is strong, stellar issues often start trading at 20 percent to 30 percent above their offering prices. A prime example is Microsoft, the software company whose disk operating systems run millions of IBM personal computers and their clones. Introduced on March 13, 1986, at $21 a share, the stock immediately traded over the counter at $25.75, up 22.6 percent. Its closing price that first day, $27.75, was 32 percent above the initial offering price. Moreover, the valuations of hot new issues are apt to be several times the average valuation of stocks in general. So buying a favorite issue that is off and running is putting your faith in the greater fool theory, which holds that there will always be a bigger fool than you around to buy the stock at a higher price.

A much more prudent policy, one that has worked well for patient and vigilant investors, is to keep track of choice new issues in hope of catching them if and when they take a tumble. A slump in the market creates such opportunities. Or a new issue may dive because the company reports disappointing earnings. For example, Floating Point

Systems, a maker of special-purpose computers, came out at $18 a share in September 1978 and dropped to $8.50 after the company reported a fourth-quarter loss; 33 months later the stock was selling at $59. Buying a previously hot issue that has turned cold works out well only if the earnings disappointment proves temporary, but the risks involved are usually lower than when you reach for winners selling at their peaks.

While the hard-to-buy issues get all the hoopla, they represent only the slim top tier of the new-issues market. Offerings that have substance but don't put stars into investors' eyes make up the middle tier. Decent middle-tier offerings are usually not difficult to buy. A sharp-eyed stock picker can find good long-term investments among them, and they tend to be less risky than top-tier ones because of their much less elevated valuations. Occasionally, they become instant winners in the aftermarket. For example, Control Resource Industries, which makes air filtration systems, was marketed on July 31, 1985 at $2.50 (adjusted for a subsequent 2-for-1 stock split) and was selling at $7.50 on December 31; in the same year, Centrafarm Group, a pharmaceuticals marketer, jumped from its offering price of $10 to $20.75 in less than a year.

The third or bottom tier of the market is the habitat of the nickel-and-dime issues, typically energy or precious metals exploration ventures. Many bottom-tier issues are Regulation A or "best efforts" offerings. Regulation A of the SEC permits companies raising no more than $1.5 million to cut through much of the red tape normally required to package a new issue. Best-efforts offerings — usually made by companies desperate for cash — allow the underwriter to take stock on consignment and return any unsold shares to the company. The risks of investing in the third tier are extraordinarily high, even by new-issue standards. But euphoric speculators figure that it's easier for a 10-cent issue to go up to 40 cents than for a $10 issue to go to $40. And when a superboom in new issues is under way, they sometimes prove to be right.

☐ Boning the Red Herring

Getting information about new issues isn't especially difficult. Some brokerage houses publish weekly calendars of forthcoming offerings, and most brokers subscribe to the *IPO Reporter,* a weekly newsletter that covers all new issues. Several advisory services devote themselves exclusively to this market, including *New Issues* (profiled in chapter 14), the biweekly *Value Line New Issues Service* (711 Third Avenue, New York, NY 10017, $330 a year), and Standard & Poor's monthly *Emerging and Special Situations* (25 Broadway, New York, NY 10004, $140 a year).

For the available facts about a new issue, you need to study the preliminary prospectus or "red herring." Your broker will send you a prospectus if he is participating in the underwriting; if he isn't, he can tell you where to get one. The red herring, unfortunately, lives up to its name; it is so filled with caveats and disclaimers that it makes all issues sound almost equally scary. The red herrings of two companies selling retirement homes, one in heaven and one in hell, would in both cases state: "There is no established market for the company's products and services, and there can be no assurance of a market in the future."

However, the prospectus does contain most of the data an investor needs to form a rough opinion of what the issue might be worth — the company's sales and earnings record, profit margins, accounting methods, competitive position, and so on. Other information with an important bearing on the merits of new issues is discussed below.

☐ The Principal Underwriter

Even the best underwriters make errors of judgment, but they won't knowingly market the stock of a company that is likely to damage their reputation. A *Who's Who* of top-echelon underwriters of new issues would include Paine Webber, Dean Witter, Goldman Sachs, Kidder Peabody & Co., L. F. Rothschild, and Shearson Lehman Brothers, all of them in New York; Alex Brown & Sons in Baltimore, Hambrecht & Quist in San Francisco, and Rotan Mosle in Houston. Over the years 1980 through 1985, the *Money* study compared the performance of all IPOs sponsored by the 25 largest underwriters. The five whose underwritings did best in the market (with the composited average annual gains in parentheses) were Paine Webber (30.2 percent), Blunt Ellis & Loewi (29.6), Advest (28.6), William Blair (26.8), and Salomon Brothers (25.5).

☐ The Holdings of Top Officers

If they are unloading much of their stock, the issue should be shunned. Such transactions are described under the headings "Use of Proceeds and Principal" and "Selling Shareholders."

☐ Financing by a Venture-Capital Firm

Strong backing by venture-capital entrepreneurs suggests that the company has been well groomed to go public and probably has genuine promise.

☐ The Balance Sheet

Are the company's finances strong enough to keep it going if profits don't meet expectations, or if profit growth is on target, to provide capital for continued expansion? If you don't trust your own judgment on this score, don't invest in new issues without reliable professional guidance.

For investors braving this market for the first time, here are a few basic precepts: avoid blockbuster offerings by large, well-known companies. These IPOs are likely to be overpriced from the start and find buyers on the sheer marketing strength of huge underwriting syndicates. If a broker makes a big effort to sell you a new issue, don't buy it without checking it out especially carefully; the good stuff doesn't need a hard sell. Beware of copycat companies — those that resemble last year's big winners; the success of those winners may well have been largely due to originality in their concept or a well-entrenched position in their field. Be wary of unproven companies that go public with little or no earnings. On the other hand, remember that companies usually plan several years in advance to go public, and they "manage" their earnings — through legitimate accounting devices — to show strong growth in the year or two preceding the offering. Be prepared to do a good deal of homework and spread your risk over several issues even if it means buying a small number of shares.

☐ A Final Point

If you can't get an alluring issue at its offering price, be a contrarian: instead of chasing after it when it is selling at more than 30 times earnings, have the courage to buy when the market has taken a nosedive.

28 Profiting from Corporate Marriages

In recent years, a boom in mergers and acquisitions has brought bonanzas to thousands of fortunate stockholders; typically, a would-be corporate buyer offers a price in cash or stock that is 25 percent to 50 percent or more above the current market value of the sought-after company's stock. It seems likely that acquisition fever will continue to run high. Nowadays, many expansion-minded corporate planners would rather buy than build; it is often cheaper and less risky. Moreover, the trend toward deregulation is prompting the Justice Department and the Federal Trade Commission to tolerate many mergers that they might once have blocked as anticompetitive. The same hands-off attitude is encouraging corporate raiders such as Carl Icahn, Oscar Wyatt, T. Boone Pickens, Ronald Perelman, and Irwin Jacobs to terrorize the managers of staid, underperforming industrial giants by buying deeply into their shares with the avowed purpose of takeover and, some say, the greedier aim of exacting greenmail — selling their holdings back to the management at an enormous profit. (Strictly speaking, "merger" and "acquisition" are not synonymous. One big difference: an acquisition is a purchase of assets for cash, and the seller's gains are taxable; a merger usually involves a nontaxable exchange of stock. But in this chapter, as in common parlance, the two terms are used interchangeably.)

Holding stock in a company that is about to be merged or acquired is usually a matter of luck, but it can sometimes be the reward of foresight. You can increase your chances by including in your portfolio stocks that are worth buying on their own merits and also have some of the earmarks of a candidate for takeover.

Corporate buyers attempt to make acquisitions for any number of reasons — to broaden their product line, enter new markets, sell off parts of the company for more than the takeover price, achieve the economies that come with greater size. Some acquisition hunters seek ably managed, well-positioned companies; others go after plodding or troubled companies, hoping to revamp them. So candidates for acquisition are of all shapes, sizes, and qualities. They have included small energy-exploration and high-technology companies and senior citizens like Nabisco and Eastern Air Lines. But despite the diversity of the acquisitions market, there are guidelines for an investor seeking to spot companies that might become takeover targets.

Look where the bargain hunters may shop. A type of company that is alluring to corporate acquirers is one whose cash holdings are large in relation to its market value (the total price of all its shares outstanding); the buyer can recoup part of the purchase price from the selling company's very own cash. Also tempting are companies whose stocks are selling appreciably below book value, and such companies abound. In April 1987, 10 percent of the 4,700 issues covered by Standard & Poor's Stockpak II, a monthly updated data base on computer disks, were selling at discounts of 55 percent or more from their book values. Many of them were losing money, and others were probably uninviting to acquirers because large investments would be needed to modernize their obsolescent plants. But among the profitable companies, there were some that might appeal to a corporate buyer. When you have acquired sufficient experience to judge whether a company might be a candidate for takeover, the *Value Line* weekly list — "Widest Discounts from Book Value" — can be a useful source of leads. (The *Value Line Investment Survey* is available in several thousand libraries, including those of brokerage houses.)

Even if a stock is selling at or slightly above book value, it can look attractive in the merger market. Book value sometimes understates the real worth of a company's assets, especially when those assets include land and natural resources Companies can also be appealing to acquirers if the price/earnings ratio of their stock is relatively depressed. (Chapter 15, "The Fundamental Approach: Judging What a Stock Is Worth," explained how to find out whether a stock's current P/E relative to the market is higher or lower than its relative P/E over the previous five years.)

Look where the owners may sell. Deal makers often search for companies whose principal owners have reasons to court, or be responsive to, a merger or takeover. Many brokers are eager to name their pet sellout candidates, *but you should consider only companies that look like intrinsically good investments, not just speculative weaklings waiting to be rescued.* One kind of attractive sellout candidate could be a flourishing company whose executives are elderly, own the controlling interest, and have most of their personal fortunes in that one corporate basket. A sale for cash would enable them to diversify their holdings, or a merger into a bigger company would give their estates a stock that is more readily marketable in large amounts. Strong motives for merger may also catch up with the youthful founder of a fast-growing company. To surmount increased competition or simply to maximize the firm's development, he may find that he needs the marketing muscle and infusions of capital that a senior corporate partner could provide.

Look where the merger action is hot. A way of narrowing down the search for acquisition candidates is to look for them in industries where merger activity is already strong. An even better way is to look for companies in which an acquisition-minded company has already made a sizable investment. Then there is a good chance that one of two things will happen: either the corporate acquirer will eventually bid for the remaining stock, or it will facilitate a takeover by agreeing to sell its shares — at a handsome profit, of course — to another suitor.

By law, acquirers of 5 percent or more of the stock in a public company must file a statement called Form 13D with the Securities and Exchange Commission within ten days after reaching that level of ownership. In this statement, the buyer must give his reasons for making the purchase, his sources of financing, and his intention, if any, to win a seat on the board of directors. Newspapers report on 13D filings by well-known raiders, and avid takeover speculators subscribe to a daily newsletter, *SEC Today,* for $205 a year and keep up with all such goings on.

Look for corporations whose managers own fewer than 10 percent of the shares while at least that many shares are held by pension funds, mutual funds and other institutional investors. Corporate executives, in fear of losing their jobs, often resist takeover if they control significant numbers of shares. On the contrary, however, institutions readily sell their holdings to takeover artists offering a fat premium over the market price.

Using the guidelines suggested above, Charles Rolo selected nine takeover candidates for an article in the August 1977 issue of *Money* magazine. Within the next five years, five of the nine companies were merged or acquired. When you invest in a company that you consider

a takeover candidate, you must be prepared to be patient. If the acquisition you are hoping for does materialize, it is far more likely to take
several years than several months.

☐ There's Many a Slip 'Twixt the Bid and the Buy

The path from takeover bid to consummated union is an obstacle
course that only a minority of runners manage to complete. When a
few large shareholders — a family or members of management — own
a controlling interest in a company, a buyer has to meet their terms.
Many deals blow up because the controlling stockholders hold out for
too high a price. There's a saying among deal makers: "All sellers think
their geese are swans." One standard defensive tactic is to obtain a
preliminary injunction barring the would-be acquirer from following
up on his proposal. The grounds for such suits are alleged violation of
the securities laws that require full disclosure of pertinent facts by
parties involved in mergers. Assuming that he wins that round, a
would-be buyer must then persuade the company's public shareholders to override management and vote for his offer. Thus a so-called
hostile takeover requires a litigious and costly compaign that only
fiercely combative acquirers are willing to undertake. A costlier and
more damaging defense for the targeted company is one called the
"poison pill"; to make a takeover prohibitively expensive, the managers put their company deeply in debt and use the money to buy its
stock on the open market or issue preferred shares that would cost the
raider a heavy premium to acquire. Still more drastically, the company
may sell some profitable subsidiaries to make itself less attractive; this
is called a "scorched earth" defense.

Finally, despite a more permissive attitude among federal agencies, some kinds of mergers will continue to encounter regulatory
roadblocks. As antitrust policemen, the Justice Department and the
Federal Trade Commission may now accept consolidations involving
major corporations where once they would have balked. But they
might still oppose mergers between large and thriving companies in
the same industry. For example, Mobil's attempt in late 1981 to take
over Ohio-based Marathon Oil was blocked on the grounds that it
would lessen competition for gasoline sales in the Midwest.

If you own a stock that has soared following a merger or takeover
offer, you may wonder whether to sell and cash in your windfall or
wait for larger gains — typically an additional 12 percent to 15 per-

cent — if the deal reaches the finish line. In the case of tender offers (firm cash offers with a set expiration date), the smart policy is not to tender your stock until the deadline is near, because another buyer may suddenly announce a higher bid. Merger proposals are harder for the stockholder to decide about, since they involve an exchange of stock, and either party to the deal could call it off. Every case is different, but the questions you must try to answer, preferably with your broker's help, are basically the same.

Is the acquiring company one you would normally invest in and, further, do you currently rate its stock a good buy? If either answer is no, sell.

How large is the risk that merger won't go through? The stakes would be discouragingly high if either the suitor or the sought-after company had a poor record for completing mergers, or if the two companies were in an industry — broadcasting, for example — where regulatory authorities might oppose consolidations.

If the deal collapses, will your stock lose all or most of what it gained after the merger announcement? It probably will, unless the merger terms weren't particularly favorable to your company and the resulting publicity has made the merits of your stock better known — or unless the chances look good that your company will eventually find another suitor.

Holders of stock in an acquiring company are usually less likely to be affected, in the short run, by the outcome of merger negotiations. The announcement of a prospective merger may give the acquirer's stock a slight lift but more often causes it to fall. For example, American Express shares dropped $2.37 to $40.75 after news of the merger proposal to Shearson Loeb Rhoades (now Shearson/American Express) on April 1981, whereas Shearson stock rose $4 just before the announcement and a further $6.37 after it, to $48.62.

The reason the acquirer's stock often slips is that the buyer is usually paying a hefty premium over the seller's market price. So it is likely to be some time before the benefits of a takeover translate into higher earnings. In fact, when a company whose stock you own has made an important merger or acquisition, you should give it another checkup. You might decide that the deal was ill-advised and that the time has come to sell your stock.

Investors sometimes wonder whether there are easy profits to be made by buying shares in companies just after they have received a merger offer. In many cases, the stock is still selling at a healthy discount from its estimated merger value. This is known as risk arbitrage, and it is a game best left to highly sophisticated investors with large amounts of money. You need to invest at least $100,000 in different merger situations to diversify your risks. Moreover, you are now dealing in an arena where once — and perhaps soon again — professional arbitrageurs dealt illegally and arrogantly in inside information. And even in the most honorable times, arbitrageurs watching the Dow Jones ticker will know when a deal has soured and unload their shares before an amateur investor reads the bad news in the newspaper; and by that time, his stock has probably been devastated.

Searching for merger and takeover candidates brings benefits even if you never succeed in picking a company that gets acquired. It will sharpen your nose for value, and it will probably lead you to discover undervalued investments that you would otherwise have missed.

VI

Conclusions

29 A Portrait of the Ideal Investor

Time overtakes all facts and most truths about the stock market. Wherever it seemed necessary, the present author has replaced outdated references with more contemporary ones and adapted stock picking strategies to changes in economic trends and tax laws. But this very personal essay by Charles Rolo needs no alteration. It comes as close as you can get to the absolute truths of investing.

Will Rogers had a nifty formula for successful investing: "Don't gamble. Take all savings and buy some good stock and hold it till it goes up, then sell it. If it don't go up, don't buy it."

During my 15 years on Wall Street, I observed that some investors have an uncanny knack for buying stocks that don't go up and not selling those that do go up until they've tumbled down. The chronic losers I knew could not be typed as dimwits: among them were doctors and dentists, successful businessmen, a magazine editor (who wrote a book about his losses), even brokers and security analysts.

After I myself had been battered by a long losing streak in the early 1970s, I began to wonder whether there was a syndrome that causes people to act self-destructively in the stock market. My own errors weren't hard to diagnose. I had drifted away from a consistent policy that for many years had brought me considerable success — investing for the long pull in growth companies I considered reasonably valued. Instead, I had slipped into buying stocks that were in fashion and not selling them when they turned sour. I had let myself be tugged this way and that by conflicting market forecasts and had become overeager to make quick profits but fearful of further losses.

Generalizing from my own mistakes, and those committed by some clients of mine who appeared to be bent on losing money, I came up with a composite portrait of the chronic loser. He is mentally lazy, gullible, apprehensive but greedy, overly impressed by authorities, and also easily infected by the emotions of the crowd. If he's not mired in indecision, he's swinging to extremes of optimism and pessimism. Consider this portrait, and you'll recognize in it Everyman with all of his human frailties hanging out. In other words, the traits that make for failure in investing are deeply rooted in human nature. An investor's worst enemy lurks within himself.

It follows that success in investing hinges on doing what does not come naturally. For example, an investor must condition himself not to sell stocks but to buy them when panic prevails, and not to buy but to sell when the market is booming and euphoria is everywhere. That's the surest way of buying low and selling high.

To do unfailingly what doesn't come naturally is not humanly possible; the ideal investor does not exist. But to set him up as a model is the best way I know to develop a winning style in the market. Here, then, is a portrait of the paragon that we can all profit by emulating.

The ideal investor has learned to be rigorously honest with himself; he knows his weaknesses and watches for signs that irrational impulses are clouding his judgment. He has also rid himself, through study and experience, of all innocence about the stock market. The ideal investor knows, for example, that the most widely recommended stocks are probably bad buys because too many people have already bought them; that the only reliable forecast of the market anyone can make was J. P. Morgan's: "It will fluctuate"; that acting on tips from the average broker is like buying hair-grower from a bald barber; that success lies not in making a bundle quickly but in making a fortune slowly.

The ideal investor knows, too, that supersuccessful investors — figures like Bernard Baruch and Joseph P. Kennedy — have been loners. So he does his homework, trusts his common sense, and charts a course of his own. He spares no effort to be well informed, because to profit from events you have to be one jump ahead of the headlines. An Irish proverb says, "Good luck beats early rising." But the men I've known who made fortunes in the market got lucky by getting places early.

There is one more ingredient, a crucial one, in the makeup of the ideal investor. It was suggested to me in an essay, "The Nature of Genius," by the late Ernest Jones, one of the pioneers of psychoanalysis. After studying the lives of Copernicus, Newton, and Freud, Jones detected in their characters a common singularity. Unlike most people, who tend to be either credulous or skeptical, each of these geniuses combined to an extraordinary degree credulity and skepticism. Jones shows how this fusion of opposite traits guided them on their journeys of discovery. His insight into the nature of genius applies to the world of investing, where great success is won by a process of discovery — the perception of future values not discounted in present market prices. Skepticism is the armor that protects investors against rumors and phony tips, á la mode "concepts," pipe dreams, or just exaggerated expectations. But chronic skepticism leads to chronic negativism and self-defeating inertia. Investors must have the credulity — I prefer to call it vision or faith in their judgment — to heed evidence that tells them a sweeping change is coming in the market or that a young company has the makings of a giant. The ideal investor maintains an interplay between skepticism and belief — an internal dialogue between his critical faculties and his creative imagination. That's something all of us can try to do. If we succeed even some of the time, we won't be chronic losers; if we succeed much of the time, we're certain to be winners.

30
Investment Vistas: Where Growth Will Be the Fastest in the Nineties

Futurology is an exercise doomed to error. On this page, in 1982, Charles Rolo asked, "Who, at the beginning of the 1970s, could have foreseen that the decade would bring a twelvefold increase in the cost of oil and make cheap energy — historically a prime source of industrial growth — a thing of the past?" At that moment the future held little hope that cheap energy would ever return. But return it did. In 1986 a barrel of oil cost as little as $13, down from $32 in 1981; oil became the engine of *deflation* instead of inflation, and the Consumer Price Index that year inched up only 1.1 percent.

Clouded though our crystal ball may be, peering into the future is a mandatory exercise for investors. Generals, it has been said, are always fighting the last war. And the same is true of investors who act without a tentative outline of the shape of things to come. In an interview with *Money* in 1980, Louis Rukeyser, host of the television program *Wall Street Week,* predicted that "the 1980s will be the decade of common stocks." John Templeton, one of the most successful fund managers of the past 30 years, was no less optimistic. In a message in 1981, Templeton said that stocks were "ridiculously cheap" and that the Dow Jones industrials could rise to 3,000 before the end of the eighties.

True forecasts are sometimes based on false premises. The thesis that the 1980s would be a great decade for common stocks rested on two related arguments: 1. A significant change in our political and economic beliefs — a so-called swing toward conservatism — would bring a much improved climate for American business and stronger incentives for the individual to save and invest. 2. In light of this favorable change, common stocks were sharply undervalued in relation to other kinds of investments. As matters turned out, the swing to conservatism almost immediately put us into a recession that was the nearest yet to the Great Depression of the 1930s and, by 1985, turned the United States into a debtor nation. Nor did Americans become better savers. Quite the opposite: we put less money away in 1985 and 1986 than in 1984. Further, the portents in 1987 pointed to "dissavings," according to F. Thomas Juster, an economist at the Institute for Social Research at the University of Michigan, as a growing cohort of the population "moves into retirement and withdraws the assets that were saved to finance consumption during their retirement years."

Yet the 1980s have indeed thus far given us a half-decade of unprecedented growth of share prices. From a closing figure of 875 in 1981, the Dow peaked on August 25, 1987, at 2,722, having more than tripled in value and having come within striking distance of Templeton's 3,000. At that point, of course, prices began to topple. On October 19, the Dow plunged 508 points, closing at 1,738.74. John J. Phelan, chairman of the New York Stock Exchange, called that day's sell-off "as close to a financial melt-down as I'd ever want to see." Without further protestations of fallibility, however, let's scan the investment vistas of the 1990s, focusing on four major themes. These are the changing structure of the U.S. economy, the forward sweep of the technological revolution, the service industries, demographic and social changes.

☐ The Rust Belt Redux

In the 1970s academics proclaimed the post-industrial society. The basic manufacturing industries that once were the mainstay of this country's growth — autos, steel, heavy machinery, textiles, and the like — had become a subeconomy beset with problems: deteriorating productivity, a worsening competitive position in world markets, an inadequate return on invested capital, and obsolescent facilities, which, because of the high cost of capital, would cost huge sums to modernize. We seemed ready to cede our smokestack businesses to countries with cheap labor and focus our future on what scholars liked to describe as "knowledge industries" — by which they meant anything from the writing of computer software to the underwriting of insurance risks. For investors seeking high long-term growth, old-line industry would remain fundamentally unattractive.

Instead of caving in to this theory, gritty corporate managers and workers at many smokestack companies have been cutting costs, accepting lower wage increases, plowing back profits into research, and generally regaining a place in world competition. The sharp decline of the U.S. dollar against the currencies of other industrialized countries abetted this revived combativeness. From 1985 to 1987 American labor costs in manufacturing industries slipped below those of West Germany and closed most of the gap between the United States and Japan.

American managers also rediscovered the work ethic. Their fortunes depended on it; mergers, acquisitions, and leveraged buyouts had taken scores of companies off the stock market, slashing jobs at high and middle levels of management. Many of those who remained in control had done so only by committing their life savings and even their homes to the repurchase of company stock from the public. Money managers who made a practice of visiting corporate headquarters in search of sound investments reported an amazing transformation. Richard Strong of the Strong Fund Group, whose research takes him to more than 400 companies a year, told *Money* magazine in 1987, "It used to be that when I tried to call the chairman of a company, he would be out on the golf course. Now those guys are working 70-hour weeks and so are all the people around them." Some of their long hours are going into new technologies and the adoption of Japanese management techniques. The quest for ways to cut costs and raise productivity occupies additional time. Their companies will slowly gain recognition as *bottom-line growth stocks.* They may even become the glamour stocks of the 1990s, in the estimation of A. Gary Shilling, an economist who heads his own consulting firm in New York City.

The first and most widely heralded beneficiaries of belt-tightening and new managerial techniques included Ford Motor, Chrysler, and Caterpillar, Inc., a much besieged maker of earthmovers and other heavy rolling stock. One of many obscurer examples on our list of 167 growth leaders in Appendix A is Philips Industries in Dayton, Ohio, a maker of windows, fans, and other components for residential and commercial construction and recreational vehicles. Philips organizes engineers, workers, and secretaries into teams to tackle manufacturing problems. Its executives claim to have saved $28 million this way from 1981 to 1987. The payoff began reaching the bottom line after a couple of years, with earnings growth averaging 18 percent a year.*

☐ Technology Triumphant

The application of technologies that came off the drawing board, or out of the laboratory, over the past three decades has assumed the force and breadth of a tidal wave. Throughout the rest of this century, the technological revolution will have a dramatic impact on industry's methods of production, on modes of doing business, and on the way America lives. The universe of high-growth technology companies is so large and complex that only a full-length book written by a team of specialists could attempt to explore it. For this squint into the future, a layman's catalogue of fast-growing sectors will suffice.

☐ Computer-Assisted Design/Computer-Aided Manufacturing

CAD/ CAM systems are used to automate graphic and production processes. Add to their ranks computer-integrated manufacturing (CIM), a type of software that monitors and controls factory production to prevent waste and avoid extra work, and computer-aided engineering systems (CAE), which are desktop computers, or work stations, used by electronic engineers to design still more computers. Computer-assisted systems have almost unbounded applications. They are used in the design and production of calculators, engineering projects, gas turbines, microwave components, molds for plastics, motors, printing presses, semiconductor integrated circuits, textiles, and typewriters.

The growth prospects of leaders in this technology quickly capture the imagination of investors, with the result that stock valuations

---

* But the stocks of companies mentioned in this chapter and in Appendix A are not, it must be stressed, investment recommendations; they are simply some of many possible candidates for investigation by interested investors.

are often exceptionally high. Sun Microsystems, in Appendix A, averaged 124 percent earnings growth from 1983 to 1987; the price/earnings ratio was at a forbidding 42. This hotly price-competitive company in Mountain View, California, makes computer-aided engineering work stations. Analysts Michael Murphy and Lissa Morgenthaler, of the *California Technology Stock Letter,* call Sun "a superb company, executing a difficult, well thought-out strategy with unbelievable speed and deftness."

□ Data Processing
This catch-all label applies to innumerable companies involved in computer technology — manufacturers of such equipment as memory systems; makers of "intelligent" data terminals linked to a central computer — for example, the cash registers used in supermarkets and department stores; firms that use computers to gather, store, process, and distribute information; and firms that provide computer programming. The tremendous growth in the use of computers of all kinds is creating an almost unlimited demand for programming. See Appendix A for names of fast-growing companies in the data processing business.

□ Instrumentation
This is a large and varied sector, which includes instruments used to automate temperature control, industrial processes and quality control; instruments used in flight and navigational systems; and instruments used for genetic engineering and scientific and medical research. Growth prospects seem particularly favorable for the companies that help to save energy and to improve industrial productivity through process and quality control. An example from Appendix A: Dionex Corp., of Sunnyvale, California, in Silicon Valley, a maker of ion chromatography systems, a technology for analyzing chemical substances in industrial and biomedical products and for monitoring acid rain and other environmental pollutants.

□ Medical Technology
This will be an area of stunning growth, powered by advances in radiology, ultrasonic diagnostic devices, improved systems for monitoring the vital functions, and other innovations. Examples from Appendix A: Bionet, a Warsaw, Indiana, maker of surgical implants such as hip and knee joints; Diagnostic Products of Los Angeles, which produces kits for testing immunological reactions and for identifying hormones, drugs, viruses, and bacteria in blood and other bodily fluids; and LyphoMed of Melrose Park, Illinois, which

prepares injectable nutrients and medications used by most hospitals. A mutual fund that invests only in companies contributing to medical progress, Medical Technology Fund, is listed in Appendix B.

☐ Small Computers, Home Computers, and Word Processors

The market for computers of less than standard size will continue to be a high-growth market — but competition will be fierce. Major producers of so-called minicomputers, which, paradoxically, are the biggest small computers, include Digital Equipment Corporation, which seized the initiative from IBM in developing and marketing "local area network" systems; Apple Computer, whose Macintosh line dominates the education market and is almost synonymous with desktop publishing, a system for preparing type, graphics, and layouts for photocopying or commercial printing. The leader in really small business computers — systems costing as little as $9,000 to $11,000 — has been Wang Laboratories. Sales of home or microcomputers took off, of course, in the 1980s, far exceeding projections of $9 billion in sales annually, worldwide, by 1990. While IBM now sets the standard to which most other machine makers claim compatibility, Apple holds a large niche, with plenty of room for cut-rate challengers such as Compaq and Tandy in this country and top-quality IBM compatibles from Korea. However, profit growth as reflected in Appendix A companies looks strongest in outfits such as Cray Research, a leader in scientific equipment labeled with the buzz word "artificial intelligence," and manufacturers and distributors of peripheral equipment, such as EMC Corp., 3COM, Tech Data, and Wyse Technology.

☐ Semiconductors/Microprocessors

American business is wedded to electronics, and semiconductors are the basic building blocks of electronics. The semiconductor industry is enormously competitive, however: profits were flat or down at most companies in the mid-1980s and are always subject to cyclical downturns. Semiconductor technology took one great stride forward when Intel Corp. pioneered the microprocessor, which has been called "a computer on a chip." The 1990s will be a period of huge expansion in the capacity of the chip — or integrated circuit. Other giants in the semiconductor industry are Motorola, National Semiconductor, and Texas Instruments. Smaller companies include Advanced Microdevices, Standard Microsystems, and Unitrode. None can claim a place on our growth stock list.

☐ Telecommunications

The label applies to communications systems that use cable, microwave, or satellite to transmit large amounts of information over long distances at reasonable costs and also to so-called interconnect systems — privately owned telephone systems that interconnect with the long-distance carriers (AT&T, MCI, and the smaller independents) and with the seven regulated regional companies created by the breakup of the Bell System. Telecommunications is yet another segment of the technology economy with seemingly unlimited growth potential. Fiber optics technology is multiplying message carrying capacity exponentially. Tiny strands of glass through which laser light transmits computer and voice impulses are replacing a billion miles of copper. By the year 2000, two such strands will handle 300,000 times as many telephone conversations as two copper wires did in 1985. Another new network, this one for cellular phones used in cars and, soon, pockets, is causing transceiver antennas to sprout on city towers everywhere; from a few thousand users in the mid-1980s, cellular phones are expected to grow in number to 2.5 million by the turn of the century. Two growth companies in the telecommunications field: Electromagnetic Sciences, which specializes in microwave components for communications and surveillance systems, and V Band Systems, specializing in special-purpose electronic key telephones.

☐ Genetics

Biotechnology, or "gene-splicing," is a new primary technology that can alter the genetic makeup of a cell to program it to perform a specific task such as the production of proteins. The potential applications of genetic engineering go far beyond its proven uses, which include making insulin and interferon, a seemingly promising substance for the treatment of cancer. Given time and capital, this new technology may revolutionize medicine and agriculture; it could also be employed in the chemical industry, food processing, pollution control, and other areas. But if biotechnology's promise is realized, it will be in the fairly distant future — more distant than was imagined by investors who rushed to buy stock in the firms that were the first to go public: Enzo Biochem, Genentech, and Cetus. As of 1986, their earnings were nominal, and it seemed unlikely that such companies would show significant profits for quite some time to come. Nevertheless, investors still valued the stocks extremely highly.

Investing in high-tech stocks can be exhilarating — some stocks double in months, some more than triple in a few years. But a caveat issued earlier needs to be repeated: beware of overpaying for expectations of growth, however dazzling they may seem to be. When something goes wrong for a high-tech issue selling at a stratospheric valuation, its price comes tumbling down. You have to try to catch a high-tech stock either before it's on the hit parade, or when it has suffered a setback, or when the general market has slumped.

☐ The Service Economy

As an area for investment, the service economy has two advantages for the layman over the universe of high technology: the companies are easy to understand, and their stocks — even those with impressive growth records — tend to sell at significantly lower valuations than the favored high-tech issues. Nobody can tell what stock valuations will be when this book is in the hands of a particular reader. What this look ahead *can* do is to suggest where some of the many investment opportunities in the service industries may lie. (This text, one hopes, will have equipped the reader to judge whether or not a stock seems reasonably valued.)

With crime ubiquitous and booming, companies that provide protection services appear to have plenty of growth in their future. Chambers Development, in Appendix A, is one of them; it makes security systems. While hospital management has become a mature industry vexed by takeover threats, specialized hospital services are still finding growth opportunities: Community Psychiatric Centers, Shared Medical Systems, and U.S. Healthcare on our list. The mutual fund industry has ballooned along with the stock market; see Eaton Vance and Franklin Resources. Other changes in the large, varied, and rapidly expanding world of financial services should make it a rewarding hunting ground for sharp-eyed investors. They should, in particular, be on the lookout for innovative companies in the financial sector that create their own base for growth by performing a specialized service. Green Tree Acceptance, which buys and sells financing contracts on mobile homes and recreational vehicles, is one example. Student Loan Marketing Association, better known as Sallie Mae, the provider of liquidity to banks that make federally guaranteed student loans, is another. A third is Telerate, a world-wide financial information network. How well these companies will do in the future is, of course, uncertain. But they had rewarded early-bird investors when this chapter was written, and they exemplify the innovativeness that generates superior growth. Other fields in which companies have won success by performing highly specialized services include pilot training (FlightSafety International), employment agencies that supply office temps (Olsten, Uniforce), and disposal of toxic wastes (Laidlaw Industries, Waste Management, and the second business of Chambers Development). Investing in the service industries, once you know the basics of stock valuation, simply requires common sense, plus a dash of prescience. The overall strategy: look for companies that have positioned themselves to exploit growing demands created by changes in American lifestyles and business techniques. You will find them in many sectors in addition to those mentioned above. You may well run across them in your daily life.

□ The New Demographics

The makeup of the American population will be substantially altered in the 1990s, according to the projections of the Census Bureau. The ranks of the 30- to 49-year-old segment will be swelled by 76 million Americans born in the baby-boom era, 1946 through 1964. Those between 40 and 50 will number 42 million by the year 2000, according to Census Bureau projections, from 26 million in 1987. Cheryl Russell, editor-in-chief of *American Demographics,* calls this the middle aging of America. Keeping pace will be the graying of America. The over-65 group will exceed 31 million, compared with 27 million in 1987. The birth rate will decline after the merest of boomlets in the early eighties. Finally, today's teenagers, members of the baby bust generation, will have their pick of entry-level jobs.

Some of the implications of these population shifts are clear. The demographics of the 1990s appear to be unfavorable for businesses with a large teenage clientele; in the major industries, these would include soft drinks, "junk" foods, and cosmetics and toiletries. The dearth of under-five-year-olds will pinch makers of food and pharmaceutical products for infants and small children, and of course makers of toys. But it won't squelch demand for day-care services: in 1990 twice as many mothers of small children will belong to the workforce as were holding jobs ten years earlier. (The two fastest-growing publicly owned companies engaged in providing this service are Kinder-Care and La Petite Academy.) The prime beneficiaries of the bulge in the elderly population will be the health-care industry — in particular hospital and nursing-home management companies and drug companies that are strong in geriatric products. Retirement communities will benefit, too, but at this writing no major publicly owned company has emerged as a promising investment in this field.

The largest surge in consumer demand will come from the 30- to 49-year-old population group, whose biggest segments will be affluent, two-income families — and have-nots. Specialists in marketing expect the spending of this huge group to be the strongest at the high end and the low end of the price spectrum. Its beneficiaries will be purveyors of luxury goods and services — and discounters. The "middle market" is likely to find the going tougher.

The demographics of the 1980s, coupled with a postponed demand for housing caused by sky-high mortgage rates, points to persistent strength in home building. In fact, housing-related companies outnumber all other fast growers in Appendix A. Demographers predict that the huge size of house payments will shape the behavior of the middle-aging boomers. In a pinch for time and funds, family life will win out over work for those who were in their thirties in 1987. Business beneficiaries: microwave ovens, VCRs, weekend vacations, financial newsletters, home photocopiers, home banking, lawn care, mail-order houses. One harbinger in Appendix A is a company called Golden Valley Microwave; from 1983 to 1986, sales of its microwave popcorn and pancakes cooked up average annual earnings gains of *614 percent.*

☐ Up the Wall of Worry

Waiting for the next bull market is hard. Waiting for a bull market to end is harder. In chapter 20, you are given a series of questions whose answers sometimes add up to a clear signal to buy or sell. Clear signals appear only about once in two years, but keep the list of questions handy and run down the answers once a month.

From August 22, 1982 to August 25, 1987, a bull market reigned supreme, the likes of which exceed living memory. By most cycle theories it should have been dethroned long before "Bloody Monday" (October 19, 1987). A few weeks earlier, John Templeton, herald of the 3,000 Dow, had contemplated a pullback to 1,500. Money managers and newsletter writers had either told their followers to lighten up on stocks or to stay in close touch with their hot lines. Howard Ruff had resumed publication of *Ruff Times,* the doomsayers bible. Alfred Malabre, the usually serene and reassuring economics editor of *The Wall Street Journal,* had warned of recession in a 1987 book, *Beyond Our Means* (Random House). Economist Ravi Batra of Southern Methodist University, a respected academic, had written a best-seller, *The Great Depression of 1990,* and was going about the country pleading for policies that he believed would make this unblessed event less severe. The numbers that fundamental analysts read like tea leaves looked ominous enough to substantiate bearish tidings: a stock market price/earnings ratio of 20 and a dividend yield of less than 3 percent — well recognized as harbingers of a price collapse. Yet the gross national product kept limping uphill, corporate profits made small, steady gains. The Dow penetrated 2,700; the S&P 500 went to a record 336.77. The market was climbing a classic wall of worry.

Conceivably, Bloody Monday was a one-day nightmare, rather than a terrible turning point in investors' fortunes. But a bear market is coming as inevitably as Eugene O'Neill's Iceman. And a bull market will follow it with equal inevitability. Templeton still holds to his expectations of 3,000, perhaps by 1990. The unknowable question as always is: When? What I hope, and what Charles Rolo would surely hope, is that the readers of this book have gained from it some useful and usable tools for living with the market — and when the times come, without it — and above all for profiting on both the upside and the downside.

To update the last words of the 1982 edition: Since it is virtually certain that the growth sectors of the next bull market will substantially outperform the Dow, the 1990s might very well turn out to be another "decade of common common stocks." I suggest, therefore, that you follow Will Rogers's advice: ". . . buy some good stock and hold it till it goes up. . . . If it don't go up, don't buy it."

Appendixes

Appendix A
A Growth Hunter's Game Preserve: 167 Stocks with Large Potential

This appendix is NOT a recommended list. It is a list of companies worthy of further investigation by investors seeking to find growth companies — small, middle-size, or large — that might be among the big winners in the next few years. Different analysts, each using his own proprietary process of elimination, could generate different lists of growth companies. This one is drawn from the July 1987 issue of *America's Fastest Growing Companies,* an investment advisory service described in chapter 14, and is printed with the permission of the publisher, John S. Herold, Inc., of Greenwich, Connecticut. The editors screened 5,500 companies in the spring of 1987 and selected only those that had reported uninterrupted earnings growth averaging 25 percent or more from 1982 through 1986, preferably while retaining a low price/earnings ratio. In addition, the earnings outlook had to be strong. The list is the cumulative result of present and past screenings. To remain on it, a company had to have continued increasing its earnings or to have demonstrated convincingly that growth soon would resume.

In the tabulation that follows, shareholders' equity indicates a company's size — the number of shares outstanding times the price per share on June 1, 1987. Represented are 21 enterprises that at the time were worth less than $100 million, small enough to qualify them as junior growth companies, and companies ranging in size to $10 billion or more, large enough to put them in the Fortune 500. The earnings per share (EPS) are for the 12 months through the company's latest reported fiscal quarter, which ended in either January, February, March, or April of 1987. Growth rates during the four years covered averaged 25 percent or greater, uncompounded, for 111 of the 167 companies on the list and ran as astonishingly high as 614 percent in the case of Golden Microwave, a packager of popcorn and pancakes for preparation in microwave ovens — the trendiest kitchen gadget of the 1980s. Keep in mind that small companies with towering growth rates were building from a small base, making such expansion unsustainable for very long. The column headed "growth rate P/E" shows the number of years it would take for earnings to equal the stock price shown, provided the company kept on growing at the same rate as in the previous 12 months. ("NA" in the "growth rate P/E" column usually indicates a profit decline in the latest 12 months.) The ROE column gives the percentage return on stockholders' equity in the latest year; 68 percent of the companies returned 20 percent or more in profits on this basis, thus meeting another eligibility requirement set by the classic growth-stock hunter. For reasons of space the description of the company's business is a broad one that simply names the sectors of industry in which it operates.

The reader scanning this list in 1988 or thereafter will enjoy benefits of hindsight that should make up for the missed opportunities. With a Standard & Poor's monthly *Stock Guide* in hand, he will quickly see which of the companies have failed to fulfill their promise and can be scratched from the performance derby. He will know which ones have sustained a high rate of growth. In comparing their mid-1987 valuations (price divided by EPS) with their current valuations, he will have a basis for judging whether or not they have climbed too high on the ladder of popularity. In short, with this list an investor who does his homework should be able to assemble a winning portfolio of growth stocks for the next three to five years.

Company and Location	Shareholders' Equity (millions)	EPS Latest 12 months	Price June 1, 1987	Exchange	Growth Rate 1983–1986 (percentage)	Growth Rate P/E	ROE (percent)	Type of Business
AAR Corp. Elk Grove Village, IL	315.0	1.44	30	NYSE	39	9	15.8	Aviation parts and service
Abbott Laboratories North Chicago, IL	13,730.3	2.42	60	NYSE	17	9	29.6	Health care products
AFG Industries Irvine, CA	455.5	2.32	27	NYSE	52	6	34.3	Flat glass products
Agency Rent-A-Car Solon, OH	460.3	0.77	21	OTC	27	8	30.9	Insurance replacement rentals
Ameribanc Investors Group, Washington, DC	61.1	1.41	10	OTC	64	6	17.7	Savings and loan holding company
American List Great Neck, NY	27.8	0.54	10	AMEX	23	5	33.8	Computerized high school student lists
American Software Atlanta, GA	154.7	0.83	15	OTC	13	3	20.5	IBM-compatible software

Anheuser-Busch St. Louis, MO	8,872.5	1.76	33	NYSE	16	8	21.9	Largest U.S. brewer; baking
Armstrong World Industries, Lancaster, PA	1,758.2	2.71	37	NYSE	26	5	17.9	Interior furnishings and building products
Arnold Industries Lebanon, PA	148.4	3.02	44	OTC	27	10	24.7	Trucking of general commodities
Arvin Industries Columbus, IN	616.6	2.48	35	NYSE	31	11	17.7	Auto parts, stereo, video, catalytic converters
Ashton-Tate Torrance, CA	573.8	1.39	24	OTC	54	5	62.1	Microcomputer software products
Autodesk, Inc. Sausalito, CA	490.5	0.61	24	OTC	275	6	58.8	Computer-aided design and drafting
Automatic Data Processing Roseland, NJ	3,617.7	1.66	47	NYSE	16	9	22.9	Computer services
Ball Corp. Muncie, IN	998.4	2.54	43	NYSE	14	25	17.6	Containers, metal, aerospace
BDM International McLean, VA	339.6	1.32	30	AMEX	23	6	30.4	Technical services for government

Company and Location	Shareholders' Equity (millions)	EPS Latest 12 months	Price June 1, 1987	Exchange	Growth Rate 1983–1986 (percentage)	Growth Rate P/E	ROE (percent)	Type of Business
Beeba's Creations San Diego, CA	54.4	0.93	14	OTC	97	NA	14.1	Distributes women's sportswear
Ben & Jerry's Homemade, Waterbury, VT	37.8	0.70	22	OTC	126	NA	16.8	Premium ice cream, franchise stores
Biomet Warsaw, IN	278.3	0.64	23	OTC	71	7	28.6	Surgical implant devices
Bolar Pharmaceutical Copiague, NY	241.8	1.08	25	AMEX	22	10	24.6	Generic prescription drugs
Bristol Myers New York, NY	14,025.6	4.32	98	NYSE	11	9	21.9	Toiletries; drugs, household products
Bruno's Birmingham, AL	670.8	0.77	17	OTC	19	NA	17.2	Self-service supermarkets in Alabama
Calmat Co. Los Angeles, CA	909.0	2.39	30	NYSE	78	1	21.6	Cement, concrete

Capital Cities/ABC New York, NY	5,753.8	12.43	357	NYSE	9	6	22.5	Radio and TV broadcasting, publishing
Chambers Development Pittsburgh, PA	363.5	0.70	33	AMEX	33	5	41.2	Waste management, security systems
Charming Shoppes Bensalem, PA	1,301.1	0.88	26	OTC	31	7	38.3	Women's specialty stores
Charter Medical Macon, GA	600.2	1.56	28	AMEX	18	10	14.8	Hospital management
Cherokee Group North Hollywood, CA	248.3	0.67	19	OTC	41	5	45.6	Women's apparel and footwear
Circle Fine Art Chicago, IL	12.0	0.37	5	OTC	32	2	14.2	Art galleries
Clayton Homes Knoxville, TN	128.3	0.71	10	NYSE	26	6	18.5	Produces and finances manufactured homes
ClothesTime Anaheim, CA	264.0	0.88	19	OTC	60	7	35.2	Young women's apparel stores
Coated Sales Laurence Harbor, NJ	189.0	0.39	11	OTC	97	6	74.5	Manufactures specialty coated fabrics
Community Psychiatric Centers, San Francisco, CA	1,150.9	1.71	38	NYSE	21	10	19.8	Acute-care hospitals; kidney dialysis centers

Company and Location	Shareholders' Equity (millions)	EPS Latest 12 months	Price June 1, 1987	Exchange	Growth Rate 1983–1986 (percentage)	Growth Rate P/E	ROE (percent)	Type of Business
Computer Associates Int'l Garden City, NY	1,338.9	0.74	27	NYSE	49	4	208.5	Systems software packages
Cray Research Minneapolis, MN	2,966.0	4.78	98	NYSE	65	3	47.4	Scientific computers, software
Crown Cork & Seal Philadelphia, PA	1,184.8	7.68	119	NYSE	25	9	13.3	Metal cans, closures; machinery
Deb Shops Philadelphia, PA	272.7	0.84	18	OTC	19	11	32.5	Women's apparel stores
Diagnostic Products Los Angeles, CA	229.8	1.16	39	OTC	27	7	32.9	Immunodiagnostic test kits
Digital Communications Alpharetta, GA	641.7	2.32	45	OTC	75	4	27.8	Datacommunications network systems

Dionex Corp. Sunnyvale, CA	266.3	0.91	29	OTC	30	12	18.2	Ion chromatography for chemical analysis
Domtar Montreal, Canada	606.0	1.64	15	NYSE	39	4	11.6	Pulp and paper, building materials, chemicals
Dress Barn Stamford, CT	399.0	0.54	18	OTC	71	9	45.7	Women's apparel stores
Duquesne Systems Pittsburgh, PA	275.4	0.67	27	AMEX	62	6	17.4	IBM-compatible software
Durakon Lapeer, MI	73.9	0.78	12	OTC	43	5	NA	Plastic truck-bed liners
Dynatech Corp. Burlington, MA	339.5	2.10	31	OTC	22	NA	24.1	Communications and medical products, scientific instruments
Eaton Vance Boston, MA	98.3	1.81	23	OTC	16	4	24.3	Adviser to mutual funds
Electromagnetic Sciences Norcross, GA	127.2	0.79	18	OTC	26	8	22.8	Microwave components and subsystems
Electrospace Systems Richardson, TX	417.2	0.75	31	NYSE	7	15	19.6	Communications, navigation equipment

Company and Location	Shareholders' Equity (millions)	EPS Latest 12 months	Price June 1, 1987	Exchange	Growth Rate 1983–1986 (percentage)	Growth Rate P/E	ROE (percent)	Type of Business
EMC Corp. Hopkinton, MA	391.6	1.26	27	OTC	157	10	153.6	Board-level computer products
Envirodyne Industries Chicago, IL	325.0	2.36	36	OTC	102	3	91.5	Plastic dining products, electrical equipment
Filtertek Cos. Hebron, IL	89.8	0.96	14	NYSE	14	9	26.1	Filtration elements
Food Lion Salisbury, NC	2,565.7	0.42	16	OTC	29	8	32.5	Supermarket chain in North Carolina
FlightSafety Int'l Flushing, NY	693.3	1.39	31	NYSE	9	8	19.0	Aircraft and marine training
Flowers Industries Thomasville, GA	558.6	1.22	24	NYSE	15	NA	19.9	Baked goods, convenience foods

Franklin Resources San Mateo, CA	657.5	2.28	31	NYSE	114	3	91.6	Mutual fund advisory services
Genuine Parts Atlanta, GA	1,748.2	1.58	33	NYSE	6	9	11.5	Distributes auto replacement parts
Golden Valley Microwave Eden Prairie, MN	266.7	0.67	24	OTC	614	3	855.9	Microwave food products
Graphic Industries Atlanta, GA	127.7	0.97	20	OTC	33	9	26.4	Commercial printing
Great Atlantic & Pacific Tea Montvale, NJ	1,293.6	1.82	34	NYSE	29	5	10.4	Supermarkets
Green Tree Acceptance St. Paul, MN	433.6	2.30	26	NYSE	31	6	20.4	Purchases and sells financing contracts on mobile homes
John H. Harland Atlanta, GA	825.9	1.11	24	NYSE	20	8	28.3	Bank stationer: checks, deposit slips, etc.
Hechinger Co. Landover, MD	307.1	1.00	22	OTC	16	6	8.1	Retail home centers
H.J. Heinz Pittsburgh, PA	5,875.5	2.38	44	NYSE	13	8	23.4	Food packager

Company and Location	Shareholders' Equity (millions)	EPS Latest 12 months	Price June 1, 1987	Exchange	Growth Rate 1983-1986 (percentage)	Growth Rate P/E	ROE (percent)	Type of Business
Houvanian Enterprises Red Bank, NJ	297.5	0.88	14	AMEX	51	3	64.9	Multifamily home builder
Hubco Union City, NJ	63.9	1.34	18	AMEX	28	6	18.8	NJ bank holding company
J. B. Hunt Transport Lowell, AR	517.9	1.09	22	OTC	39	9	55.6	Trucking: general freight
Huntingdon Int'l Holdings Huntingdon, U.K.	185.1	1.09	23	OTC	47	4	NA	Biological safety evaluation
IMS International New York, NY	1,270.6	0.94	31	OTC	32	11	34.1	Syndicated market research reports
Intermet Corp. Atlanta, GA	306.7	0.92	17	OTC	49	11	329.4	Auto parts

Int'l Lease Finance Beverly Hills, CA	539.7	1.14	18	OTC	28	4	153.8	Leasing and sale of jet aircraft
Jacobson Stores Jackson, MI	191.6	2.70	35	OTC	31	6	26.3	Specialty department stores
Jim Walter Tampa, FL	1,587.5	4.89	50	NYSE	21	5	14.0	Major manufacturer of home-building materials
JP Industries Ann Arbor, MI	217.1	1.15	20	NYSE	21	8	9.0	Pumping products and transportation parts
Juno Lighting Des Plaines, IL	169.2	1.74	37	OTC	38	7	31.3	Recessed and track lighting
Kellogg Co. Battle Creek, MI	7,537.3	2.81	61	NYSE	18	6	25.1	Convenience food products
Kellwood Co. St. Louis, MO	371.2	3.22	34	NYSE	16	10	26.8	Apparel for Sears, Roebuck
Kinder-Care, Inc. Montgomery, AL	715.7	0.85	16	OTC	30	4	6.0	Day care centers, life insurance, thrifts
King World Productions Summit, NJ	739.3	0.90	24	NYSE	214	4	63.3	Distributor of syndicated TV programs

Company and Location	Shareholders' Equity (millions)	EPS Latest 12 months	Price June 1, 1987	Exchange	Growth Rate 1983–1986 (percentage)	Growth Rate P/E	ROE (percent)	Type of Business
Ladd Furniture High Point, NC	403.9	1.26	21	OTC	15	5	29.0	Manufactures and markets furniture
Laidlaw Industries Hinsdale, IL	526.1	0.90	26	OTC	14	NA	14.7	Solid waste management services
Land's End Chicago, IL	429.4	1.66	43	OTC	23	5	61.0	Markets men's and women's apparel
La Petite Academy Kansas City, MO	268.2	0.53	17	OTC	34	7	21.0	Preschool and day-care centers
Leggett & Platt Carthage, MO	559.6	2.14	34	NYSE	17	8	66.5	Springs for furniture and beds
P. Leiner Nutritional Products Torrance, CA	59.0	1.01	17	OTC	10	8	17.7	Vitamins and nutritional supplements
Eli Lilly Indianapolis, IN	12,376.0	4.21	89	NYSE	9	8	21.4	Ethical drugs, agricultural chemicals

The Limited Columbus, OH	7,734.6	1.28	41	NYSE	45	9	59.8	Women's and men's apparel stores
Lin Broadcasting New York, NY	2,079.3	1.24	39	OTC	29	7	21.0	Radio and TV stations
Liz Claiborne New York, NY	2,640.0	2.21	61	OTC	55	6	38.6	Designer of women's apparel
Longview Fibre Longview, WA	621.7	4.18	56	OTC	24	2	19.8	Logs, boards, paper products
Luby's Cafeterias San Antonio, TX	564.9	1.27	31	NYSE	16	10	21.0	Operates cafeterias in Texas
LyphoMed Inc. Melrose Park, IL	806.4	0.58	27	OTC	64	9	19.4	Critical-care nutritional products
Manor Care Silver Spring, MD	719.8	1.03	18	NYSE	17	9	23.8	Operates nursing homes and motels
Marion Labs Kansas City, MO	5,386.4	0.52	36	NYSE	57	6	37.4	Markets ethical drugs and health products
Masco Corp. Taylor, MI	4,580.1	1.63	35	NYSE	17	9	21.8	Building and home-improvement products
Mayfair Supermarkets Elizabeth, NJ	132.9	2.03	34	OTC	35	6	41.9	Foodtown supermarkets in New Jersey

Company and Location	Shareholders' Equity (millions)	EPS Latest 12 months	Price June 1, 1987	Exchange	Growth Rate 1983–1986 (percentage)	P/E	ROE (percent)	Type of Business
McDonalds Oak Brook, IL	10,193.0	3.84	80	NYSE	13	10	20.0	Fast food restaurants; franchising
Merry Land Development Augusta, GA	69.0	1.04	11	OTC	42	5	25.3	Real estate investment
Microsoft, Inc. Redmond, WA	2,883.8	2.30	113	OTC	74	8	42.2	Software for microcomputers
J. P. Morgan New York, NY	7,864.0	4.68	44	NYSE	21	13	20.4	Money-center bank holding company
Mylan Labs Pittsburgh, PA	536.8	0.65	15	NYSE	70	7	49.0	Pharmaceutical products
Neutrogena Corp. Los Angeles, CA	661.1	0.85	48	OTC	35	5	NA	Skin care products

New York Times Co. New York, NY	3,362.0	1.71	41	AMEX	17	9	23.9	Newspapers, magazines, TV, and cable TV stations
Nordstrom Seattle, WA	2,590.7	1.94	64	OTC	20	8	25.0	Shoe and apparel retailer
N. V. Homes, L. P. McLean, VA	242.4	0.81	12	AMEX	129	5	281.1	Builder of single-family homes
Oil Dri Corp. America Chicago, IL	128.2	1.34	32	OTC	44	11	19.6	Absorbent minerals, cat litter
Olsten Corp Westbury, NY	228.2	1.20	28	NYSE	32	7	23.1	Provides temporary work forces
Oracle Systems Belmont, CA	770.4	0.40	27	OTC	90	4	33.8	Database management software
Oshkosh B'Gosh Oshkosh, WI	503.2	3.18	69	OTC	35	5	48.8	Clothing manufacturer
Oshkosh Truck Oshkosh, WI	261.2	3.00	29	OTC	65	7	54.5	Specialized heavy-duty trucks
Oxford First Philadelphia, PA	59.4	1.26	16	NYSE	36	4	15.8	Financial services
Pall Corp. Glen Cove, NY	1,099.1	1.25	30	AMEX	13	8	20.7	Fine filters, fluid control equipment
Pansophic Systems Oak Brook, IL	375.5	0.93	22	NYSE	28	7	17.7	Standardized system software programs

Company and Location	Shareholders' Equity (millions)	EPS Latest 12 months	Price June 1, 1987	Exchange	Growth Rate 1983–1986 (percentage)	P/E	ROE (percent)	Type of Business
Par Pharmaceutical Spring Valley, NY	248.1	0.72	23	NYSE	25	9	24.6	Generic prescription drugs
Patten Corp. Stamford, VT	185.1	1.10	17	NYSE	108	5	80.9	Sells undeveloped rural land
Paul Harris Stores Indianapolis, IN	115.0	1.02	20	OTC	10	8	16.2	Apparel specialty stores
PCS, Inc. Scottsdale, AZ	377.0	0.53	26	OTC	43	6	100.2	Processes prescription drug claims
Philips Industries Dayton, OH	486.9	1.17	18	NYSE	18	8	20.8	Housing and recreational vehicle components
Price Co. San Diego, CA	2,102.1	1.37	43	OTC	54	11	41.6	Wholesale cash-and-carry merchandise
Puerto Rican Cement San Juan, PR	67.4	4.02	34	NYSE	44	2	17.5	Largest manufacturer of cement in Puerto Rico

Quebecor Montreal, Canada	202.7	1.16	13	NYSE	23	4	28.0	Newspapers, printing, film
Ralston Purina St. Louis, MO	6,174.5	7.18	81	NYSE	27	9	54.8	Pet food, bakery products, batteries
Reebok International Avon, MA	2,118.0	2.75	40	NYSE	395	5	164.2	Markets athletic footware
Rule Industries Gloucester, MA	21.9	0.67	9	OTC	28	4	22.8	Marine, hardware products; export services
Russ Berrie Co. Oakland, NJ	549.9	2.18	37	NYSE	24	6	33.2	Markets a variety of gift items
Ryan's Family Steak Houses Greenville, SC	727.5	0.24	14	OTC	61	6	18.4	Cafeteria-style restaurants
Safety-Kleen Elgin, IL	908.2	0.92	28	NYSE	19	8	26.2	Auto and farm machinery parts cleaning service
Sage Software Rockville, MD	85.5	0.42	19	OTC	144	5	11.5	Software tools for IBM equipment
Salem Carpet Mills Winston-Salem, NC	80.1	0.99	10	OTC	17	5	16.7	Manufactures tufted carpets
Sara Lee Chicago, IL	4,484.1	2.27	42	NYSE	12	9	21.0	Processed foods, consumer products

Company and Location	Shareholders' Equity (millions)	EPS Latest 12 months	Price June 1, 1987	Exchange	Growth Rate 1983–1986 (percentage)	Growth Rate P/E	ROE (percent)	Type of Business
Sbarro Commack, NY	183.5	0.61	21	OTC	68	10	37.0	Italian fast-food restaurants
SCI Systems Huntsville, AL	414.5	1.10	30	OTC	20	11	13.3	Electronic products and systems
Sealed Air Saddle Brook, NJ	333.2	2.31	46	NYSE	18	6	18.0	Protective packaging materials
Seaman Furniture Carle Place, NY	326.8	1.05	24	OTC	40	7	68.1	Retail furniture stores
Service Corp. Int'l Houston, TX	1,210.4	1.20	27	NYSE	19	10	18.0	Funeral services, cemetery
ServiceMaster LP Downers Grove, IL	935.5	1.22	30	NYSE	9	3	50.2	Health care and cleaning services
Shared Medical Systems Malvern, PA	704.4	2.10	28	OTC	22	8	29.8	Hospital computer services

Sherwin Williams Cleveland, OH	1,498.7	2.34	34	NYSE	26	11	22.2	Largest paint and varnish manufacturer
Shoney's Nashville, TN	978.7	1.19	27	OTC	18	10	19.9	Restaurants in the Southeast
Steel Technologies Louisville, KY	145.2	0.94	31	OTC	29	7	21.9	Processes flat rolled steel
Student Loan Marketing Washington, DC	2,706.4	3.32	71	AMEX	31	6	30.8	Student loan financing program
Sun Microsystems Mountain View, CA	1,411.0	1.04	44	OTC	124	4	30.6	Markets 32-bit work stations
Super Food Services Dayton, OH	169.4	1.58	25	AMEX	17	11	15.4	Wholesaler to IGA and others
Sysco Corp. Houston, TX	1,559.0	1.41	35	NYSE	11	13	15.8	Food distribution and service systems
Tech Data Corp. Clearwater, FL	50.9	0.43	16	OTC	141	4	14.6	Wholesaler of computer hardware products
Telerate New York, NY	1,982.7	0.97	42	NYSE	22	6	31.2	Computerized financial information network
Telex Corp. Tulsa, OK	1,096.7	5.28	75	NYSE	28	5	28.6	Computer peripherals, audio equipment

Company and Location	Shareholders' Equity (millions)	EPS Latest 12 months	Price June 1, 1987	Exchange	Growth Rate 1983–1986 (percentage)	Growth Rate P/E	ROE (percent)	Type of Business
Telxon Corp. Akron, OH	157.1	0.91	22	OTC	46	8	11.9	Hand-held microcomputer systems
3COM Corp. Santa Clara, CA	301.9	0.71	20	OTC	73	5	32.8	Computer networking products
Tyson Foods Springdale, AR	1,279.3	0.93	20	OTC	60	6	21.1	Integrated poultry business
Uniforce Temporary Personnel New Hyde Park, NY	31.6	0.42	11	OTC	30	9	13.4	National network of temporary-personnel agencies
U.S. Healthcare Blue Bell, PA	595.4	1.49	12	OTC	174	7	54.8	Health maintenance organizations
USG Corp. Chicago, IL	1,940.1	4.38	37	NYSE	43	2	23.5	Gypsum-base building products
UST Inc. Boston, MA	1,451.1	1.91	26	NYSE	15	7	33.0	Massachusetts bank holding company

Company							Description
V Band Systems Yonkers, NY	183.6	1.06	28	OTC	106	3	62.7	Telecommunications terminal equipment
Valspar Corp. Minneapolis, MN	321.3	1.44	29	AMEX	21	4	21.4	Paints and coatings
Vanguard Technology Fairfax, VA	60.2	0.68	18	AMEX	73	4	84.0	Provides data processing services
Versa Technologies Racine, WI	70.8	1.37	23	OTC	21	4	34.9	Silicone rubber, fluid power
VM Software Vienna, VA	184.2	0.79	23	OTC	59	15	24.2	Software for IBM mainframe
Wallace Computer Services Hillside, IL	408.0	2.49	40	NYSE	13	10	16.1	Business forms, printing
Wal-Mart Stores Bentonville, AR	16,632.1	1.72	59	NYSE	31	7	37.9	Operates discount stores
Waste Management Oak Brook, IL	9,032.5	1.86	42	NYSE	41	8	35.2	Solid and chemical waste management services
Waxman Industries Bedford Heights, OH	65.5	0.56	10	OTC	77	6	24.4	Home electrical and plumbing supplies

Company and Location	Shareholders' Equity (millions)	EPS Latest 12 months	Price June 1, 1987	Exchange	Growth Rate 1983–1986 (percentage)	P/E	ROE (percent)	Type of Business
Weis Markets Sunbury, PA	917.0	1.47	30	NYSE	9	9	11.0	Supermarkets in Pennsylvania, Maryland, and New York
Westwood One Culver City, CA	301.0	0.67	24	OTC	54	9	29.9	Produces national radio programs
A. L. Williams Duluth, GA	445.0	1.22	18	OTC	43	4	25.1	Life insurance agency holding company
Wolohan Lumber Saginaw, MI	82.1	1.10	14	OTC	57	3	18.1	Building supply centers
F. W. Woolworth New York, NY	3,141.9	3.38	48	NYSE	20	7	14.9	Variety, discount, and shoe stores
Wyse Technology San Jose, CA	403.6	1.50	34	OTC	70	8	24.7	Video display terminals, workstations, personal computers

Appendix B
A Guide to No-Load and
Low-Load Mutual Funds

(Reproduced by permission from the 1987
No-Load Mutual Fund Association Inc. Directory)

The list that follows includes all types of funds except money market funds, whose sales charges (loads), if any, are 3% or less. Also excluded are funds with less than $10 million of assets and funds requiring an initial investment of more than $10,000.

☐ Aggressive Growth Funds — for Maximum Long-Term Gain Through Investment in Common Stocks

Fund Name (Adviser) Address and Telephone Number	Investment Objective and Policy
BABSON ENTERPRISE FUND (Jones & Babson, Inc.) 3 Crown Center 2440 Pershing Road Kansas City, MO 64108 800-821-5591	Long-term growth by investing in smaller faster-growing companies.
BOSTON COMPANY SPECIAL GROWTH FUND (The Boston Company Advisors) 1 Boston Place Boston, MA 02106 800-225-5267	Above-average growth without regard to income through investments principally in securities of issues thought to have significant growth potential.
EQUITY PORTFOLIO: GROWTH (Fidelity Investments) 82 Devonshire Street Boston, MA 02109 800-544-6666/617-523-1919	Capital appreciation through investments in common stocks with above-average growth potential.

Fund Name (Adviser) Address and Telephone Number	Investment Objective and Policy
FIDELITY FREEDOM FUND (Fidelity Investments) 82 Devonshire Street Boston, MA 02109 800-544-6666/617-523-1919	Capital appreciation usually through common stocks. Only open to tax-qualified investors since short-term gains may be realized without limitation.
FIDELITY GROWTH COMPANY (Fidelity Investments) 82 Devonshire Street Boston, MA 02109 800-544-6666/617-523-1919	Aggressive growth by investment in stock and convertible securities with above-average growth characteristics. 3% load
FIDELITY MAGELLAN FUND (Fidelity Investments) 82 Devonshire Street Boston, MA 02109 800-544-6666/617-523-1919	Capital appreciation primarily through investments in common stock and convertible securities. 3% load
FIDELITY OTC PORTFOLIO (Fidelity Investments) 82 Devonshire Street Boston, MA 02109 800-544-6666/617-523-1919	Invested in companies whose securities are traded on the over-the-counter markets. 3% load
FIDELITY OVERSEAS FUND (Fidelity Investments) 82 Devonshire Street Boston, MA 02109 800-544-6666/617-523-1919	Long-term growth of capital primarily through investments in foreign securities. 3% load
FIDELITY SPECIAL SITUATIONS FUND (Fidelity Investments) 82 Devonshire Street Boston, MA 02109 800-544-6666/617-523-1919	Capital appreciation by investing in securities believed to involve special situations. 3% load
FINANCIAL DYNAMICS FUND (Financial Programs, Inc.) P.O. Box 2040 Denver, CO 80201 800-525-8085/800-525-9769 (CO)/303-779-1233 (Denver)	For the aggressive investor seeking capital growth through aggressive investment policies.

Fund Name (Adviser) Address and Telephone Number	Investment Objective and Policy
44 WALL STREET EQUITY FUND (Forty Four Management) One State Street Plaza New York, NY 10004 800-221-7836/212-344-4224 800-522-2033 (NY State)	Long-term capital appreciation — using a limited number of relatively small common stock companies with above-average potential and which are fundamentally attractive. 1% load
GINTEL CAPITAL APPRECIATION FUND (Gintel Equity Management) Greenwich Office Park #6 Greenwich, CT 06830 800-243-5808/203-622-6400	Open-end no-load nondiversified fund whose goal is long-term capi- tal appreciation.
HARTWELL GROWTH FUND (Hartwell Management Co.) 515 Madison Avenue New York, NY 10022 800-645-6405/212-308-3355	Invests in high-quality growth stocks with above-average appreci- ation potential.
HARTWELL LEVERAGE FUND (Hartwell Management Co.) 515 Madison Avenue New York, NY 10022 800-645-6405/212-308-3355	Seeks to achieve its objective through a program based on sub- stantially full investments in emerg- ing growth stocks and does not rely on market timing.
JANUS VENTURE FUND (Janus Capital Corp.) 100 Filmore Street Denver, CO 80206 800-525-3713/303-333-3863	Capital appreciation through in- vestments in stocks of smaller com- panies anticipated to experience strong growth in revenue, earnings, and assets.
LEHMAN CAPITAL FUND (Lehman Management Co., Inc.) 55 Water Street New York, NY 10041 800-221-5350/212-668-4308	Capital appreciation; essentially common stocks with above-average market appreciation potential.
LEHMAN OPPORTUNITY FUND (Lehman Management Co., Inc.) 55 Water Street New York, NY 10041 800-525-5350/212-668-4308	Long-term capital appreciation, in- come secondary, through common- stock investment.

Fund Name (Adviser) Address and Telephone Number	Investment Objective and Policy
NAESS & THOMAS SPECIAL FUND (Schroder Capital Management) The Vanguard Group P.O. Box 2600 Valley Forge, PA 19482 800-662-SHIP	Seeks long-term capital growth by investing in small, rapidly growing companies.
NEUWIRTH FUND (Wood, Struthers & Winthrop Management) 140 Broadway New York, NY 10005 800-221-5672/212-902-4396	A diversified investment company seeking growth of capital by emphasizing investments in common stocks and convertible securities with the possibility of capital appreciation.
T. ROWE PRICE CAPITAL APPRE-CIATION (T. Rowe Price Associates, Inc.) 100 E. Pratt Street Baltimore, MD 21202 800-638-5660/301-547-2308	To maximize capital appreciation through investment primarily in common stocks.
QUEST FOR VALUE FUND (Oppenheimer Capital Corp.) Oppenheimer Tower World Financial Center New York, NY 10281 800-525-7048/212-667-7587	Capital appreciation through investment in securities believed to be undervalued in relation to such factors as the company's assets, earnings, or growth potential.
STEINROE DISCOVERY FUND (Stein Roe & Farnham) 300 W. Adams Street Chicago, IL 60606 800-621-0320/312-368-7700	Long-term capital appreciation; investment in smaller or newer companies having prospects for rapid growth due to new products or services or technological developments.
STRONG OPPORTUNITY FUND (Strong/Corneliuson Capital Management) 815 E. Mason Street Milwaukee, WI 53202 800-368-3863/414-765-0620	Capital appreciation achieved by short-term trading. Invests in a diversified portfolio of common stock and equity-type securities. 2% load

Fund Name (Adviser) Address and Telephone Number	Investment Objective and Policy
TUDOR FUND (Tudor Management Co., Inc.) One New York Plaza New York, NY 10004 800-223-3332/212-908-9582	Capital appreciation. Writes covered-call options.
TWENTIETH CENTURY GROWTH (Investors Research Corp.) P.O. Box 200 Kansas City, MO 64141 800-345-2021/816-531-5575	Capital growth. Common stocks believed to have above-average appreciation potential.
TWENTIETH CENTURY ULTRA (Investors Research Corp.) P.O. Box 200 Kansas City, MO 64141 800-345-2021/618-531-5575	Capital growth. Common stocks believed to have above-average appreciation potential. 0.5% load
TWENTIETH CENTURY VISTA INVESTORS (Investors Research Corp.) P.O. Box 200 Kansas City, MO 64141 800-345-2021/618-531-5575	Capital growth. Common stocks believed to have above-average appreciation potential. 0.5% load
VALUE LINE CENTURION FUND (Value Line Inc.) 711 Third Avenue New York, NY 10017 800-223-0818	Tax-deferred growth through annuity (Value Guard II) offered with Guardian Insurance & Annuity Co.
VALUE LINE CONVERTIBLE FUND (Value Line Inc.) 711 Third Avenue New York, NY 10017 800-223-0818	Current income plus capital appreciation.

Fund Name (Adviser) Address and Telephone Number	Investment Objective and Policy
VALUE LINE LEVERAGED GROWTH (Value Line Inc.) 711 Third Avenue New York, NY 10017 800-223-0818	Noteworthy to the aggressive investor is this fund's ability to borrow up to 30% of its net assets to increase buying power. Most closely follows the Value Line Ranking System.
VANGUARD EXPLORER FUND (Wellington Management Co.) The Vanguard Group P.O. Box 2600 Valley Forge, PA 19482 800-662-SHIP	Long-term capital growth by investing in high-tech stocks of relatively small, unseasoned, or embryonic companies. Currently closed to new accounts.
VANGUARD EXPLORER II (Granahan Investment Management Inc.) The Vanguard Group P.O. Box 2600 Valley Forge, PA 19482 800-662-SHIP	Long-term capital growth by investing in high-tech stocks of small, unseasoned, or embryonic companies.

☐ Growth Funds — for Long-Term Growth of Capital Through Common Stocks

Fund Name (Adviser) Address and Telephone Number	Investment Objective and Policy
AMA GROWTH FUND, INC. (AMA Advisers, Inc.) 5 Sentry Parkway West P.O. Box 1111 Blue Bell, PA 19422 800-523-0864/215-825-0400	Invests primarily in common stocks believed by management to have potential for capital appreciation.

Fund Name (Adviser) Address and Telephone Number	Investment Objective and Policy
ACORN FUND (Harris Associates, Inc.) 2 N. La Salle Street, Suite 500 Chicago, IL 60602-3703 312-621-0630	We identify important trends, define investment concepts, and select appropriate smaller growth companies for long-term investment.
AFUTURE FUND (Carlisle-Asher Management) Legal Arts Building Front and Lemon Streets Media, PA 19063 800-523-7594/215-565-3131	Seeks growth of capital through investment in superior earnings companies with reasonable valuations.
AMERICAN INVESTORS FUND (American Investors Corp.) P.O. Box 2500 Greenwich, CT 06836 800-243-5353/203-531-5000	Growth of investment capital. Emphasis is on timing and selecting securities believed to have best potential for capital appreciation.
AMEV SPECIAL FUND (Amev Advisers, Inc.) Box 64284 St. Paul, MN 55164 800-872-2638	Appreciation of capital and the realization of both long- and short-term capital gains.
ARMSTRONG ASSOCIATES (Portfolios Inc.) 311 N. Market Street Dallas, TX 75202 214-744-5558	Capital growth by investing primarily in common stocks and securities convertible into common stock.
BABSON GROWTH FUND (Jones & Babson, Inc.) 3 Crown Center 2440 Pershing Road Kansas City, MO 64108 800-821-5591	Long-term growth of both capital and dividend income.
BENHAM TARGET MATURITIES TRUST (Benham Management Corp.) 755 Page Mill Road Palo Alto, CA 94304 800-4-SAFETY/800-348-0002 (AK and HI only)	First Treasury zero coupon bond fund; 6 series seeking the highest possible investment return on immunized portfolio of U.S. Treasury securities.

Fund Name (Adviser) Address and Telephone Number	Investment Objective and Policy
BOSTON COMPANY CAPITAL APPRECIATION (The Boston Company Advisors) One Boston Place Boston, MA 02106 800-225-5267	Long-term growth of capital with current income secondary. Invests primarily in common stock.
BULL & BEAR CAPITAL GROWTH (Bull & Bear Group, Inc.) 11 Hanover Square New York, NY 10005 800-847-4200/212-363-1100	Invests in emerging growth companies and special situations for long-term capital appreciation.
DE VEGH MUTUAL FUND (Wood Struthers & Winthrop Management) 140 Broadway New York, NY 10005 800-221-5672/212-902-4396	A diversified investment company seeking long-term capital appreciation through investment in common stocks and other equity securities.
ENERGY FUND INCORPORATED (Neuberger & Berman Management) 342 Madison Avenue New York, NY 10173 800-367-0770/212-850-8300	Long-term capital appreciation, primarily investing in common stocks whose activities are related to the field of energy.
FIDELITY CONTRAFUND (Fidelity Investments) 82 Devonshire Street Boston, MA 02109 800-544-6666/617-523-1919	Growth from contrarian strategy; seeks solid investment values among stocks currently out of favor with other investors.
FIDELITY TREND FUND (Fidelity Investments) 82 Devonshire Street Boston, MA 02109 800-544-6666/617-523-1919	Growth. Seeks long-term growth by considering market, industry, and company trends.
FIDELITY VALUE FUND (Fidelity Investments) 82 Devonshire Street Boston, MA 02109 800-544-6666/617-523-1919	Capital appreciation by investing in companies with valuable fixed assets or securities undervalued with respect to the company's assets, earnings, or growth potential.

Fund Name (Adviser) Address and Telephone Number	Investment Objective and Policy
FLEX RETIREMENT GROWTH FUND (R. Meeder & Assoc., Inc.) 6000 Memorial Drive Dublin, OH 43017 800-325-FLEX/614-766-7000 (OH)	Long-term growth. Fund is intended primarily for tax-exempt investors. Fund will not seek to avoid incurring ordinary income or capital gains.
GINTEL FUND (Gintel Equity Management) Greenwich Office Park #6 Greenwich, CT 06830 800-243-5808/212-931-5300/ 203-622-6400	An open-end, no-load mutual fund whose primary goal is capital appreciation. It is nondiversified with a cap at $150 million.
G. T. GLOBAL GROWTH FUNDS (G. T. Capital Management) 601 Montgomery Street, Suite 1400 San Francisco, CA 94111 800-824-1580/415-392-6181	A series of four growth funds: Pacific (formerly G. T. Pacific), Japan, Europe, and International. Invested in non-U.S. equity securities, seeking long-term growth and international diversification.
GREENSPRING FUND, INC. (Key Equity Management Corp.) Suite 322, Quadrangle, Village of Cross Keys Baltimore, MD 21210 301-435-9000	Long-term capital appreciation, primarily invests in common and preferred stocks and bonds that are undervalued, with emphasis on special situations.
GROWTH INDUSTRY SHARES (William Blair & Company) 135 S. La Salle Street Chicago, IL 60603 312-346-4830	Long-term appreciation of capital by investing in well-managed companies in growing industries.
IVY GROWTH FUND (Hingham Management, Inc.) 40 Industrial Park Road Hingham, MA 02043 800-235-3322/617-749-1416	Growth and income. The fund seeks to achieve long-term growth of capital primarily through investment in equity securities. Consideration of current income is secondary to this principal objective.

Fund Name (Adviser) Address and Telephone Number	Investment Objective and Policy
JANUS FUND (Janus Capital Corp.) 100 Filmore Street Denver, CO 80206 800-525-3713/303-333-3863	The only investment objective is capital appreciation. Will invest substantially all assets when market conditions warrant, otherwise takes a defensive position in interest-bearing securities.
JANUS VALUE FUND (Janus Capital Corp.) 100 Filmore Street Denver, CO 80206 800-525-3713/303-333-3863	The fund intends to buy stocks with strong current financial positions and future potential for growth which may not be recognized by the market.
KLEINWORT BENSON INVESTMENT STRATEGIES: TRANSATLANTIC GROWTH (Kleinwort Benson Int'l) 200 Park Avenue, Suite 5610 New York, NY 10166 800-233-9164/212-687-2515	Long-term growth through foreign equities.
LEXINGTON GROWTH FUND (Lexington Management Corp.) P.O. Box 1515 Saddle Brook, NJ 07662 800-526-0057	Capital appreciation; invests in common stocks believed to be undervalued and offering better than average growth possibilities.
LINDNER FUND (Lindner Management Corp.) 200 S. Bemiston, P. O. Box 11208 St. Louis, MO 63105 314-727-5305	Growth. Seeks optimum combination of low price/earnings ratio and growth.
MANHATTAN FUND (Neuberger & Berman Management) 342 Madison Avenue New York, NY 10173 800-367-0770/212-850-8300	Capital appreciation.

Fund Name
(Adviser)
Address and Telephone Number

Investment Objective
and
Policy

MATHERS FUND
  (Mathers and Company, Inc.)
  125 S. Wacker Drive
  Chicago, IL 60606
  312-236-8215

Long-term capital appreciation — emphasis on security selection using proprietary valuation model and special situation analysis.

MERIDIAN FUND
  (Aster Capital Management)
  60 E. Sir Francis Drake Boulevard,
  #306
  Larkspur, CA 94939
  415-461-6237

Long-term growth through common stock investments of small- and medium-size companies experiencing above-average growth in revenues and earnings.

"NEW BEGINNING" GROWTH
FUND
  (Sit Investment Associates, Inc.)
  1714 First Bank Place West
  Minneapolis, MN 55402
  612-332-3223

Maximize long-term capital appreciation by investing primarily in small emerging-growth companies. May invest in larger companies which offer growth possibilities.

NEWTON GROWTH FUND
  (M & I Investment Management
  Corp.)
  330 E. Kilbourn Avenue
  Two Plaza East, Suite 1150
  Milwaukee, WI 53202
  800-247-7039/800-242-7229
  (WI)/414-347-1141 (Milwaukee)

Long-term growth of capital, through a diversified portfolio of companies situated to benefit from changes in political, social, and economic trends.

NICHOLAS FUND, INC.
  (Nicholas Company, Inc.)
  700 N. Water Street, Suite 1010
  Milwaukee, WI 53202
  414-272-6133

Growth. Concentrates in common stocks of small- and medium-size companies.

NICHOLAS II
  (Nicholas Company, Inc.)
  700 N. Water Street, Suite 1010
  Milwaukee, WI 53202
  414-272-6133

Long-term growth — small companies in general.

Fund Name (Adviser) Address and Telephone Number	Investment Objective and Policy
NORTH STAR APOLLO FUND (Investment Advisers, Inc.) 1100 Dain Tower P. O. Box 357 Minneapolis, MN 55440 612-371-2884	Long-term capital appreciation. Invests in securities believed to be undervalued and considered to offer unusual opportunities for capital growth.
NORTH STAR REGIONAL FUND (Investment Advisers, Inc.) 1100 Dain Tower P. O. Box 357 Minneapolis, MN 55440 612-371-2884	The objective is capital appreciation. Invests 80% of its equities in companies headquartered in a seven-state midwest region.
NOVA FUND (Nova Advisors) Two Oliver Street Boston, MA 02109 800-572-0006/617-439-6126	Long-term growth. Emphasizes growth through investments in science technology and undervalued special situations.
THE ONE HUNDRED FUND (Berger Associates, Inc.) 899 Logan Street Denver, CO 80203 303-837-1020	Managed investments in successful and highly profitable corporations, with emphasis upon retained earnings.
THE PARTNERS FUND (Neuberger & Berman Management) 342 Madison Avenue New York, NY 10173 800-367-0770/212-850-8300	Capital growth. Emphasis on common stocks with a portion of assets in stocks selected for short-term gain potential.
PENNSYLVANIA MUTUAL FUND (Quest Advisory Group) 1414 Avenue of the Americas New York, NY 10019 800-221-4268/212-355-7311	Capital appreciation. Invests in common stocks with special emphasis on securities of small companies purchased on value basis. Currently closed to all new accounts except IRA and 403(b).

**Fund Name
(Adviser)
Address and Telephone Number**

**Investment Objective
and
Policy**

T. ROWE PRICE GROWTH
STOCK FUND
    (T. Rowe Price Associates, Inc.)
    100 E. Pratt Street
    Baltimore, MD 21202
    800-638-5660/301-547-2308

Long-term capital appreciation and
increased future income through
investment in well-established
growth companies.

T. ROWE PRICE NEW AMERICA
GROWTH
    (T. Rowe Price Associates, Inc.)
    100 E. Pratt Street
    Baltimore, MD 21202
    800-638-5660/301-547-2308

Seeks long-term growth of capital
through investment primarily in
common stocks of U.S. companies
operating in the service sector of
the economy.

T. ROWE PRICE NEW HORIZONS
FUND
    (T. Rowe Price Associates, Inc.)
    100 E. Pratt Street
    Baltimore, MD 21202
    800-638-5660/301-547-2308

Long-term capital appreciation
through investment in small, rapidly growing companies.

THE RIGHTIME FUND
    (Rightime Econometrics, Inc.)
    The Benson East Office Plaza
    Jenkintown, PA 19046
    800-242-1421/215-927-7880

High total return consistent with
reasonable risk.

ROYCE FUND — VALUE SERIES
    (Quest Advisory Corp.)
    1414 Avenue of the Americas
    New York, NY 10019
    800-221-4268/212-355-7311

Capital appreciation. Invests in
common stocks with special emphasis on securities of small companies purchased on value basis.

SAFECO GROWTH FUND
    (Safeco Asset Management Co.)
    Safeco Plaza T15
    Seattle, WA 98185
    800-426-6730

Seeks to provide growth of capital
and increased income that ordinarily follows such growth.

SELECTED SPECIAL SHARES
    (Prescott Asset Management)
    230 W. Monroe
    Chicago, IL 60606
    800-621-7321/800-572-4437 (IL
    only)

Growth of capital. Invests primarily
in common stocks. Investment income is only incidental.

Fund Name (Adviser) Address and Telephone Number	Investment Objective and Policy
STEINROE & FARNHAM CAPITAL OPPORTUNITIES FUND (Stein Roe & Farnham) 300 W. Adams Street Chicago, IL 60606 800-621-0320/312-368-7700	Long-term capital appreciation. Invests in selected companies with the potential for rapid growth.
STEINROE & FARNHAM STOCK FUND (Stein Roe & Farnham) 300 W. Adams Street Chicago, IL 60606 800-621-0320/312-368-7700	Long-term capital appreciation. Invests primarily in companies having strong promise of increased earnings and dividends at an above-average rate over the long term.
STEINROE SPECIAL FUND (Stein Roe & Farnham) 300 W. Adams Street Chicago, IL 60606 800-621-0320/312-368-7700	Maximum capital appreciation. Invests in companies expected to benefit from special factors or trends.
STEINROE UNIVERSE FUND (Stein Roe & Farnham) 300 W. Adams Street Chicago, IL 60606 800-621-0320/312-368-7700	Maximum capital appreciation through investing in an unusually broad spectrum of common stocks utilizing a proprietary computerized selection process.
TWENTIETH CENTURY SELECT (Investors Research Corp.) P.O. Box 200 Kansas City, MO 64141 800-345-2021/816-531-5575	Capital growth. Common stocks believed to have above-average appreciation potential and pay dividends.
UNIFIED GROWTH FUND (Unified Management Corp.) Guaranty Building Indianapolis, IN 46204 800-862-7283/317-634-3300	Capital appreciation. Medium to smaller companies with above-average growth in sales and earnings. Attention to timing.
UNITED SERVICES GROWTH FUND (United Services Advisors, Inc.) Box 29467 San Antonio, TX 78229-0467 800-824-4653/512-696-1234	Growth. Income. Invested in common stocks of companies that show an excellent potential for capital appreciation.

Fund Name (Adviser) Address and Telephone Number	Investment Objective and Policy
USAA GROWTH FUND (USAA Investment Management) P.O. Box 33277 San Antonio, TX 78265 800-531-8181	Long-term growth of capital, income secondary; diversified and flexible — can take a defensive position.
USAA SUNBELT ERA FUND (USAA Investment Management) P.O. Box 33277 San Antonio, TX 78265 800-531-8181	Capital appreciation; invests in common stocks of emerging companies located in Sunbelt region of U.S. that have high potential for future growth.
VALUE LINE SPECIAL SITUATIONS FUND (Value Line, Inc.) 711 Third Avenue New York, NY 10017 800-223-0818/800-522-5217 (NY only)	For aggressive investors, stressing appreciation potential from less-seasoned, emerging companies. Maximum capital appreciation with no consideration given to current income is this fund's goal.
VANGUARD/W.L. MORGAN GROWTH (Wellington Management Co.) The Vanguard Group P. O. Box 2600 Valley Forge, PA 19482 800-662-SHIP	Seeks long-term growth of capital by investing in companies believed to have above-average growth potential.
VANGUARD WORLD FUND — U.S. GROWTH PORTFOLIO (Wellington Management Co.) The Vanguard Group P.O. Box 2600 Valley Forge, PA 19482 800-662-SHIP	A no-load mutual fund seeking long-term capital appreciation by investing in common stocks of U.S.-based companies.
VANGUARD WORLD FUND — INTERNATIONAL GROWTH PORTFOLIO (Schroder Capital Management) P.O. Box 2600 Valley Forge, PA 19482 800-662-SHIP	A no-load mutual fund seeking long-term capital appreciation by investing in common stocks of companies based outside the United States.

☐ Specialty Funds — for Investment in a Specific Industry Through Common Stocks

Fund Name (Adviser) Address and Telephone Number	Investment Objective and Policy
CENTURY SHARES TRUST (Internally Managed) One Liberty Square Boston, MA 02109 800-321-1928/617-482-3060	Long-term growth of principal and income from investment in common stocks of insurance companies and banks.
FIDELITY SELECT PORTFOLIOS (Fidelity Investments) 82 Devonshire Street Boston, MA 02109 800-554-6666/617-523-1919	Growth. Group of 35 equity-based sector portfolios plus money market. 2% load and 1% redemption
FINANCIAL STRATEGIC PORTFOLIOS, INC. (Financial Programs, Inc.) P.O. Box 2040 Denver, CO 80201 800-525-8085/800-525-9769 (CO)/303-779-1233 (Denver)	A sector fund seeking capital appreciation through nine portfolios: energy, gold, health sciences, leisure, Pacific Basin, European, financial services, technology, utilities.
GOLCONDA INVESTORS LTD. (Bull & Bear Group, Inc.) 11 Hanover Square New York, NY 10005 800-847-4200/212-363-1100	Specialized; invests in gold bullion and internationally diversified portfolio of gold mining shares.
LEXINGTON GOLD FUND (Lexington Management Corp.) P.O. Box 1515 Saddle Brook, NJ 07662 800-526-0057	Capital appreciation, income secondary. Invests exclusively in gold bullion and gold mining stocks.
MEDICAL TECHNOLOGY FUND (AMA Advisers, Inc.) 5 Sentry Parkway West P.O. Box 1111 Blue Bell, PA 19422 800-523-0864/215-825-0400	Growth through companies engaged in products or services related to technology for medicine or health care.

Fund Name (Adviser) Address and Telephone Number	Investment Objective and Policy
T. ROWE PRICE INTERNATIONAL BOND FUND (Rowe Price Fleming) 100 E. Pratt Street Baltimore, MD 21202 800-638-5660/800-IRA-5000	Seeks to achieve high income by investing in international high-quality, fixed-income securities. Capital appreciation is a secondary objective.
T. ROWE PRICE INTERNATIONAL STOCK FUND (Rowe Price Fleming) 100 E. Pratt Street Baltimore, MD 21202 800-638-5660/301-547-2308	Total return from long-term growth of capital and income through investment in foreign securities.
T. ROWE PRICE NEW ERA FUND (T. Rowe Price Associates, Inc.) 100 E. Pratt Street Baltimore, MD 21202 800-638-5660/301-547-2308	Long-term capital appreciation through investment primarily in companies that own or develop natural resources.
UNITED SERVICES GOLD SHARES FUND (United Services Advisors, Inc.) P.O. Box 29467 San Antonio, TX 78229-0467 800-824-4653/512-696-1234	Growth. Income. Invested primarily in South African gold shares.
UNITED SERVICES NEW PROSPECTOR FUND (United Services Advisors, Inc.) P.O. Box 29467 San Antonio, TX 78229-0467 800-824-4653/512-696-1234	Long-term growth. Income. Invested primarily in North American gold mines and other precious metals.
UNITED SERVICES PROSPECTOR FUND (United Services Advisors, Inc.) P.O. Box 26467 San Antonio, TX 78229-0467 800-824-4653/512-696-1234	Long-term growth. Income. Invested primarily in North American gold mines and other precious metals. Closed to new accounts.

Fund Name (Adviser) Address and Telephone Number	Investment Objective and Policy
USAA CORNERSTONE FUND (USAA Investment Management) P.O. Box 33277 San Antonio, TX 78265 800-531-8181	Positive inflation adjusted return by investing assets equally in gold, foreign, real estate, and basic value stocks and government securities.
USAA GOLD FUND (USAA Investment Management) P.O. Box 33277 San Antonio, TX 78265 800-531-8181	Long-term capital appreciation and protection of purchasing power against inflation by investing assets primarily in gold-mining stocks.
VANGUARD SPECIALIZED PORT-FOLIO (Wellington Management Co.) The Vanguard Group P. O. Box 2600 Valley Forge, PA 19482 800-662-SHIP	Offers series of portfolios each concentrating in common stocks of a particular industry or group of related industries. Energy, gold and precious metals, health care, service economy, technology.
WORLD OF TECHNOLOGY (Financial Programs, Inc.) P.O. Box 2040 Denver, CO 80201 800-525-8085/800-525-9769 (CO)/303-779-1223 (Denver)	Seeks long-term capital appreciation through a portfolio of worldwide high-tech companies.

☐ Growth and Income Funds — for Long-Term Current Income and Capital Growth Through Investments in Stocks and Bonds

Fund Name (Adviser) Address and Telephone Number	Investment Objective and Policy
ANALYTIC OPTIONED EQUITY FUND (Analytic Investment Management) 2222 Martin Street, Suite 230 Irvine, CA 92715 714-833-0294	To earn the long-term return of higher quality stocks with much less risk by hedging with options.

Fund Name (Adviser) Address and Telephone Number	Investment Objective and Policy
COPLEY TAX-MANAGED FUND (Copley Financial Services Corp.) 109 Howl Street Fall River, MA 02769 617-674-8459	Safety of principal. Purchases stocks of companies with a history of increasing dividends; banks.
FIDELITY FUND (Fidelity Investments) 82 Devonshire Street Boston, MA 02109 800-544-6666/617-523-1919	Growth with income. Invests primarily in dividend-paying common stocks and convertible securities of blue chip companies.
FIDELITY GROWTH & INCOME FUND (Fidelity Investments) 82 Devonshire Street Boston, MA 02109 800-544-6666/617-523-1919	Capital growth, current income and growth of income. 2% load
FIDELITY PURITAN FUND (Fidelity Investments) 82 Devonshire Street Boston, MA 02109 800-544-6666/617-523-1919	Primary emphasis on income growth from high-yielding common stocks, convertibles, and fixed-income securities.
FINANCIAL INDUSTRIAL FUND (Financial Programs, Inc.) P.O. Box 2040 Denver, CO 80201 800-525-8085/800-525-9769 (CO)/303-779-1233 (Denver)	Primary focus on long-term capital growth, with income a secondary strategy.
GENERAL SECURITIES (Craig-Hallum, Inc.) 701 4th Avenue So., 10th floor Minneapolis, MN 55415-1655 612-332-1212	Capital appreciation and security of principal. Flexible to use stocks and sometimes fixed-income securities, also covered options.
GINTEL ERISA FUND (Gintel Equity Management) Greenwich Office Park #6 Greenwich, CT 06830 800-243-5808/212-931-5300/ 203-622-6400	Nondiversified fund restricted to investors whose assets are qualified as tax-exempt. Objective to maximize return through long-term appreciation, investment income, and short-term gains.

Fund Name (Adviser) Address and Telephone Number	Investment Objective and Policy
GUARDIAN MUTUAL FUND (Neuberger & Berman Management) 342 Madison Avenue New York, NY 10173 800-367-0770/212-850-8300	Capital appreciation with income secondary; common stocks of seasoned companies, flexibility to shift to fixed income securities.
LEPERCQ-ISTEL FUND (Lepercq, de Neufize & Co.) 345 Park Avenue New York, NY 10154 212-702-0174	Seeks possible long-term growth of capital and reasonable current income.
LEHMAN INVESTORS FUND (Lehman Management Co., Inc.) 55 Water Street New York, NY 10041 800-221-5350/212-668-4308	Long-term growth of capital; income secondary, through common-stock investment.
LEXINGTON RESEARCH FUND (Lexington Management Corp.) P.O. Box 1515 Saddle Brook, NJ 07662 800-526-0057	Long-term capital appreciation; invests in common stocks of large, ably managed, well-financed companies.
LMH FUND, LTD. (Heine Management Group) 253 Post Rd. W., Suite 1010 P.O. Box 830 Westport, CT 06881 800-442-2564/800-522-2564 (in CT)	Seeks capital appreciation and current income by selecting equity securities through a valuation analysis approach.
LOOMIS-SAYLES MUTUAL FUND (Loomis, Sayles & Co.) Box 449, Back Bay Annex Boston, MA 02117 617-578-4200	Flexibly managed portfolio of stocks and bonds aiming at reasonable long-term capital appreciation and current income return without undue risk.

Fund Name
(Adviser)
Address and Telephone Number

Investment Objective
and
Policy

MUTUAL QUALIFIED INCOME
FUND
  (Heine Securities Corp.)
  26 Broadway
  New York, NY 10004
  800-457-0211/212-908-4048

Primary objective is capital appreciation without regard to holding period for individual portfolio positions and, secondarily, the receipt
of income.

MUTUAL SHARES CORP.
  (Heine Securities Corp.)
  26 Broadway
  New York, NY 10004
  800-457-0211/212-908-4048

Primary objective is long-term capital appreciation primarily pursued
through investments in common,
preferred, and debt securities available at less than intrinsic value. Second objective is receipt of income.

NORTH STAR STOCK FUND
  (Investment Advisers, Inc.)
  1100 Dain Tower, Box 357
  Minneapolis, MN 55440
  612-371-2884

Primary objective is capital appreciation, with income being its secondary objective. The portfolio
consists primarily of common
stocks.

PENN SQUARE MUTUAL FUND
  (Penn Square Management)
  2650 Westview Drive
  Wyomissing, PA 19610
  800-523-8440/215-670-1031

Long-term capital growth with income. Investments principally in
common stocks of larger companies considered undervalued on a
fundamental basis.

PINE STREET FUND
  (Wood, Struthers & Winthrop
  Management)
  140 Broadway
  New York, NY 10005
  800-221-5672/212-902-4396

A diversified investment company
seeking continuity of income and
the opportunity for growth through
investments in common stocks and
other equity securities.

T. ROWE PRICE GROWTH &
INCOME FUND
  (T. Rowe Price Associates, Inc.)
  100 E. Pratt Street
  Baltimore, MD 21202
  800-638-5660/301-547-2308

Long-term capital growth, reasonable current dividend level, and
growth of future income through
investment in income-producing
common stocks.

Fund Name (Adviser) Address and Telephone Number	Investment Objective and Policy
SAFECO EQUITY FUND (Safeco Asset Management Co.) Safeco Plaza T15 Seattle, WA 98185 800-426-6730	Seeks to provide long-term capital growth and a reasonable current income.
SAFECO INCOME FUND (Safeco Asset Management Co.) Safeco Plaza T15 Seattle, WA 98185 800-426-6730	Income is the primary objective, but investments may also be selected with a view to long-term capital growth.
SELECTED AMERICAN SHARES (Prescott Asset Management Inc.) 230 W. Monroe Chicago, IL 60606 800-621-7321/800-572-4437 (IL)	Combination of growth of capital and income. Investment among common stocks and fixed-income securities in varying proportions.
STEINROE TOTAL RETURN FUND (Stein Roe & Farnham) 300 W. Adams Street Chicago, IL 60606 800-621-0320/312-368-7700	Current income and capital appreciation. Seeks maximum total return consistent with reasonable investment risk through a combination of equities, convertibles, and fixed-income securities.
STRATTON GROWTH FUND (Stratton Management Co.) Butler & Skippack, Box 550 Blue Bell, PA 19422 215-542-8025	Growth — primary; income — secondary. All common stocks.
STRONG INVESTMENT FUND (Strong/Corneliuson Capital Management Inc.) 815 E. Mason Street Milwaukee, WI 53202 800-368-3863/414-765-0620	Invests in stocks and interest-paying securities, depending upon market conditions. Maximum 65% stocks. Seeks capital growth and income. Strives to maintain principal. 1% load

Fund Name (Adviser) Address and Telephone Number	Investment Objective and Policy
STRONG TOTAL RETURN FUND (Strong/Corneliuson Capital Management Inc.) 815 E. Mason Street Milwaukee, WI 53202 800-368-3863/414-765-0620	Invests in stocks and interest-bearing securities, depending upon market conditions. Flexible portfolio striving for highest total return in all market conditions. 1% load
UMB STOCK FUND (Jones & Babson, Inc.) 3 Crown Center, 2400 Pershing Road Kansas City, MO 64108 800-821-5591	Long-term growth of capital and dividend income.
UNIFIED MUTUAL SHARES (Unified Management Corp.) Guaranty Building Indianapolis, IN 46204 800-862-7283/317-634-3300	Capital growth and current income. Flexible with emphasis on high-quality stocks and convertibles; uses covered-option writing.
UNITED SERVICES GOOD AND BAD TIMES FUND (United Services Advisors, Inc.) Box 29467 San Antonio, TX 78229-0467 800-824-4653/512-696-1234	Preservation of capital and capital appreciation. Invested in the common stock of conservative, financially sound, and well-managed companies.
VALUE LINE FUND (Value Line, Inc.) 711 Third Avenue New York, NY 10017 800-223-0818	Best suited for investors whose primary goal is capital appreciation. Income is secondary objective.
VANGUARD INDEX TRUST (Vanguard Group) The Vanguard Group P.O. Box 2600 Valley Forge, PA 19482 800-662-SHIP	Seeks to provide investment results that correspond to the price and yield performance of the S&P 500 index, by owning all stocks in the S&P 500.

Fund Name (Adviser) Address and Telephone Number	Investment Objective and Policy
VANGUARD STAR FUND (Vanguard Group) The Vanguard Group P.O. Box 2600 Valley Forge, PA 19482 800-662-SHIP	Provides balanced return of growth and income through investing in four other Vanguard funds. Designed specifically for tax advantaged accounts, e.g., IRAs and Keoghs.
VANGUARD WINDSOR FUND (Wellington Management Co.) The Vanguard Group P.O. Box 2600 Valley Forge, PA 19482 800-662-SHIP	Long-term growth of capital and income by investing in companies with favorable prospects but currently undervalued in the market. Currently closed to new accounts.
VANGUARD WINDSOR II (Barrow, Hanley, Mewhinney & Strauss, Inc.) P.O. Box 2600 Valley Forge, PA 19482 800-662-SHIP	Long-term growth of capital and income by investing in companies with favorable prospects but currently undervalued in the market.
WPG FUND (WPG Advisers, Inc.) One New York Plaza New York, NY 10004 800-223-3332/212-908-9582 (NY only)	To achieve a return consisting of capital appreciation and current income.
WPG GOVERNMENT SECURITIES FUND (WPG Advisers, Inc.) One New York Plaza New York, NY 10004 800-223-3332/212-908-9582 (NY only)	To achieve a high current return consistent with capital preservation.

☐ Fixed-Income Funds — for Steady Current Income Through Corporate Bonds and U.S. Government-Backed Securities, Such as GNMA's and FNMA's

Fund Name (Adviser) Address and Telephone Number	Investment Objective and Policy
AMA INCOME FUND (AMA Advisers, Inc.) 5 Sentry Parkway West P.O. Box 1111 Blue Bell, PA 19422 800-523-0864/215-825-0400	Income: seeks the highest investment income available consistent with preservation of capital.
AMERICAN INVESTORS INCOME (American Investors Corp.) P.O. Box 2500 Greenwich, CT 60836 800-243-5353/203-531-5000	High current income. Capital appreciation secondary. Diversified investments in generous yielding lower-rated bonds and preferred stocks.
BABSON BOND TRUST (Jones & Babson, Inc.) 3 Crown Center 2440 Pershing Road Kansas City, MO 64108 800-821-5591	Provide maximum current income and stability of principal.
BENHAM GNMA INCOME FUND (Benham Management Corp.) 755 Page Mill Road Palo Alto, CA 94304 800-4-SAFETY/800-348-0002 (AK and HI)	For high current income, safety and liquidity; invests in GNMA certificates guaranteed by the U.S. government.
BOSTON COMPANY MANAGED INCOME FUND (The Boston Company Advisors) One Boston Place Boston, MA 02106 800-225-5267	High current income consistent with prudent risk of capital; invests at least 65% of total assets in U.S. government obligations and corporate obligations in the four highest ratings of S&P and Moody's; invests at least 65% in obligations with maturities of 10 years or less.

Fund Name (Adviser) Address and Telephone Number	Investment Objective and Policy
BULL & BEAR HIGH YIELD FUND (Bull & Bear Group, Inc.) 11 Hanover Square New York, NY 10005 800-847-4200/212-363-1100	To provide its shareholders with the highest monthly income over the long term from a diversified portfolio of debt securities.
CALVERT INCOME FUND (Calvert Asset Management Co.) 1700 Pennsylvania Avenue N.W. Washington, D.C. 20006 800-368-2748/301-951-4820	A high level of current income through investment in corporate bonds and other income producing securities.
CAPITAL PRESERVATION TREA-SURY NOTE TRUST (Benham Management Corp.) 755 Page Mill Road Palo Alto, CA 94304 800-4-SAFETY/800-848-0002 (AK and HI)	For high yields and longer maturities; invests exclusively in U.S. Treasury notes.
FIDELITY FLEXIBLE BOND FUND (Fidelity Investments) 82 Devonshire Street Boston, MA 02109 800-544-6666/617-523-1919	Income. At least 80% of assets in investment-grade (rated BBB or better) debt securities. Some consideration of growth characteristics of securities.
FIDELITY GINNIE MAE PORTFO-LIO (Fidelity Investments) 82 Devonshire Street Boston, MA 02109 800-544-6666/617-523-1919	Income. Invests primarily in Ginnie Maes and only in securities backed by the U.S. government.
FIDELITY GOVERNMENT SECURI-TIES LTD. (Fidelity Investments) 82 Devonshire Street Boston, MA 02109 800-544-6666/617-523-1919	Income from obligations issued by the U.S. government, its agencies or instrumentalities; income is exempt from state and local income taxes in all states.

**Fund Name
(Adviser)
Address and Telephone Number**

**Investment Objective
and
Policy**

FIDELITY HIGH INCOME
(Fidelity Investments)
82 Devonshire Street
Boston, MA 02109
800-544-6666/617-523-1919

High current income from a diversified portfolio of high-yielding, fixed-income corporate securities. Growth will also be considered in selecting securities.

FIDELITY MORTGAGE SECURITIES
(Fidelity Investments)
82 Devonshire Street
Boston, MA 02109
800-544-6666/617-523-1919

Income from investments in A or better quality mortgage backed instruments such as Fannie Maes, Ginnie Maes, and Freddie Macs.

FIDELITY THRIFT TRUST
(Fidelity Investments)
82 Devonshire Street
Boston, MA 02109
800-544-6666/617-523-1919

Income. Corporate obligations (A or better), government securities, and money market instruments; maturity not to exceed ten years.

FINANCIAL HIGH YIELD PORTFOLIO
(Financial Programs, Inc.)
P.O. Box 2040
Denver, CO 80201
800-525-8085/800-525-9769
(CO)/303-779-1233 (Denver)

Higher yielding income from bonds rated medium-quality or lower by industry rating services, convertible and nonconvertible issues, and preferred stocks.

FINANCIAL SELECT INCOME PORTFOLIO
(Financial Programs, Inc.)
P.O. Box 2040
Denver, CO 80201
800-525-8085/800-525-9769
(CO)/303-779-1233 (Denver)

High current income consistent with preservation of capital through high-quality corporate and government bonds and other debt securities.

LEXINGTON GNMA INCOME FUND
(Lexington Management Corp.)
P.O. Box 1515
Saddle Brook, NJ 07662
800-526-0057

High current income, liquidity, safety; invests in mortgage-backed Ginnie Mae certificates guaranteed by U.S. government.

Fund Name (Adviser) Address and Telephone Number	Investment Objective and Policy
LIBERTY FUND (Neuberger & Berman Management Inc.) 342 Madison Avenue New York, NY 10172 800-367-0770/212-850-8300	High level of current income, diversified portfolio of high-yielding, lower-rated, fixed-income securities.
NEWTON INCOME FUND (M & I Investment Management) 330 E. Kilbourn Avenue Two Plaza East, Suite 1150 Milwaukee, WI 53202 800-247-7039/800-242-7229 (WI)/414-347-1141 (Milwaukee)	Above-average current income consistent with preservation of capital; investing in a diversified portfolio of fixed-income securities.
NICHOLAS INCOME FUND (Nicholas Co., Inc.) 700 N. Water Street, Suite 1010 Milwaukee, WI 53202 414-272-6133	High current income consistent with conservation of capital.
NORTH STAR BOND FUND (Investment Advisers, Inc.) 1100 Dain Tower, Box 357 Minneapolis, MN 55440 612-371-2884	High level of current income consistent with preservation of capital through investment in a diversified portfolio of investment grade bonds and other debt securities.
NORTH STAR RESERVE FUND (Investment Advisers, Inc.) 1100 Dain Tower, Box 357 Minneapolis, MN 55440 612-371-2884	Provide shareholders with high levels of capital stability and liquidity and, to the extent consistent with these primary objectives, a high level of current income.
T. ROWE PRICE GNMA FUND (T. Rowe Price Associates) 100 E. Pratt Street Baltimore, MD 21202 800-638-5660/301-547-2308	Highest current income consistent with capital preservation, maximum credit protection. Invests exclusively in securities backed by the full faith and credit of the U.S. government.

Fund Name (Adviser) Address and Telephone Number	Investment Objective and Policy
T. ROWE PRICE HIGH YIELD FUND (T. Rowe Price Associates) 100 E. Pratt Street Baltimore, MD 21202 800-638-5660/301-547-2308	High current income through a diversified portfolio of high-yielding, medium- and lower-quality fixed-income securities.
T. ROWE PRICE NEW INCOME FUND (T. Rowe Price Associates) 100 E. Pratt Street Baltimore, MD 21202 800-638-5660/301-547-2308	High current income with reasonable stability through investment grade fixed-income securities.
T. ROWE PRICE SHORT-TERM BOND FUND (T. Rowe Price Associates) 100 E. Pratt Street Baltimore, MD 21202 800-638-5660/301-547-2308	Minimum fluctuation in principal value, liquidity, and consistent with these objectives, the highest level of income.
ROYCE FUND — HIGH YIELD SERIES (Quest Advisory Corp.) 1414 Avenue of the Americas New York, NY 10019 800-221-4268/212-355-7311	High current income. Invests primarily in a diversified portfolio of high yield fixed-income securities.
STEINROE GOVERNMENT PLUS (Stein Roe & Farnham) 300 W. Adams St. Chicago, IL 60606 800-621-0320/312-368-7700	High current income by investing principally in debt securities supported by the U.S. government.
STEINROE HIGH-YIELD BONDS (Stein Roe & Farnham) 300 W. Adams Street Chicago, IL 60606 800-621-0320/312-368-7700	High current income by investing in medium-quality debt securities.

Fund Name (Adviser) Address and Telephone Number	Investment Objective and Policy
STEINROE MANAGED BONDS (Stein Roe & Farnham) 300 W. Adams Street Chicago, IL 60606 800-621-8320/312-368-7700	High current income consistent with preservation of capital. Diversified portfolio of high-quality, marketable debt securities, U.S. government and corporate bonds.
STRONG INCOME FUND (Strong/Corneliuson Capital Management) 815 E. Mason Street Milwaukee, WI 53202 800-368-3863/414-765-0620	Highest level of current income consistent with reasonable risks. Diverse portfolio of fixed income securities and dividend-paying stocks.
TWENTIETH CENTURY U.S. GOVERNMENT (Investors Research Corp.) P.O. Box 200 Kansas City, MO 64141 800-345-2021/816-531-5575	Seeks income by investing in securities of the U.S. government and its agencies.
UMB BOND FUND (Jones & Babson, Inc.) 3 Crown Center, 2440 Pershing Road Kansas City, MO 64108 800-821-5591	Maximum current income with quality and maturity standards.
USAA INCOME (USAA Investment Management) P.O. Box 33277 San Antonio, TX 78265 800-531-8181	Maximum current income without undue risk to principal. Flexible, diversified portfolio, high yields relative to risk.
VALUE LINE AGGRESSIVE INCOME TRUST (Value Line, Inc.) 711 Third Avenue New York, NY 10017 800-223-0818	Maximum current income. Capital appreciation is a secondary objective that will only be sought when consistent with primary objective.

Fund Name **(Adviser)** **Address and Telephone Number**	**Investment Objective** **and** **Policy**
VALUE LINE U.S. GOVERNMENT SECURITIES FUND (Value Line, Inc.) 711 Third Avenue New York, NY 10017 800-223-0818	Seeks high-grade bonds for yield, safety, and capital appreciation in the event of falling interest rates.
VANGUARD GNMA PORTFOLIO (Wellington Management Co.) The Vanguard Group P.O. Box 2600 Valley Forge, PA 19482 800-662-SHIP	Current income, primarily from mortgage-backed securities, whose timely payment of interest and principal is guaranteed by the U.S. government.
VANGUARD HIGH YIELD BOND (Wellington Management Co.) The Vanguard Group P.O. Box 2600 Valley Forge, PA 19482 800-662-SHIP	Current income, primarily from high-yielding, medium-grade quality bonds.
VANGUARD INVESTMENT GRADE BOND (Wellington Management Co.) The Vanguard Group P.O. Box 2600 Valley Forge, PA 19482 800-662-SHIP	High current income by investing in top-quality bonds from the four highest investment ratings.
VANGUARD SHORT TERM BOND (Vanguard Group) The Vanguard Group P.O. Box 2600 Valley Forge, PA 19482 800-662-SHIP	High current income through short-term bonds with an average maturity of less than four years.

☐ Equity Income Funds — for High Current Yields from Equity Securities with High Dividends

FIDELITY EQUITY-INCOME FUND (Fidelity Investments) 82 Devonshire Street Boston, MA 02109 800-544-6666/617-523-1919	Yield exceeding composite yield of S&P 500 and some capital appreciation. 2% load

Fund Name (Adviser) Address and Telephone Number	Investment Objective and Policy
FINANCIAL INDUSTRIAL INCOME FUND (Financial Programs, Inc.) P.O. Box 2040 Denver, CO 80201 800-525-8085/800-525-9769 (CO)/303-779-1233 (Denver)	Emphasis on current income, with capital growth given additional consideration.
GATEWAY OPTION INCOME FUND (Gateway Investment Advisers) P.O. Box 458167 Cincinnati, OH 45245 513-248-2700	Earns a high current return with less risk by owning all 100 stocks in the S&P 100 stock index and selling call options on the index.
LINDNER DIVIDEND FUND (Lindner Management Corp.) 200 S. Bemiston P.O. Box 11208 St. Louis, MO 63105 314-727-5305	Primary objective is the production of current income. Capital appreciation is a secondary objective of fund. Currently closed to new accounts.
T. ROWE PRICE EQUITY-INCOME FUND (T. Rowe Price Associates, Inc.) 100 E. Pratt Street Baltimore, MD 21202 800-638-5660/301-547-2308	Seeks high current income and potential for capital appreciation by investing in dividend-paying common stocks of established companies.
STRATTON MONTHLY DIVIDEND SHARES (Stratton Management Co.) Butler & Skippack, Box 550 Blue Bell, PA 19422 215-542-8025	Seeks high rate of return from common stocks. Monthly dividend payments.
UNIFIED INCOME FUND (Unified Management Corp.) Guaranty Building Indianapolis, IN 46204 800-862-7283/317-634-3300	Current income and capital appreciation. Invests without quality restrictions. May buy stock and write options.

Fund Name (Adviser) Address and Telephone Number	**Investment Objective** and Policy

VALUE LINE INCOME FUND
(Value Line, Inc.)
711 Third Avenue
New York, NY 10017
800-223-0818

May be of interest to investors seeking a combination of current income and moderate capital appreciation.

VANGUARD QUALIFIED DIVIDEND I
(Wellington Management Co.)
The Vanguard Group
P.O. Box 2600
Valley Forge, PA 19482
800-662-SHIP

Maximize income that qualifies for the 85% corporate dividend exclusion, by investing in common stocks. Currently closed to new accounts.

VANGUARD QUALIFIED DIVIDEND II
(Wellington Management Co.)
The Vanguard Group
P.O. Box 2600
Valley Forge, PA 19482
800-662-SHIP

Maximize income (from all sources) that qualifies for the 85% corporate dividend exclusion, by investing in preferred stocks.

VANGUARD QUALIFIED DIVIDEND III
(Wellington Management Co.)
The Vanguard Group
P.O. Box 2600
Valley Forge, PA 19482
800-662-SHIP

Maximize income (from all sources) that qualifies for the 85% corporate dividend exclusion, by investing in adjustable rate preferred stocks.

VANGUARD/WELLESLEY INCOME FUND
(Wellington Management Co.)
The Vanguard Group
P.O. Box 2600
Valley Forge, PA 19482
800-662-SHIP

Seeks as much current income as is consistent with reasonable risk; 60% to 70% fixed-income securities; balance in high-yielding stocks.

VANGUARD WELLINGTON FUND
(Wellington Management Co.)
The Vanguard Group
P.O. Box 2600
Valley Forge, PA 19482
800-662-SHIP

Conservation of principal; reasonable income; profits without undue risk; 60% to 70% in common stocks; balance in fixed-income securities.

□ Municipal Bond Funds — for Current Income Exempt from Federal Taxes

Fund Name (Adviser) Address and Telephone Number	Investment Objective and Policy
BENHAM NATIONAL TAX-FREE TRUST (Benham Management Corp.) 755 Page Mill Road Palo Alto, CA 94304 800-4-SAFETY/800-348-0002 (AK and HI)	Federal tax-free income for investors outside of California; three portfolios — money market, intermediate, and long-term.
THE BOSTON COMPANY TAX-FREE BOND FUND (The Boston Company Advisors) One Boston Place Boston, MA 02106 800-225-5267	Maximum current income exempt from federal income taxes through investment in a diversified portfolio of municipal obligations.
BULL & BEAR TAX-FREE INCOME FUND (Bull & Bear Group, Inc.) 11 Hanover Square New York, NY 10005 800-847-4200/212-363-1100	To provide its shareholders with the highest monthly income exempt from federal income tax from a diversified portfolio of municipal bonds.
CALVERT TAX-FREE RESERVES: LIMITED-TERM (Calvert Asset Management Co.) 1700 Pennsylvania Avenue, N.W. Washington, D.C. 20006 800-368-2748/301-951-4820	Higher tax-free yields than could be achieved by a money fund through investment in intermediate-term municipal obligations.
CALVERT TAX-FREE RESERVES: LONG-TERM (Calvert Asset Management Co.) 1700 Pennsylvania Avenue, N.W. Washington, D.C. 20006 800-368-2748/301-951-4820	High tax-exempt interest income. Invests in long-term investment grade municipal obligations. Maintains an average maturity of 20 years.

Fund Name
(Adviser)
Address and Telephone Number

Investment Objective
and
Policy

FIDELITY AGGRESSIVE TAX-FREE PORTFOLIO
(Fidelity Investments)
82 Devonshire Street
Boston, MA 02109
800-544-6666/617-523-1919

Seeks the highest tax-free yields by investing in long-term municipal bonds of below investment-grade quality.

FIDELITY HIGH-YIELD MUNICI-PALS
(Fidelity Investments)
82 Devonshire Street
Boston, MA 02109
800-544-6666/617-523-1919

High tax-free income. Carefully selected long-term municipal bonds of medium quality.

FIDELITY INSURED TAX-FREE PORTFOLIO
(Fidelity Investments)
82 Devonshire Street
Boston, MA 02109
800-544-6666/617-523-1919

Combines high tax-free yields with the safety of long-term bonds that are insured to guarantee timely payment of principal and interest.

FIDELITY LIMITED TERM MUNICI-PALS
(Fidelity Investments)
82 Devonshire Street
Boston, MA 02109
800-544-6666/617-523-1919

High tax-free income consistent with preserving capital; high-quality tax-exempt obligations maturing in 15 years or less, with average maturity of 12 years or less.

FIDELITY MUNICIPAL BOND FUND
(Fidelity Investments)
82 Devonshire Street
Boston, MA 02109
800-544-6666/617-523-1919

As high a level of tax-free income as is consistent with capital preservation; invests primarily in high-grade or upper-medium-grade municipal bonds.

FINANCIAL TAX-FREE INCOME SHARES
(Financial Programs, Inc.)
P.O. Box 2040
Denver, CO 80201
800-525-8085/800-525-9769
(CO)/303-779-1233 (Denver)

As high a level of interest income exempt from federal income taxes as is consistent with preservation of capital.

Fund Name (Adviser) Address and Telephone Number	Investment Objective and Policy
T. ROWE PRICE TAX-FREE IN-COME FUND (T. Rowe Price Associates, Inc.) 100 E. Pratt Street Baltimore, MD 21202 800-638-5660/301-547-2308	High income exempt from federal income taxes through investment-grade municipal bonds.
T. ROWE PRICE TAX-FREE HIGH YIELD FUND (T. Rowe Price Associates, Inc.) 100 E. Pratt Street Baltimore, MD 21202 800-638-5660/301-547-2308	Provide high level of current income exempt from income taxes by investing in long-term, medium- and lower-quality municipal bonds.
T. ROWE PRICE TAX-FREE SHORT-INTERMEDIATE FUND (T. Rowe Price Associates, Inc.) 100 E. Pratt Street Baltimore, MD 21202 800-638-5660/301-547-2308	High income exempt from federal income taxes, investing in short- and intermediate-term municipal securities.
SAFECO MUNICIPAL-BOND FUND (Safeco Asset Management Co.) Safeco Plaza T-15 Seattle, WA 98185 800-426-6730	Provide high level of current interest income, exempt from federal income tax, to the extent consistent with relative stability of capital.
STEINROE HIGH YIELD MUNICI-PALS (Stein Roe & Farnham) 300 W. Adams Street Chicago, IL 60606 800-621-0320/312-368-7700	Maximum current income exempt from federal income tax by investing in medium-quality, long-term municipal bonds.
STEINROE INTERMEDIATE MUNI-CIPALS (Stein Roe & Farnham) 300 W. Adams Street Chicago, IL 60606 800-621-0320/312-368-7700	To seek high current yield exempt from federal income tax, consistent with preservation of capital.

Fund Name
(Adviser)
Address and Telephone Number

Investment Objective
and
Policy

STEINROE MANAGED MUNI
(Stein Roe & Farnham)
300 W. Adams Street
Chicago, IL 60606
800-621-0320/312-368-7700

High current income which is exempt from federal income taxes and consistent with the preservation of capital. Invests in high-quality, long-term municipal bonds.

USAA TAX EXEMPT HIGH YIELD
(USAA Investment Management)
P.O. Box 33277
San Antonio, TX 78265
800-531-8181

Invests primarily in investment-grade, tax-exempt securities; no limit on maturity of these securities.

USAA TAX EXEMPT/
INTERMEDIATE-TERM
(USAA Investment Management)
P.O. Box 33277
San Antonio, TX 78265
800-531-8181

Invests primarily in investment-grade, tax-exempt securities having a maturity of no more than 12 years.

USAA TAX EXEMPT/SHORT-TERM
(USAA Investment Management)
P.O. Box 33277
San Antonio, TX 78265
800-531-8181

Invests primarily in investment-grade, tax-exempt securities having a maturity of no more than five years.

UST INTERMEDIATE TERM TAX-EXEMPT FUND
(U.S. Trust Company)
P.O. Box 9110
Boston, MA 02205-9110
800-233-1136

Higher level of income generally exempt from federal income taxes. Invests mostly in muni bonds with average maturity of ten years or less.

VALUE LINE TAX-EXEMPT FUND
(Value Line, Inc.)
711 Third Avenue
New York, NY 10017
800-223-0818

Offers the investor long-term, high-yield bonds (average maturity: ten to 40 years) exempt from federal income tax.

Fund Name (Adviser) Address and Telephone Number	Investment Objective and Policy
VANGUARD HIGH-YIELD MUNI BOND (Vanguard Group) The Vanguard Group P.O. Box 2600 Valley Forge, PA 19482 800-662-SHIP	Tax-free income, primarily from medium-grade-quality municipal bonds with an average maturity of more than 25 years.
VANGUARD INSURED LONG-TERM MUNI BOND (Vanguard Group) The Vanguard Group P.O. Box 2600 Valley Forge, PA 19482 800-662-SHIP	Tax-free income from high-quality insured long-term municipal bonds with an average maturity of more than 20 years.
VANGUARD INTERMEDIATE-TERM MUNI BOND (Vanguard Group) The Vanguard Group P.O. Box 2600 Valley Forge, PA 19482 800-662-SHIP	Tax-free income, primarily from high-quality municipal bonds with an average maturity of seven to 12 years.
VANGUARD LONG-TERM MUNI BOND (Vanguard Group) The Vanguard Group P.O. Box 2600 Valley Forge, PA 19482 800-662-SHIP	Tax-free income, primarily from high-quality municipal bonds with an average maturity of more than 25 years.
VANGUARD SHORT-TERM MUNI BOND (Vanguard Group) The Vanguard Group P.O. Box 2600 Valley Forge, PA 19482 800-662-SHIP	Tax-free income, primarily from high-quality municipal bonds with average maturity of four years or less.

☐ Double and Triple Tax-Exempt Bond Funds — for Current Income Exempt from City, State, and Federal Taxes

Fund Name (Adviser) Address and Telephone Number	Investment Objective and Policy
BENHAM CALIFORNIA TAX-FREE TRUST (Benham Management Corp.) 755 Page Mill Road Palo Alto, CA 94304 800-4-SAFETY/800-348-0002 (AK and HI)	Double tax-free income for California residents: three portfolios to choose from — money market, intermediate, and long-term.
CALIFORNIA TAX-FREE INCOME FUND (CCM Partners) 44 Montgomery Street, #2265 San Francisco, CA 94104 415-398-2727	Double tax-free income for California residents. Three highest quality ratings in portfolio.
FIDELITY CAL TAX-FREE FUND (Fidelity Investments) 82 Devonshire Street Boston, MA 02109 800-544-6666/617-523-1919	Current income exempt from federal and California income taxes from a portfolio of municipal obligations. Two portfolios — short-term (A) and muni-bond (B).
FIDELITY MASS. TAX-FREE FUND (Fidelity Investments) 82 Devonshire Street Boston, MA 02109 800-544-6666/617-523-1919	Current income exempt from federal and Massachusetts income taxes from a nondiversified portfolio of municipal obligations. Two funds — money market (A) and muni-bond (B).
FIDELITY MICHIGAN TAX-FREE PORTFOLIO (Fidelity Investments) 82 Devonshire Street Boston, MA 02109 800-544-6666/617-523-1919	Current income exempt from federal tax and Michigan income taxes from a portfolio of long-term, primarily investment-grade municipal obligations.

Fund Name (Adviser) Address and Telephone Number	Investment Objective and Policy
FIDELITY MINNESOTA TAX-FREE PORTFOLIO (Fidelity Investments) 82 Devonshire Street Boston, MA 02109 800-544-6666/617-523-1919	Current income exempt from federal tax and Minnesota income taxes from a portfolio of long-term, primarily investment-grade municipal obligations.
FIDELITY NEW YORK TAX-FREE FUND (Fidelity Investments) 82 Devonshire Street Boston, MA 02109 800-544-6666/617-523-1919	Current income exempt from federal and New York State and City income taxes from a portfolio of municipal obligations. Three portfolios — short-term (A), muni-bond (B), and insured (C).
FIDELITY OHIO TAX-FREE PORTFOLIO (Fidelity Investments) 82 Devonshire Street Boston, MA 02109 800-544-6666/617-523-1919	Current income exempt from federal tax and Ohio income taxes from a portfolio of long-term municipal obligations.
FIDELITY TEXAS TAX-FREE PORTFOLIO (Fidelity Investments) 82 Devonshire Street Boston, MA 02109 800-544-6666/617-523-1919	Current income free from federal and Texas income taxes from a portfolio of long-term municipal obligations.
NEW YORK MUNI FUND (Investors Portfolio Management) Suite 8407, One World Trade Center New York, NY 10048 212-775-0043	Tax-free income exempt from federal and New York State taxes.
T. ROWE PRICE CALIFORNIA TAX-FREE BOND FUND (T. Rowe Price Associates, Inc.) 100 E. Pratt Street Baltimore, MD 21202 800-638-5660/800-IRA-5000	Invests in longer-term, high-quality municipal securities exempt from federal and California State income tax.

Fund Name (Adviser) Address and Telephone Number	Investment Objective and Policy
SAFECO CALIFORNIA TAX-FREE INCOME FUND (Safeco Asset Management Co.) Safeco Plaza T-15 Seattle, WA 98185 800-426-6730	Provide high level of current interest income exempt from federal and California State income taxes while maintaining capital stability.
VANGUARD CALIFORNIA INSURED TAX-FREE FUND (Vanguard Group) The Vanguard Group P.O. Box 2600 Valley Forge, PA 19482 800-662-7447	High current income exempt from federal and California income taxes.
VANGUARD NEW YORK INSURED TAX-FREE FUND (Vanguard Group) The Vanguard Group P.O. Box 2600 Valley Forge, PA 19482 800-662-7447	High current income exempt from federal, New York State, and New York City income tax.
VANGUARD PENNSYLVANIA INSURED TAX-FREE FUND (Vanguard Group) The Vanguard Group P.O. Box 2600 Valley Forge, PA 19482 800-662-7447	High current income exempt from federal and Pennsylvania income tax.

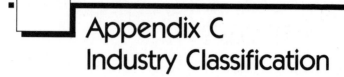

Appendix C
Industry Classification

☐ **Highly Cyclical**
▬▬▬▬▬▬▬▬▬▬ Agricultural equipment, airlines, aluminum, apparel, appliances, automobile and truck manufacturers, home building, home furnishings, iron, machinery (heavy), nonferrous metals (copper, lead, zinc), oil refining, oil-field equipment and services, railroads, real-estate investment trusts, semiconductors, steel, sugar, textiles, tires and rubber, trucking.

☐ **Cyclical Growth**
▬▬▬▬▬▬▬▬▬▬ Advertising, aerospace and defense, banks, broadcasting, brokerage houses, cement, chemicals, forest and paper products, department stores, health care, insurers (life, property, and casualty), lodging/leisure, machine tools, oil and gas production, packaging and containers, photography, precious metals, restaurants, savings and loans.

☐ **Relatively Stable**
▬▬▬▬▬▬▬▬▬▬ Auto parts, beverages, convenience stores, cosmetics, food, drugstores, grocery chains, insurance (multiline), publishing, tobacco, toys, utilities (electric, gas, telephone).

☐ **Growth**
▬▬▬▬▬▬▬▬▬▬ Automation (robotics, word-processing), computers, consumer electronics, drugs (ethical and proprietary), environmental services, fast food service, recreation, telecommunications.

☐ **High Growth**
▬▬▬▬▬▬▬▬▬▬ Biotechnology and other emerging technologies, computer software and services (computer-assisted design/computer-aided manufacturing, data processing), medical technology, instruments (process control and scientific).

Source: Rauscher Pierce Refsnes Inc., Dallas, Texas

Appendix D
The Language of Investing: A Glossary

The language spoken in America's investment world may sound like a strange tongue to the newcomer. Any glossary of this special language involves certain problems. Some words and phrases cannot be defined completely without going into related background material; others have nuances of meaning that even the experts may dispute. We have tried to define terms simply and easily, trimming subtle shades of meaning in the interest of brevity and readability. Many terms covered in the glossary are more fully explained in the text.

Accelerated Depreciation: writing off the cost of an asset faster than under the straight-line method, which, for example, would depreciate a $10 million asset over a 10-year period by $1 million each year.

Accounts Payable: all monies owed by the firm for materials or services purchased and due for payment at the date of the balance sheet.

Accounts Receivable: all monies owed to the firm for products or services and still unpaid at the date of the balance sheet.

Accrued Interest: interest accrued on a bond since the last interest payment was made. The buyer of the bond pays the market price plus accrued interest.

Advance-Decline Line: a charted line showing the number of stocks that have advanced compared with the number that have declined.

Amortization: periodic repayment of a debt. Includes various specific practices such as depreciation, depletion, write-off of intangibles.

Arbitrage: buying a stock in one market and simultaneously selling it in another to take advantage of a price difference between the two markets.

Asked Price: *see* Offer, also Bid and Asked.

Assets: everything that a corporation owns or that is due to it — cash, investments, materials and inventories, which are called current assets; buildings and machinery, which are known as fixed assets; and patents and goodwill, called intangible assets.

At the Market: an order to buy or sell a stock "at the market" will be automatically executed at the best price available when the order reaches the floor of the exchange (or, in the case of OTC stocks, the best price obtainable from the dealers who make a market in the issue). *See* Limit Order, Market Order.

Averaging Down: adding to one's existing holdings of a stock that has declined in order to lower one's average cost.

Balance Sheet: a condensed statement showing the nature and amount of a company's assets, liabilities, and capital on a given date. In dollar amounts, the balance sheet shows what the company owned, what it owed, and the ownership interest in the company of its stockholders.

Bankers' Acceptances: short-term obligations issued and guaranteed by banks and sold in denominations of $100,000.

Bear: someone who believes that the market will decline. A bear market is one in which stock prices are dropping.

Bearer Bond: a bond that does not have the owner's name registered on the books of the issuing company and that is payable to the holder.

Beta: a measure of a stock's volatility in relation to that of Standard & Poor's 500-stock index. *See* chapter 12.

Bid and Asked: often referred to as a quotation or a quote. The bid is the highest price anyone has offered for a security at a given time; the asked is the lowest price anyone will accept.

Big Board: a popular term for the New York Stock Exchange.

Block: a large amount of stock, usually 10,000 shares and over.

Blue Chip: the common stock of a company known nationally for the quality and wide acceptance of its products and services, and for its ability to make profits and pay dividends.

Blue Sky Laws: a popular name for laws that various states have enacted to protect the public against securities frauds. The term is believed to have originated when a judge ruled that a particular stock had about the same value as a patch of blue sky.

Board Room: a room for customers in a broker's office where the action of the market can be seen on an electronic board.

Boiler Room: a sleazy firm that uses high-pressure salesmanship to peddle, over the telephone, stocks, gold or other investments of questionable value. A typical boiler room is simply a room lined with desks or cubicles, each with a salesman and a telephone. The salesmen call what are known in the trade as sucker lists.

Bond: basically an I.O.U. or promissory note of a corporation, usually issued in multiples of $1,000. A bond is evidence of a debt on which the issuing company promises to pay the bond-holders a specified amount of interest for a specified length of time, and to repay the loan on the expiration date. A bond-holder is a creditor of the corporation and not a part owner, as is a shareholder.

Book Value: an accounting term. The book value of a stock is determined by adding all assets (generally excluding such intangibles as goodwill), then deducting all debts and other liabilities, plus the liquidation price of any preferred issues. The sum arrived at is divided by the number of common shares outstanding, and the result is book value per common share. Book value may have little or no significant relationship to market value.

Breadth (Market): breadth has to do with the total number of stocks advancing and declining on the New York Stock Exchange. Most technical analysts use four principle breadth indexes, all derived and computed from the same data carried in the *Wall Street Journal.* The basic index is a straight advance-decline line. Two indexes are concerned with increasing and decreasing volume. The fourth is a composite breadth index.

Breakout: a term used in technical analysis to signify a decisive move up or down on substantial volume out of a consolidation area. For example, if a stock has been trading for a time in the 32–36 area, a move on volume to 37 or 31 would be termed a breakout.

Bull: one who believes that the market will rise. A bull market is one in which stock prices are advancing.

Call: *see* Options, also chapter 26.

Callable: a bond issue that, under specified conditions, may be redeemed wholly or in part by the issuing corporation before the maturity date. The term also applies to preferred stock.

Capital Gain or Capital Loss: profit or loss from the sale of a capital asset. Under the Tax Reform Act of 1986, a net capital gain is taxed at the reporting individual's full income-tax rate. Up to $3,000 of net capital loss is deductible from the individual's taxable income during the year reported. If the capital loss is more than $3,000, as much as $3,000 is deductible annually thereafter until all of the loss has been accounted for.

Capitalization: the total amount of the stocks and bonds issued by a corporation.

Cash Flow: the reported net income of a corporation plus the amounts charged off for depreciation, depletion, amortization, and extraordinary charges to reserves, all of which are bookkeeping deductions and not paid out in actual dollars. A company's cash flow often offers a better indication of its ability to pay dividends and finance expansion from self-generated cash than the reported net-income figure.

Certificate: the actual piece of paper that is evidence of ownership of stock in a corporation. Loss of a certificate may at the least cause a great deal of inconvenience — at the worst, financial loss.

Certificate of Deposit (CD): a negotiable receipt, issued by a bank, for time deposits in the bank. CDs have maturities ranging from 1 month up to 1 year, and their minimum denomination is $100,000.

Churning: a broker who overtrades a discretionary account or encourages a customer to overtrade is guilty of churning, which is a punishable offense under the securities laws but is often difficult to prove.

Commercial Paper: short-term, unsecured promissory notes issued by major corporations in denominations of $100,000 and up.

Common Stock: securities that represent an ownership interest in a corporation.

Consolidated Balance Sheet: a balance sheet showing the financial condition of a corporation and its subsidiaries.

Convertible: a bond or preferred stock that may be exchanged by the owner for common stock of the same company, in accordance with the terms of the issue.

Coupon Bond: a bond with interest coupons attached. The coupons are clipped as they come due and are presented by the holder through a bank or broker for payment of interest.

Covering: buying a security that has previously been sold short. *See* Short Sale.

Cumulative Preferred: a stock having a provision that if one or more dividends are omitted, the omitted dividends must be paid before dividends may be paid on the company's common stock.

Current Assets: assets, including inventory and receivables, that are expected to be converted into cash within a year, plus cash on hand and readily marketable securities.

Current Liabilities: obligations that a company must meet and pay for in cash within a year.

Customers' Man: *see* Registered Representative.

Customers' Net Debit Balances: the net amount owed to the New York Stock Exchange by customers who have borrowed from the Exchange to help finance purchases of stocks, bonds, or commodities.

Day Order: an order to buy or sell that, if not executed, expires at the end of the trading day on which it was entered.

Dealer: an individual or firm in the securities business acting as a principal rather than as an agent. Typically, a dealer buys for his own account and sells to a customer from his own inventory. The same individual or firm may function, at different times, either as a broker or dealer.

Debenture: a promissory note backed by the general credit of a company and usually not secured by a mortgage or lien on any specific property. *See* Bond.

Depletion: the consumption of natural resources such as metals, timber, oil, and gas, which conceivably can be reduced to zero over the years. Depletion is a charge against earnings based on the amount of the asset taken out of the total reserves in the accounting period. It does not represent any cash outlay or setting aside of cash reserves; it is simply a bookkeeping entry.

Depreciation: charges against earnings to write off the cost of an asset over its estimated useful life. It is a bookkeeping entry and does not represent any cash outlay, nor are any funds earmarked for the purpose.

Dilution: actual or potential reduction of earnings per share because of stock options, warrants, and/or convertible issues outstanding.

Director: a person elected by the shareholders at the annual meeting of a company to establish company policies. The directors appoint the president, vice presidents, and all other operating officers. Directors decide, among other matters, if and when dividends shall be paid.

Discretionary Account: an account in which an investor gives the broker or someone else discretion (which may be complete or within specified limits) to buy and sell securities or commodities on his behalf.

Discretionary Order: the customer instructs the broker to use his judgment as to the price at which a security will be bought or sold. If the broker is unable to buy or sell at the price he is seeking, he cannot be held accountable for not executing the order.

Distribution: the sale of a large block of stock to a large group of investors.

Diversification: spreading investments among different companies in different fields. A company that is in many different lines of business is said to be diversified. Such companies are usually described as "conglomerates" or "multiform" companies.

Dividend: the payment designated by the board of directors to be distributed pro rata among the shares outstanding. On preferred shares, it is generally a fixed amount. On common shares, the dividend varies with the fortunes of the company and its available cash, and may be omitted if business is poor or the directors decide to withhold earnings to invest in plant and equipment. Sometimes a company that is not currently operating at a profit will pay a dividend out of past earnings. *See also* Stock Dividend.

Dividend Payout: the percentage of earnings per share paid to stockholders in dividends.

Dollar Cost Averaging: investing a fixed amount at regular intervals in a selected security. *See* chapter 19.

Dual-Purpose Fund: a closed-end investment company with two classes of stock. One class entitles shareholders to receive all of the fund's income; owners of the other class receive all of the fund's capital gains.

Earnings Report: a statement issued by a company showing its earnings or losses over a given period.

Econometrics: the branch of economics that expresses economic theory in mathematical terms and seeks to verify it by statistical methods.

Equity: the ownership interest of common and preferred stockholders in a company. Also refers to the amount by which the value of securities in a margin account exceeds the debit balance.

Ex-dividend: a synonym for "without dividend." The buyer of a stock selling ex-dividend does not receive the recently declared dividend. Every dividend is payable on a fixed date to shareholders recorded on the company's books as of a previous date of record. For example, a dividend may be declared as payable to holders of record on a given Friday. Since five business days are allowed for delivery of stock in a "regular way" transaction on the New York Stock Exchange, the Exchange would declare the stock "ex-dividend" as of the opening of the market on the preceding Monday. This means that anyone who bought the stock on and after the Monday would not be entitled to that dividend.

Extra: the short form of "extra dividend." This is a dividend in the form of stock or cash in addition to the regular dividend the company has been paying.

Face Value: the value of a bond that appears on the face of the bond. Face value, or "par," is the amount the issuing company promises to pay at maturity.

Fiscal Year: a corporation's accounting year. Because of the nature of their particular business, some companies do not use the calendar year for their bookkeeping. A typical example is department stores, which find December 31 too early a date to close their books after the Christmas rush. For that reason, many stores wind up their accounting year on January 31. The fiscal year of other companies may run from July 1 through the following June 30. Most companies, though, operate on a calendar-year basis.

Fixed Charges: a company's fixed expenses — for example, bond interest, which it has agreed to pay whether or not the interest due is covered by earnings. These charges are deducted from income before earnings on equity capital are computed.

Floor: the huge trading area — about two-thirds the size of a football field — where stocks and bonds are bought and sold on the New York Stock Exchange.

Floor Broker: a member of the stock exchange who executes orders on the floor of the exchange to buy or sell listed securities.

Formula Investing: a method of investing under which purchases and sales are made automatically, in accordance with a hard-and-fast formula. One formula calls for the shifting of funds from common stocks to money-market securities when the market has risen a predetermined percentage, and the switching of funds into common stocks when the market drops a predetermined percentage.

Funded Debt: usually interest-bearing bonds of a company. The term could include long-term bank loans, but not short-term loans.

Gilt-edged: a high-grade bond issued by a company that has demonstrated its ability to earn a comfortable profit over a period of years and pay its bond-holders their interest without interruption is called gilt-edged.

Glamour Stocks: the stocks of companies whose prospects investors consider particularly exciting. Such stocks tend to sell at the highest prevailing P/E ratios.

Good till Canceled Order (GTC), or Open Order: an order to buy or sell that remains in effect until it is either executed or canceled.

Head-and-Shoulders: a term used by technical analysts to describe a chart pattern (resembling a human head and shoulders) that is taken as signaling the reversal of a trend.

Holding Company: a corporation that owns the securities of other companies, usually with voting control.

Hypothecation: the pledging of securities as collateral for a loan.

Indenture: a written agreement under which debentures are issued, setting forth maturity date, interest rate, security, and other terms.

Index: a statistical yardstick expressed in terms of a base year or years. For instance, Standard & Poor's 500-stock index is based on 1941–1943 as 10. An index is not an average, but the two terms are popularly treated as synonymous.

Investment Banker: also known as an underwriter. He is the middle-

man between the corporation issuing new securities and the public. The usual practice is for one or more investment bankers to buy outright from a corporation a new issue of stocks or bonds. The group forms a syndicate to sell the securities to individuals and institutions. Investment bankers also distribute very large blocks of stocks or bonds — perhaps held by an estate.

Investment Counsel: a professional money manager who handles accounts for institutions or individuals on a fee basis.

Investment Trust: the two principal types are closed-end and open-end mutual funds. Shares in closed-end investment trusts, most of which are listed on the New York Stock Exchange, are bought and sold like other shares. The capitalization of these companies remains the same. Open-end funds issue new shares to investors and stand ready to buy back their old shares at their net asset value; they are not listed on an exchange. These funds are called open-end because their capitalization is not fixed.

Keogh Plan and IRA: tax-sheltered retirement plans. Keogh allows self-employed persons to defer taxation on up to 20 percent of their annual income (but not more than $30,000 a year) by contributing to a tax-sheltered pension fund for themselves and their employees. An employed person who is or is not covered by a company retirement plan may contribute up to $2,000 each year to a tax-deferred Individual Retirement Account. Contributions are tax-deferred if the employee is ineligible for a company pension plan or if he earns less than a specified amount: $50,000 for taxpayers who file jointly and $35,000 for single filers.

Leverage: the effect on the per-share earnings of the common stock of a company when large sums must be paid for bond interest or preferred stock dividends, or both, before the common stock is entitled to share in earnings. Leverage is advantageous for the common stock holder when earnings are good but damaging when earnings decline.

Liabilities: everything a company owes. Current liabilities include wages and salaries payable, declared dividends payable, and accrued taxes. Fixed or long-term liabilities consist of bonds, bank loans, lease commitments, and certain pension obligations.

Limit Order: an order to buy a stock at not more than a specified price or to sell a stock at not less than a specified price.

Liquidation: the process of converting securities into cash. Also, the dissolution of a company.

Liquidity: the ability of the market in a particular security to absorb a reasonable amount of buying or selling without sharp price changes. Liquidity is the hallmark of a good market.

Listed Stock: a stock that is traded on a securities exchange. To qualify for listing, companies have to meet certain requirements in regard to market value, net income, number of shares publicly held, and number of shareholders.

Load and No-Load: a load is the portion of the offering price of shares in open-end mutual funds that covers sales commissions; it is typically 4½ to 8½ percent. There may also be a charge when shares are redeemed. No-load funds are those whose shares are sold directly to investors at their net asset value with no commission added.

Long: signifies ownership of securities. "I am long 100 Mobil" means that the speaker owns 100 shares.

Management: the board of directors, elected by the stockholders, and the officers of the corporation, appointed by the board of directors.

Manipulation: an illegal operation. Buying or selling a security to create a false or misleading appearance of active trading or for the purpose of raising or depressing the price to induce purchase or sale by others.

Margin: the amount put up by a customer when he borrows from his broker to buy a security. The margin requirement, which is set by the Federal Reserve Board, has, over the past 25 years, ranged from 40 percent of the purchase price all the way to 100 percent.

Margin Account: an account that permits the customer to use a brokerage firm's credit to buy securities. To open a margin account the customer must sign a margin agreement, which authorizes his brokerage house to lend to itself or to other brokers any securities carried in the account.

Margin Call: brokerage firms issue a margin call when a customer's equity in a margin account declines below a minimum standard set by the firm or the New York Stock Exchange. If an investor cannot put up the amount required in cash (or securities whose marginable value equals that amount), the brokerage firms sells stock in his account. A steep decline in stock prices can cause an avalanche of margin calls, and the resulting forced liquidations drive prices down still farther.

Market Order: an order to buy or sell a stated amount of a security at the best price obtainable when the order reaches the floor of the exchange.

Market Price: the last reported price at which a stock or bond sold.

Maturity: the date on which a bond comes due for redemption.

Mortgage Bond: a bond secured by a mortgage on property.

Municipal Bond: a bond issued by a state or political subdivision, such as a county, city, town, or village. The term also designates bonds issued by state agencies or authorities. In general, interest paid on municipal bonds is exempt from federal income taxes. But the 1986 tax law created two new classes of municipals. One is taxable to all bond-holders; the other is subject to the alternative minimum tax.

NASD: the National Association of Securities Dealers, Inc., an association of brokers and dealers in the over-the-counter securities business. One of the NASD's functions is to "administer and enforce rules of fair practice and to prevent fraudulent and manipulative acts."

NASDAQ: the NASD's automated quotation system, which provides quotes and other data on about 3,400 over-the-counter stocks.

Negotiable: refers to a security the title to which is transferable by delivery.

Net Asset Value: an investment trust (mutual fund) computes its assets daily by totaling the market value of all its security holdings. After all liabilities have been deducted, the balance is divided by the number of shares outstanding; the resulting figure is the net asset value per share.

Net Change: the change in the price of a security from the closing price on one day to the closing price on the following trading day. In the case of a stock that is entitled to a dividend one day but is traded "ex-dividend" the next, the dividend is considered in computing the change. The same applies to stock splits. A stock selling at $100 before a 2-for-1 split and closing the next day at $50 would be considered unchanged. The net change is ordinarily the last figure in a newspaper stock table.

New Issue: a stock or bond sold by a corporation for the first time; also called an initial public offering or IPO.

Odd Lot: an amount of stock less than the normal 100-share unit of trading.

Offer: the price at which a security is offered for sale; also referred to as the asked price.

Open Order: *see* Good till Canceled.

Options: contracts that give the holder the right to buy (in the case of a "call") or sell (in the case of a "put") a specified number of shares of a particular stock within a specified time at a specified price. *See* chapter 26.

Overbought: when a stock or the market has advanced vigorously for some time on heavy trading volume and without any appreciable setbacks, it is often said to be overbought. The term reflects the opinion that investors no longer have the buying power required to sustain a further advance and that prices will go down, at least temporarily. "Oversold" means that a wave of selling has probably run its course and that prices are due for at least a temporary rebound.

Over-the-Counter: the market where securities not listed on the regular exchanges are traded. *See* chapter 1.

Paper Profit or Loss: an unrealized profit or loss on a security that one is still holding.

Penny Stocks: low-priced issues, nearly always highly speculative ones, that are selling at less than $1 a share.

Pink Sheets: the prices of thousands of small stocks traded over the counter are not published in newspapers. But bid and asked prices for all OTC stocks can be found in the Pink Sheets (so-called because of their color), a service to which brokerage houses subscribe. The service also gives the names of the market-makers for each stock — the firms that stand ready to buy the stock from investors or sell it to them from their own inventory. An OTC market-maker sometimes performs functions somewhat similar to those of a specialist on a regular exchange.

Point: in the case of shares of stock, a point means $1; in the case of bonds it means $10, since a bond is quoted as a percentage of $1,000. A bond that rises 3 points gains 3 percent of $1,000, or $30, in value.

Point-and-Figure: one of the two main types of charts used by technical analysts, the other being the "bar" chart.

Portfolio: holdings of securities by an individual or institution.

Preferred Stock: a class of stock that has priorities over common stock, both in regard to dividends and to claims on the company's assets if it goes into bankruptcy. Preferred stockholders must receive specified dividends before any dividends may be paid on the common.

Premium: the amount by which a preferred stock or bond is selling about its par value. In the case of a new stock or bond issue, the premium is the amount by which the market price rises over the original selling price. When the shares of a closed-end mutual fund are selling above their net asset value, they are said to be selling at a premium.

Price/Earnings Ratio: the current market price of a share of stock divided by the company's earnings per share for a 12-month period. *See* chapter 4.

Prime Rate: the rate of interest that commercial banks charge their most creditworthy customers for short-term loans.

Principal: the investor for whom a broker executes an order, or a dealer buying or selling for his own account. The term *principal* may also refer to a person's capital or to the face value of a bond.

Profit-Taking: selling to realize a profit; the process of converting paper profits into cash.

Prospectus: a circular, required by the Securities Act of 1933, that describes securities that are being offered for sale to the public.

Proxy: written authorization given by a shareholder to someone else to represent him and vote his shares at a shareholders meeting.

Proxy Statement: a circular containing information that, under SEC regulations, must be given to stockholders when their proxies are being solicited.

Put: *see* Options, also chapter 26.

Quotation, Quote: the highest bid to buy, and the lowest offer to sell, a security in a given market at a given time.

Rally: a brisk rise following a decline in the market or in an individual stock.

Red Herring: an advance copy of the prospectus that will be filed with the SEC by a company intending to go public or issue new securities. *See* chapter 27.

Registered Bond: a bond that is registered on the books of the issuing company in the name of the owner. It can be transferred only when endorsed by the registered owner. *See* Bearer Bond.

Registered Representative: a stockbroker, also known as an account executive. In a New York Stock Exchange member firm, a registered representative is a full-time employee who has met the requirements of the Exchange as to background and knowledge of the securities business.

Registered Trader: a member of the New York Stock Exchange who trades in stocks on the floor for his own account.

Registration: before a public offering may be made of new securities by a company, or of outstanding securities by controlling stockholders — through the mails or in interstate commerce — the securities must be registered under the Securities Act of 1933. A registration statement filed with the SEC by the issuer must disclose information relating to the company's business, sales, and earnings (or losses), financial condition, management, and the purpose of the public offering. Before a security can be traded on a national securities exchange, it must be registered under the Securities Exchange Act of 1934. The application for registration must be filed with the SEC by the company issuing the securities.

Regular Way Delivery: unless otherwise specified, securities (other than government bonds) must be delivered to the buying broker by the selling broker, and payment made to the selling broker by the buying broker, on the fifth business day after the transaction. Regular way delivery for government bonds is the business day following the transaction.

Regulation T: the federal regulation governing the amount of margin credit that may be advanced by brokers and dealers to customers for the purchase of securities.

Round Lot: a unit of trading or a multiple thereof. The unit of trading is generally 100 shares for stocks and $1,000 par value for bonds.

Rule of 72: a simple formula for determining approximately how long it will take for money to double at a fixed rate of interest that is reinvested and compounded; just divide the number 72 by the rate of interest. For example, if the interest rate is 8 percent compounded annually, your money will double in 9 years.

Seat: a figure of speech for a membership in a securities or commodities exchange.

SEC: the Securities and Exchange Commission, established by Congress to regulate the securities industry and protect the investing public's interests. The SEC administers the Securities Act of 1933, the Securities Exchange Act of 1934, the Trust Indenture Act, the Investment Company Act, the Investment Advisers Act, and the Public Utility Holding Company Act.

Secondary Distribution: a sale of a large block of previously issued stock at a fixed price by a securities firm or group of firms. A "secondary" — often a sale by a large shareholder — must be registered with the SEC.

Short Sale: a short sale is a sale of borrowed stock — the borrowing is done by your broker — made in the expectation that the stock's price will go down. Eventually, the short seller has to buy the stock and return it to its owner, an action known as covering his short. If he buys it at a price lower than the sale price, he makes a profit; if the stock rises and he buys it at a higher price, he suffers a loss. Short sales are made in a margin account, and a short sale is subject to the same margin requirements as a purchase; if the margin requirement is 50 percent and you sell short $6,000 worth of stock, you have to put up $3,000. The proceeds of the sale — $6,000 — are credited to your margin account, but you cannot draw on them unless the price of the stock drops, causing your equity in the account to rise. A short sale can be made only on an "uptick" or "zero-plus" tick. An uptick means that the stock has traded at a price higher than the previous transaction. A zero-plus tick describes a transaction made at the same price as the preceding trade or trades but higher than the most recent different price at which the stock changed hands. Short selling is basically a speculative tactic and a very risky one if the stock is volatile. When you buy a stock at $15, the worst possibility is a drop to zero, which hardly ever happens. But if you sell a $15 stock short and you have to cover at $40, you lose $25; your liability when you go short is unlimited.

Sinking Fund: money regularly set aside by a company to redeem its bonds or preferred stock from time to time, as specified in the indenture or charter.

Specialist: a member of the New York Stock Exchange who has two functions. One is to maintain an orderly market, insofar as is reasonably practicable, in the stocks in which he is registered as a specialist. To maintain an orderly market, the specialist engages in "stabilizing" transactions, which bridge temporary gaps between supply and demand; he buys for his own account when supply exceeds demand, and he sells short when demand is appreciably greater than supply. The specialist's second function is to act as a brokers' broker. When a commission broker on the exchange floor receives a limit order — an order, say, to buy at $58 a stock then selling at $60 — he cannot wait at the particular post where the stock is traded until the price reaches the specified level. So he leaves the order with the specialist, who enters it in his "book" and will execute it in the market if and

when the stock declines to the specified price. There are about 350 specialists on the New York Stock Exchange, and there are specialists on the other stock exchanges.

Split: the division of the outstanding shares of a corporation into a larger number of shares. A 3-for-1 split by a company with 1 million shares outstanding results in 3 million shares outstanding; each holder of 100 shares before the split winds up with 300 shares. But his proportionate equity in the company remains exactly the same, and the split in itself doesn't change the market value of his investment.

Stock Ahead: sometimes an investor who has entered an order to buy or sell a stock at a certain price will see transactions at that price reported on the electronic ticker while his own order has not been executed. His broker will explain that there was "stock ahead," which means that other buy and sell orders at the same price reached the specialist ahead of his and had priority.

Stock Clearing Corporation: a subsidiary of the New York Stock Exchange, which acts as a central agency for security deliveries and money payments between member firms of the exchange.

Stock Dividend: a dividend paid in shares of stock rather than in cash.

Stop Order: an order to buy or sell a stock when it reaches a specified price. A stop order to buy becomes a market order when a transaction in the security, which has been trading at a lower price, occurs at or above the stop price; short sellers often use such orders to protect themselves against potentially large losses. A stop order to sell becomes a market order when a transaction in the security, which has been trading at a higher price, takes place at or below the stop price. Such orders are used to protect a paper profit or to limit losses. But since any stop order becomes an "at-the-market" order when the stop price is reached, a stop sell order may be executed at a lower price, and a stop buy order at a higher price.

Street Name: securities held in the name of a brokerage firm instead of the customer's name are said to be carried in "street name." This procedure is mandatory when the securities have been bought on margin. An investor may keep his securities at a brokerage house in his own name, but he is an active trader there are advantages in having the securities registered in street name.

Syndicate: a group of investment bankers who together underwrite and distribute a new issue of securities or a large block of an outstanding issue.

Tax Selling: securities sales made, usually late in the year, to realize gains or losses for income-tax purposes.

Thin Market: the term — which generally applies to an individual stock but can refer to the market in general — means that there are comparatively few bids to buy, or

offers to sell, or both. In a thin market, relatively small changes in supply and demand can cause sharp price changes. A thin market is the opposite of a liquid market.

Ticker: a machine that reports the prices and the volume of security transactions. The action of the ticker is usually displayed on an electronic board in brokerage house board rooms.

Topping Out: this term can be applied to the general market, to a group of stocks, or to an individual issue. It signifies that an uptrend is, or appears to be, coming to an end. The opposite term is Bottoming Out.

Trader: one who buys and sells for his own account for short-term profit.

Trading Crowd: members of a stock exchange assembled at a trading post to execute buy and sell orders.

Trading Post: one of 14 horseshoe-shaped trading locations on the floor of the New York Stock Exchange at which stocks assigned to that location are bought and sold. About 75 stocks are traded at each post.

Transfer Agent: a transfer agent — normally a bank — keeps a record of the name of each registered shareowner, his or her address, and the number of shares owned, and sees to it that certificates presented to his office for transfer are properly canceled and new certificates issued in the name of the transferee.

Transfer Tax: a tax imposed by New

York State, Florida, South Carolina, and Texas on transactions that occur on exchanges or between dealers within the state. New York bases its tax on the selling price; the other three states, on the par value. There is no tax on transfers of bonds.

Treasury Stock: stock issued by a company but later reacquired. It may be held in the company's treasury indefinitely, reissued to the public, or retired. Treasury stock receives no dividends and has no vote while held by the company.

Underwriter: *see* Investment Banker.

Warrant: a certificate giving the holder the right to purchase a security at a stipulated price within a specified time limit or perpetually. Sometimes warrants are included in a securities offering as an inducement to buy.

When Issued: a short form of "when, as, and if issued." For example, after a stock split has been announced, trading on the split stock usually begins on a "when issued" basis before the split has occurred. All "when issued" transactions are on an "if" basis; they are settled if and when the actual security is issued and the exchange on which the stock is traded or the NASD rules that the transactions are to be settled.

Wire House: a national brokerage firm with a communications network linking its branch offices throughout the country. *See* chapter 13.

Yield: also known as Return. The annual dividends or interest paid by a company divided by the current price of the stock or bond, or, if you already own the security, by the price you originally paid.

Index